D0908125

**Basic Documents
of
American
Public Administration
Since 1950**

Basic Documents
of
American
Public Administration
Since 1950

Selected and edited
by
Richard J. Stillman II

Holmes & Meier
Publishers, Inc.
New York   London

First published in the United States of America 1982 by
Holmes & Meier Publishers, Inc.
30 Irving Place
New York, N.Y. 10003

Great Britain:
Holmes & Meier Publishers, Ltd.
131 Trafalgar Road
Greenwich, London SE10 9TX

Copyright © 1982 by Holmes & Meier, Publishers, Inc.
All rights reserved

Book design by Rose Jacobowitz

Library of Congress Cataloging in Publication Data
Main entry under title:

Basic documents of American public administration since
    1950.

    Continues: Basic documents of American public adminis-
tration, 1776–1950/selected and edited by Frederick C.
Mosher.
    1. United States—Politics and government—1945–
—Sources.   2. United States—Executive departments—
Management—History—Sources.   3. Administrative
agencies—United States—Management—History—Sources.
4. Civil service—United States—History—Sources.
I. Stillman, Richard Joseph, 1943–
JK411.B32   1982   353   82-11726
ISBN 0-8419-0818-4
ISBN 0-8419-0819-2 (pbk.)

Manufactured in the United States of America

*Dedicated to
students, scholars, and
practitioners of
American public administration
who have sought to make
government more
responsible and responsive
in the postwar era*

Contents

PART II

The Quest for Improved Public Personnel Systems: Key Values in Conflict

PART III

The Quest for Improved Budgeting and Financial Management: New Layers of Reform

PART IV
Strategies for Achieving Administrative Accountability:
New "Checks" on the Bureaucracy

Preface

This volume contains important postwar public documents in public administration including legislative acts, executive commission reports, executive orders, and statements by public figures and thereby serves as a continuation of Frederick C. Mosher's *Basic Documents of American Public Administration, 1776–1950* (New York: Holmes & Meier, 1976). Like the Mosher volume, this text is designed to have several purposes: First, it provides in a single volume many of the critical documents that have shaped American postwar administrative processes and institutions. Many of these documents cannot be found in a public library. Some have never been published in a collection before. Second, this volume not only permits readers to examine the text of the documents but offers explanatory information regarding their origins, impact, and significance to public administration. In other words, each document is placed within the overall historical development of the field. Third, the book can serve as either a reference for scholars and general readers or as a supplementary textbook to enrich the standard fare of classroom readings in public administration, public affairs, or government courses. Finally, it is the editor's belief that a firsthand appreciation of the major postwar public documents will give both undergraduate and graduate students of the field a far broader, more comprehensive, and realistic picture of American administration as well as deeper awareness of the institutional complexity, historical trends, and value problems confronting the field today.

Whereas Professor Mosher's *Basic Documents* was organized in a chronological fashion—sequentially according to the dates of their enactment or publication—readers should note that the postwar documents in this volume have been arranged thematically—on the basis of four basic categories: those that outline important patterns of organization and management for postwar public sector enterprises (Part I); those that deal primarily with personnel systems and practices (Part II); those that pertain to budgeting and financial issues (Part III); and those that are concerned mainly with administrative accountability (Part IV). Readers should note that in two cases, both taken from the First Hoover Report of 1949, 1949 documents appear. The overlap, which is not significant, is due to a few critical post-1950 "themes" beginning one year before 1950, and this text uses 1950 as the starting benchmark date (to be consistent with Mosher's volume).

An enormous number of public documents were prepared during this thirty-year period—estimated to be enough paper annually to rise to the moon and return. The decision as to what to include was largely based upon the following criteria:

1. A document had to be a *public* document—an official government report, executive order, legislative act, or major pronouncement by a public official during the *postwar era*. Those pieces written by individuals or groups not in official governmental capacities were omitted.

2. A document had to have a *significant* impact on shaping public administration since 1950 *in general*. While there were numerous acts and reports deemed important, such as aspects of foreign affairs or urban development, these more specialized functional or area items were not included unless they related to the overall field of study.

3. Documents or parts of documents written in complex technical or legal language were also not used. The aim was to use written works that could make sense to a *layman* or *nonspecialist*.

4. Finally, documents that focused upon *central and enduring issues* in the field were included. In part, the decision to organize the book under such subject headings as "organization and management," "personnel," "budgeting," and "administrative accountability" was an effort to be responsive to "mainline" scholar, practitioner, and student interests in these ongoing public administration problems and issues.

The editor spent more than three years reading, collecting, and analyzing documents from many sources including some previously unpublished. Further, to double-check the accuracy of his selections, the editor sent a letter to more than 150 senior American scholars and practitioners of the field, members of the National Academy of Public Administration, soliciting their views about what should be covered in this volume. Their help was indeed useful, and the editor is very grateful to a number of individuals who took time from their busy schedules to write lengthy replies including: Wayne Anderson, Executive Director, Advisory Commission on Intergovernmental Relations; Professor Lynton K. Caldwell, Arthur F. Bently Professor of Political Science, University of Indiana; Dr. Mark W. Cannon, Administrative Assistant to the Chief Justice, U.S. Supreme Court; William D. Carey, Executive Director, American Association for the Advancement of Science; Frank C. Carlucci, Deputy Secretary of Defense; Dr. Morris W.H. Collins, John C. Stennis Chair in Political Science, Mississippi State University; Dr. Ruth M. Davis, Assistant Secretary, Department of Energy; Professor Emeritus Marshall E. Dimock; Dr. Lyle C. Fitch, President, Institute of Public Administration; Professor Nesta M. Gallas, John Jay University; Bernard L. Gladieux, Consultant; General Andrew J. Goodpaster, Superintendent, U.S. Military Academy; Matthew Holden, Jr., Commissioner, Federal Energy Regulatory Commission; Professor Tobe Johnson, Political Science Dept., Morehouse College; Dr. Robert R. Nathan, President, Robert R. Nathan Associates; Dr. James ("Dolph") Norton, Institute of

Government, University of Virginia; Elsa A. Porter, Assistant Secretary for Administration, Department of Commerce; Dean Don K. Price, John F. Kennedy School of Government, Harvard University; Professor Emmette S. Redford, Ashbel Smith Professor of Government and Public Affairs, University of Texas; Professor Wendell G. Schaeffer, Herman Brown Professor of Political Science, Texas Christian University; Harvey Sherman, Director, Port Authority of New York and New Jersey; Professor Donald C. Stone, Carnegie-Mellon University; Dr. Jule M. Sugarman, Deputy Director, Office of Personnel Management; Dr. David B. Walker, Assistant Director, Advisory Commission on Intergovernmental Relations; Graham Watt, County Administrator, Fort Lauderdale, Florida; James E. Webb, Attorney at Law, Washington, D.C.; and Professor York Wilbern, University Professor of Government, Indiana University.

Special thanks must go to Professor Frederick C. Mosher, University of Virginia, and Nathan Laks and Emily Granrud, editors at Holmes & Meier Publishers, for originating and sustaining my interest in this project as well as to my faculty colleagues at George Mason University, Professors Robert Clark and Harold Gortner, for their helpful suggestions and support on this volume. Deborah Marriott provided the invaluable labor for much of the manuscript typing and preparation.

Ultimately, the final product must remain the author's responsibility. It is hoped that readers may find this volume and its selected documents useful, instructive, and of assistance to their understanding of modern Public Administration.

PART I

Postwar Patterns of Organization and Management in the Public Sector: Ways of Doing the People's Business

Postwar Patterns of Organization and Management in the Public Sector: Ways of Doing the People's Business

In the thirty-year period between 1950 and 1981, annual federal government expenditures jumped from 70 billion dollars to almost 700 billion or a tenfold increase. This dramatic expansion in the scope, content, and level of American governmental activities was fueled by two decisive changes, which Samuel P. Huntington calls "The Defense Shift" and "Welfare Shift."[1] The first occurred in the late 1940s and early 1950s and spawned a rapid rise in defense expenditures necessitated by both the perceived and very real threats of Soviet expansionism abroad. Between 1948 and 1953 defense expenditures grew from 20 percent to 28 percent of the nation's total Gross National Product (GNP). The rise of these expenditures resulted from the new varieties of foreign and military aid spent to meet Soviet challenges overseas through such instruments as the Marshall Plan, the North Atlantic Treaty Organization, armed troop interventions in Korea, and the Berlin airlift. The level and pattern of this international security involvement continued throughout the Eisenhower and Kennedy administrations as America became increasingly involved in Vietnam.

However, a second surge of expenditures resulted from President Johnson's "Great Society" and Richard Nixon's "New Federalism," which fueled, in Huntington's words, "the Welfare Shift." Rapidly, new forms of categorical grants, block grants, and general revenue sharing monies exploded over a broad range of domestic social fields such as education, job training, health, housing, and other public services. Between 1965 and 1974 nondefense expenditures rose from 20 percent of the GNP to 27 percent (and defense expenditures dropped to 6 percent of the GNP in 1974). In 1953 at the height of the Korean buildup, defense accounted for nearly one-half of the federal budget; by 1972 it was only 15 percent of the total. The federal government further witnessed a precipitous decline in its total share of overall public expenditures vis-à-vis states and localities. In 1960 the

---

1. Samuel P. Huntington, "The United States" in Michael Crozier, *The Crisis of Democracy* (New York: New York University Press, 1975).

federal share accounted for 59.7 percent of the total (virtually the same percentage it had been since 1950), but that figure dropped to less than half of total governmental outlays by 1980 due to the mushrooming social expenditures at the local levels.

Both the Defense Shift—(due to external foreign threats) and the Welfare Shift (due to internal social demands) promulgated numerous new public programs at all levels of government. How were these programs organized and administered in the postwar era? What ways were selected to do "the people's business" in an era that sharply increased in an unprecedented manner the level and scope of public activities?

While numerous patterns of public sector organization and management were discussed in postwar scholarly and popular literature, a surprisingly limited range of basic patterns of public sector organization and management were put into actual practice during this era:

First, there was the continuation of what many specialists in the field refer to simply as the "classical orthodox model." The classical model was articulated in its clearest and most persuasive format in the pre-World War II era by the Brownlow Commission Report (The Report of the President's Committee on Administrative Management, 1937).[2] Its basic theme was that the "President needs help" and that he should be given the management tools as the "General Manager of Government" to manage the executive branch in a positive and effective manner. This argument translated into a series of recommendations: (1) strengthening the president's staff in the areas of budgeting, personnel, and planning; (2) limiting his span of control by integrating a diverse range of programs and activities under a dozen major cabinet departments; (3) vesting the president with greater authority to reorganize government and (4) extending civil service "upward" and "downward" throughout public employment. The classical model fundamentally believed in the efficacy of a strong chief executive—à la Alexander Hamilton—one expected to do a big job for a big nation.

While the classical model was never as forcefully nor as clearly articulated in the documents of the postwar period as in the "Brownlow Report" (found in Mosher's *Basic Documents*), certainly documents contained in Part I of this book reveal that there were several postwar "classical offspring" of Brownlow. None was more effusive of this classical perspective than the massive Hoover Commission Report produced in the late 1940s by several task forces of prominent experts under the leadership of former President Hoover. As Herman Finer pointed out some time ago, "The Hoover Commission and many of its collaborators are Mr.

2. Richard Polenberg, *Reorganizing Roosevelt's Government: The Controversy over Executive Reorganization, 1936–1939* (Cambridge: Harvard University Press, 1966).

3. Herman Finer, "The Hoover Commission Reports," *Political Science Quarterly* (September 1949), p. 412.

Brownlow's children . . ."³ Brownlow's ideas permeated other prominent postwar documents as well. President Eisenhower's message to Congress in 1953 advocated the creation of a new "super-cabinet department" of Health, Education, and Welfare (HEW), and later the President's Task Force on Governmental Reorganization in 1964 (the "Price Report") made significant recommendations to President Johnson for organizing the Great Society programs. Both reflected important attributes of classical perspectives. Both called for rationalizing hierarchical lines of control of the bureaucracy, reducing the number of agencies reporting to the chief executive, strengthening administrative oversight capabilities of the chief executive, and fundamentally improving managerial economy and effectiveness. Certainly one could find many, many other examples of classical doctrine outlined by government publications, but these three postwar documents expressed classical ideals in a most sophisticated and influencial form.

A second important managerial pattern for public sector enterprises might be termed "the coordinative model," that is, the development of intergovernmental councils to serve as arenas for discussion, bargaining, negotiation, development, resolution, and implementation of policy. On the national level, the National Security Council (NSC) created by the National Security Act of 1947 was an early and highly successful example of this coordinative model (see Frederick C. Mosher's *Basic Documents of American Public Administration, 1776–1950,* for the National Security Act). NSC has proved to be one of the most influencial bodies for formulating America's international security policies at the highest levels of federal government. However, this managerial approach achieved its broadest and most pervasive application on the intergovernmental level in the United States. The establishment of the Advisory Commission on Intergovernmental Relations in 1959, the creation of Councils of Governments (COGs) in virtually all metropolitan areas of the United States by 701 federal grants, and the regionalized clearance process developed by Bureau of the Budget Circular A–95 (1969) institutionalized this style of management at the very heart of American government. Reorganization Plan 2 of 1970, based on Nixon's Advisory Council on Executive Organization (the Ash Council's) recommendation, also exemplified important attributes of this coordinative model.

A third model, the "neoclassical model"—something of a mixture of the classical and coordinative models—used executive staff members for "pushing" targeted programs and activities that have high priority on the president's agenda. Of course, this neoclassical managerial approach is not new to postwar America. One finds many prewar examples in, say, President Woodrow Wilson's use of Colonel Edward House in World War I or President Franklin Roosevelt's reliance upon Harry Hopkins or former Justice James Byrnes in numerous capacities throughout his tenure in office. However, what is *new* is the explicit and enthusiastic justification *for* this manner of doing the public business in this manner in some postwar documents. One can find the most lively and persuasive argument for this approach in the Final Report of the President's Task Force on Governmental Organization (Heineman Commission Report, 1967).

On the opposite end of the "managerial spectrum" is the "decentralized model." This fourth public management model stresses "grass-roots" participation of the citizenry at the lowest levels of government in the planning, formulation, development, and implementation of public policies that affect their lives. So, the theory runs, the best way to organize and manage public affairs is through close, direct, active, and continued involvement of the citizenry in policies affecting their lives. While there have long been strong tendencies toward Jeffersonian "home rule" in America dating from colonial New England "town meetings," the 1960s and early 1970s saw a fresh resurgence of this participatory enthusiasm. The Economic Opportunity Act of 1964 was perhaps the best reflection of this particular mode of governance with its primary requirements placed upon "maximum feasible participation" of the concerned local residents. Later block grant programs like the Law Enforcement Assistance Act (1968) and the Comprehensive Employment Training Act (1972) or the State and Local Fiscal Assistance Act (1972) (Revenue Sharing Act) that funnelled federal funds directly to states and localities were justified on much the same grounds (though not necessarily for the same results) of getting key public decisions made back "at the grass roots" (see Part III of this volume for a discussion of revenue sharing).

The fifth model of public management used in government might best be termed "the corporate model." Here organization and management is patterned after the ideal of the modern business corporation. Again, the corporate ideal, like Jeffersonian home rule, has had a long historical tradition and strong attraction in America. In part, the appeal of the corporate design has been due to the public's association of the term *business* with the three *e*'s—efficiency, economy, and effectiveness. Whatever the reasons, the attraction to using business models for doing the public's business grew after the turn of the century. The rise of council-manager government across America is a good example of the widespread grass-roots appeal of this corporate ideal. The ideal was equally potent at the federal level with the creation by Congress of more than forty government corporations prior to 1945. While government corporations come in many varieties today—from the Communication Satellite Corporation (COMSAT), a private for-profit government corporation, to the Inter-American Foundation, a wholly government controlled and financed not-for-profit corporation for promoting inter-American cooperation—they contain common elements such as an attempt to set up a separate organization free from government oversight, authority derived from an independent board of directors, a degree of independence from federal budgetary, personnel, and other statutory requirements that are common for most public organizations. These and other elements of their uniqueness are outlined in the Government Corporation Control Act of 1945 (found in Mosher's *Basic Documents*), which sought to standardize their operations and is still the basic law today outlining their fundamental organizational structure and procedures.[4]

THE "CLASSICAL MODEL"

1. *Report of the Commission on Organization of the Executive Branch of the Government* (First Hoover Commission Report, 1949)

The massive growth of the federal government, stimulated in large part during World War II, led to a postwar reaction by a Republican-controlled Congress—to cut back the size of the federal government. In 1947 Congress passed the Lodge-Brown Act creating a commission to study the executive branch in order to "limit expenditures," "eliminate duplication," and "consolidate services" and "abolish services." The commission, under the direction of former President Herbert Hoover, was composed of twelve members, with equal representation from the two political parties as well as a balanced number from the government and business worlds. Its major work was done by twenty-four task forces that focused upon twenty-four of the most critical problem areas deemed important by the commission. After sixteen months of work, the task forces produced a multivolume, 2.5-million-word collection of facts, figures, and recommendations—perhaps the most ambitious and thorough review of the executive branch ever undertaken. In the end, the Hoover Commission had a remarkably high success rate in that more than two-thirds of its recommendations were eventually implemented. Furthermore, it stimulated the establishment of many "little Hoover Commissions" in states and cities across the nation. The introduction to the Hoover Commission Report offers quite succinctly its basic philosophical perspectives by articulating clearly its "classical orthodox management" frame of reference.

2. *Creation of the Department of Health, Education, and Welfare (1953)*

HEW was the second so-called superdepartment created in the federal government (the first being the Department of Defense) that merged many disparate federal agencies. In this case, agencies involved with matters of health, education,

---

4. For an outstanding discussion of the varieties and complexities of public corporations, see LLoyd D. Musolf and Harold Seidman, "The Blurred Boundaries of Public Administration," *Public Administration Review* (March/April 1980), pp. 124–130. For an excellent overall discussion relative to the significance of organization and management to the "outcomes" of federal programs, read Harold Seidman, *Politics, Position and Power* (3rd ed.) New York: Oxford University Press, 1980).

and welfare were brought into the giant "umbrella organization" of HEW. Reorganization Plan No. 1 submitted by President Eisenhower early in his first term created this new cabinet-level department. The president's message to Congress covering the transmittal of the Reorganization Plan that is contained here in Part I justifies the reorganization on very distinctly "classical" grounds: that is, "to give leadership in the Departmental organization and management activities" and "to centralize services and activities common to the several agencies of the Department." The "superdepartment" model has in recent years continued to be a popular form of federal government organization.

3. *Report of the President's Task Force on Government Reorganization* ("Price Report," 1964)

Prior to the 1964 election President Lyndon Johnson assembled a group of distinguished public administration scholars headed by Dean Don K. Price of Harvard University to examine the federal government organization with an eye to implementing most effectively the president's Great Society programs. As the introduction to the Price Report indicates in the opening sentence, "The primary issue of organization . . . is how to focus the efforts of the government and the attention of the country on the purpose of building the Great Society." Reminiscent of the Brownlow Report (see Mosher's *Basic Documents of American Public Administration, 1776–1950*) the Price Report endorsed the president's programs unequivocally. The report sought the organizational means to put them into action most effectively. The report saw the president as "A General Manager" of government, but it also emphasized that operation of the federal programs should be left to several key new cabinet-level departments in order better to focus the implementation of important aspects of the president's agenda. Apparent in this influencial and well-written report were many classical themes of rationalized lines of authority, a limitation on the chief executive's span of control, a generalized management role for the president, a concern that operational details should be left to line agencies. Many of the report's recommendations were eventually implemented, several long after Johnson and his Great Society were gone.

THE "COORDINATIVE MODEL"

4. *The Commission on Intergovernmental Relations* "Kestnbaum Report," June 1955)

5. *The Act to Establish an Advisory Commission on Intergovernmental Relations*, (September 24, 1959)

6. *Washington, D.C., Metropolitan Region*, (June 27, 1960)

The decade of the 1950s was an especially rich period for intergovernmental innovation. The Kestnbaum Commission (named for its chairman, Meyer Kestnbaum) was created by President Eisenhower in 1953, in the words of the president, "to study the means of achieving a sounder relationship between Federal, State and local governments." The "Kestnbaum Report," released June 1955, though "conservative" in its tone and approach (at least by today's standards) was well written, thoughtful, and well received when it was published. It essentially called for using the level of government closest to the community for public functions it can handle "and utilizing operative intergovernmental arrangements where appropriate to attain economical performance and popular approval. . . ." One of its most important specific recommendations was that "an advisory board on Intergovernment Relations should be appointed on a permanent basis." Within four years Congress created the permanent "Advisory Commission on Intergovernmental Relations" (ACIR) in order to gain the "fullest cooperation and coordination of activities between levels of government" and "to give continuing attention to intergovernmental problems." ACIR's members represent equal portions of representatives from federal, state, and local units of government. Over the years since its creation, ACIR has played a key role in the identification of critical intergovernmental problems, the development of policy solutions to these issues as well as offering innovative collaborative efforts in terms of technical assistance for various levels of government. Of equal importance during the late 1950s, with the encouragement of the Kestnbaum study and 701 grants, the first metropolitan regions were established, the first in Washington, D.C. Today, all metropolitan areas in the United States have Councils of Governments (COGs), following the Washington, D.C., pattern. COGs play an important "brokering" role at the local level by providing common forums for various representatives of governmental units within metropolitan regions to meet, discuss, plan and decide upon a wide range of issues affecting the development of their regions.

7. *Bureau of the Budget Circular A–95* (July 24, 1969)

The proliferation of Great Society domestic programs coupled with the increasing problems associated with coordination *between* these new federal programs at both the field and headquarters levels led to the adoption of Bureau of the Budget (BOB) Circular A–95 in July 1969. This circular established critically new procedures for "project notification and review." The A–95 proposal was first put forward by several Brookings Institution scholars concerned with the effective implementation of the Great Society, but the circular was drafted and signed by the first budget director of the Nixon administration, Robert P. Mayo, who viewed the proposal more as a means to reduce costs, duplication, and overlapping federal services than as a way to implement the Great Society. The circular required state and regional plans for social programs within their regional areas and created metropolitan, statewide, and regional "clearinghouses" to insure that future program development using federal funds would be in accordance with these plans. The clearinghouses were also to provide regular reports on the progress of the development and coordination between governmental projects. Circular A–95 remains in place today as an important and highly successful "coordinative" device for federal-state-local program implementation and planning.[5]

8. *Reorganization Plan No. 2 of 1970,* (March 12, 1970)

Early in his new administration, President Richard Nixon became enormously impressed with Henry Kissinger's vigorous leadership and oversight of foreign policy matters as a presidential assistant heading the National Security Council. The NSC had been created in Title I of the National Security Act of 1947 (with important amendments in 1949). The NSC Act designated the makeup of the council, which was to be composed of senior civilian officials in government who would provide overall direction and coordination to national security affairs. According to the act, the NSC "shall advise the President with respect to the integration of domestic, foreign and military policy relating to national security. . . ." While every president since Harry Truman used the NSC extensively, Henry Kissinger brought it to the highest pinnacles of influence in giving decisive direction of United States foreign policy from the White House during Nixon's first term. Might this coordinative mechanism be applied with equal success to domestic affairs?

The president appointed an Advisory Council on Executive Organization, under the chairmanship of Roy Ash, then president of Litton Industries, to come up with the answer. The Ash council's proposals, which were incorporated in Nixon's Reorganization Plan No. 2 issued on March 12, 1970, created the Domestic Council and changed the Bureau of the Budget (BOB) into the Office of Management and Budget (OMB). The creation of the new Domestic Council, combined with the upgrading of OMB's responsibilities to include *management* as well as budgetary oversight, was explained in the words of the Reorganization Plan No. 2—"The Domestic Council will be primarily concerned with *what* we do, the Office of Management and Budget will be primarily concerned with *how* we do it, and *how well* we do it." The plan further explicitly pointed out that the Domestic Council would be "a domestic counterpart of the National Security Council." Every President since Richard Nixon has utilized *both* the Domestic Council and OMB to

5. Harvey C. Mansfield, "Federal Executive Reorganization: Thirty Years of Experience," *Public Administration Review* (July/August 1969), p. 342.

provide direction, leadership, and coordination over a broad range of domestic policy issues—though their influence has tended to wax and wane according to each president's individual emphases and interests in these matters. Recently the Domestic Council was renamed Office of Policy Development, which retains essentially the same functions as the Domestic Council.

THE "NEOCLASSICAL MODEL"

9. The Organization and Management of Great Society Programs, A Final Report of the President's Task Force on Government Organization, ("Heineman Report," June 15, 1967)

Within a few years after the start of the Great Society programs, enormously complex organizational problems began to appear—disunity of purpose, fragmentation of activities, lack of coordination and control of programs. President Johnson commissioned a major examination of these organization and management issues by appointing a presidential commission chaired by industrialist Ben W. Heineman and composed of several prominent leaders from the New Frontier–Great Society era including McGeorge Bundy, Charles Schultze, Robert McNamara, and Kermit Gordon. Their report, which was highly critical of the implementation of the Great Society programs, was never released due to the approaching 1968 presidential campaign. While the report therefore had little impact upon restructuring government, the Heineman Report did uniquely recommend "a neo-classical" approach to organization and management of the executive branch with its call for the creation of an Office of Program Coordination within the Executive Office of the President to "mediate and settle disputes," "to spur and insure cooperation," "to provide a focal point" for "pushing" the president's programs—in short, key White House staff aides to "move" the president's targeted programs into action at the local level; i.e., a combination of the "classical" and "coordinative" management models.

THE "DECENTRALIZED MODEL"

10. The Economic Opportunity Act of 1964

One of the most novel—or, at the very least, different—approaches to public organization and management was contained in the Economic Opportunity Act of 1964 (EOA). The EOA was the centerpiece of Johnson's "War on Poverty" and included several important social programs such as Head Start, Job Corps, and Neighborhood Youth Corps. The unusual managerial feature central to EOA was its insistence upon "community action" in order to "provide stimulation and incentives for urban and rural communities to mobilize their resources to combat poverty . . ." In essence, "community action" was defined in Title II of EOA as "the maximum feasible participation of residents of the areas and members of the groups served. . . ." Federal funds were to be channeled through the states, generally on the basis of population or need, and the local "lead agencies" could be designated from public, private, or nonprofit organizations. Overall direction from Washington came from the Office of Economic Opportunity, but from its beginning, the emphasis of EOA was upon "grassroots participation" in program planning, development, direction, and implementation.

This grass-roots concept for EOA grew out of the work of Paul Ylvisaker, director of the Public Affairs Department at the Ford Foundation, as well as of Richard Cloward and Lloyd Ohlin at the Columbia University's School of Social Work in the late 1950s and was translated into public policy recommendations by President Kennedy's Committee on Youth, Crime, and Delinquency and later EOA in the 1960s. The concept of "Maximum Feasible Participation" generated considerable political and scholarly debate during the 1960s and became a central element of other federal programs such as "model cities" during this decade.[6] While little in the way of the EOA's "neighborhood governance" concept remains in practice today (at least on the federal level), several of the social programs begun by EOA, such as Job Corps and Head Start, continue as viable federal programs. However, later block grant and federal revenue sharing programs were designed in part to "decentralize" national program decision making down to the grass roots, thus continuing in a different format the "decentralized model" of public management.

6. For two lively discussions of this act, read Daniel P. Moynihan, *Maximum Fesible Misunderstanding: Community Action in the War on Poverty* (New York: Free Press, 1969) and Peter Marris and Martin Rein, *Dilemmas of Social Reform: Poverty and Community Action in the United States,* 2nd ed. (Chicago: Aldine Publishers, 1973).

1. Report of the Commission on Organization of the Executive Branch of the Government (Introduction to the First Hoover Commission Report, 1949)

In this part of its report, the Commission on Organization of the Executive Branch of the Government deals with the essentials of effective organization of the executive branch. Without these essentials, all other steps to improve organization and management are doomed to failure.

The President, and under him his chief lieutenants, the department heads, must be held responsible and accountable to the people and the Congress for the conduct of the executive branch.

Responsibility and accountability are impossible without authority—the power to direct. The exercise of authority is impossible without a clear line of command from the top to the bottom, and a return line of responsibility and accountability from the bottom to the top.

The wise exercise of authority is impossible without the aids which staff institutions can provide to assemble facts and recommendations upon which judgment may be made and to supervise and report upon the execution of decisions.

Definite authority at the top, a clear line of authority from top to bottom, and adequate staff aids to the exercise of authority do not exist. Authority is diffused, lines of authority are confused, staff services are insufficient. Consequently, responsibility and accountability are impaired.

To remedy this situation is the first and essential step in the search for efficiency and economy in the executive branch of the Federal Government.

The critical state of world affairs requires the Government of the United States to speak and act with unity of purpose, firmness, and restraint in dealing with other nations. It must act decisively to preserve its human and material resources. It must develop strong machinery for the national defense, while seeking to construct an enduring world peace. It cannot perform these tasks if its organization for development and execution of policy is confused and disorderly, or if the Chief

Introduction to the Report of The Commission on Organization of the Executive Branch of the Government (Washington, D.C.; U.S. Government Printing Office, 1949), chapter 1, "General Management of the Executive Branch." pp. 3–8.

Executive is handicapped in providing firm direction to the departments and agencies.

If disorder in the administrative machinery makes the executive branch of the Government work at cross purposes within itself, the Nation as a whole must suffer. It must suffer—if its several programs conflict with each other and executive authority becomes confused—from waste in the expenditure of public funds, and from the lack of national unity that results from useless friction.

An energetic and unified executive is not a threat to free and responsible government, as Alexander Hamilton pointed out in "The Federalist" (No. 70). He declared that the ingredients of "safety in the republican sense" are "first, a due dependence on the people; secondly, a due responsibility." Strength and unity in an executive make clear who is responsible for faults in administration and thus enable the legislature better to enforce accountability to the people.

FINDINGS

The Commission has found that violation of these principles results from the conditions stated in the following findings.

FIRST FINDING. The executive branch is not organized into a workable number of major departments and agencies which the President can effectively direct, but is cut up into a large number of agencies, which divide responsibility and which are too great in number for effective direction from the top.

Thousands of Federal programs cannot be directed personally by the President. They must be grouped by related function and divided among a small number of principal assistants who are the heads of departments.

If the number gets too large, the President cannot control or supervise them. Yet, at the present time, we have a large number of agencies subject to no direction except that of the President. In many cases several agencies each have a small share in carrying out a single major policy which ought to be the responsibility of one department. Until these dispersed units are pulled together, and authority is placed in department heads as chief assistants to the President, there will be conflict, waste, and indecisiveness in administration.

SECOND FINDING. The line of command and supervision from the President down through his department heads to every employee, and the line of responsibility from each employee of the executive branch up to the President, has been weakened, or actually broken, in many places and in many ways.

That line of responsibility still exists in constitutional theory, but it has been worn away by administrative practices, by political pressures, and by detailed statutory provisions. Statutory powers often have been vested in subordinate officers in such a way as to deny authority to the President or a department head.

For example, the statute governing the sale of helium to a foreign nation gave the Secretary of the Interior the authority to control such sales regardless of the opinion of the President. The Corps of Engineers of the United States Army, in another case, has the statutory duty of preparing river development plans, and the Secretary of the Army is not responsible for its selection of projects.

Some administrative or operating tasks are given to boards instead of to single executives, and the President's authority to appoint and remove the members of those boards is restricted. The United States Maritime Commission, which has a high degree of independence as a Commission because of its regulatory functions, also has statutory authority to conduct a great business enterprise and to make executive decisions affecting our foreign policy.

On some occasions the responsibility of an official to his superior is obscured by laws which require him, before acting, to clear his proposals with others. This breaks the line of responsibility, and encourages indecision, lack of initiative, and irresponsibility.

THIRD FINDING. The President and the heads of departments lack the tools to frame programs and policies and to supervise their execution.

No executive, public or private, can manage a large and complex establishment without staff assistance. Staff agencies must keep the President informed on the way in which the various departmental programs are related to each other, assist in defining specific programs pursuant to the instructions of the Congress, and help him supervise the execution of these programs.

Staff agencies do this by helping the President control the common requirements of all Government programs—funds spent, legislation requested, personnel required, the relation of each program to others and to the national interest. The President's staff agencies can best help him by keeping in close touch with their counterparts in the departments.

Despite improvements during the past decade, these staff agencies are still less effective than they should be. Detailed recommendations on this subject appear in our report on The Executive Office of the President.

FOURTH FINDING. The Federal Government has not taken aggressive steps to build a corps of administrators of the highest level of ability with an interest in the program of the Government as a whole.

Recommendations on this subject appear in our report on Personnel Management.

FIFTH FINDING. Many of the statutes and regulations that control the administrative practices and procedures of the Government are unduly detailed and rigid.

It is impossible to secure efficiency of administration unless administrators have enough authority and discretion to seize opportunities for economical and effective operation. Present laws and regulations establish patterns so detailed and rigid that department heads are granted almost no operational discretion or flexibility necessary to give real effect to the purpose of the Congress.

Instead of being unified organizations, many departments and agencies are but loose federations of bureaus and subdivisions, each jealously defending its own jurisdiction. Department heads will not be able effectively to aid the President in the coordination of administration unless reorganizations produce unity and integration in fact as well as in appearance.

Recommendations on this problem appear in our report on Departmental Management.

SIXTH FINDING. Likewise, the budgetary processes of the Government need improvement, in order to express the objectives of the Government in terms of the work to be done rather than in mere classifications of expenditures.

Recommendations on budgeting are presented in our report on Budgeting and Accounting.

SEVENTH FINDING. The accounting methods in the executive branch require standardization and simplification and accounting activities require decentralization if they are to become effective tools of management and if great expense and waste are to be eliminated.

Accounting recommendations also are presented in our report on that subject.

EIGHTH FINDING. General administrative services for various operating agencies—such as purchasing of supplies, maintenance of records, and the operation of public buildings—are poorly organized or coordinated.

At present some of these services are unduly centralized. Decentralization to operating departments, under proper performance standards, would achieve improvements. Moreover, some of these services are illogically scattered among independent agencies, or located in subdivisions of executive departments.

Recommendations appear in our report on The Office of General Services.

SUMMARY

Any systematic effort to improve the organization and administration of the Government, therefore, must:

1. Create a more orderly grouping of the functions of Government into major departments and agencies under the President.

2. Establish a clear line of control from the President to these department and agency heads and from them to their subordinates with correlative responsibility from these officials to the President, cutting through the barriers which have in

many cases made bureaus and agencies partially independent of the Chief Executive.

3. Give the President and each department head strong staff services which should exist only to make executive work more effective, and which the President or department head should be free to organize at his discretion.

4. Develop a much greater number of capable administrators in the public service, and prepare them for promotion to any bureau or department in the Government where their services may be most effectively used.

5. Enforce the accountability of administrators by a much broader pattern of controls, so that the statutes and regulations which govern administrative practices will encourage, rather than destroy, initiative and enterprise.

6. Permit the operating departments and agencies to administer for themselves a larger share of the routine administrative services, under strict supervision and in conformity with high standards.

Only by taking these steps can the operations of the executive branch be managed effectively, responsibly, and eonomically.

2. Creation of the Department of Health, Education, and Welfare (March 12, 1953)

To the Congress of the United States:

I transmit herewith Reorganization Plan No. 1 of 1953, prepared in accordance with the provisions of the Reorganization Act of 1949, as amended.

In my message of February 2, 1953, I stated that I would send to the Congress a reorganization plan defining a new administrative status for Federal activities in health, education, and social security. This plan carries out that intention by creating a Department of Health, Education, and Welfare as one of the executive departments of the Government and by transferring to it the various units of the Federal Security Agency. The Department will be headed by a Secretary of Health, Education, and Welfare, who will be assisted by an Under Secretary and two Assistant Secretaries.

The purpose of this plan is to improve the administration of the vital health, education, and social-security functions now being carried on in the Federal Security Agency by giving them departmental rank. Such action is demanded by the importance and magnitude of these functions, which affect the well-being of millions of our citizens. The programs carried on by the Public Health Service include, for example, the conduct and promotion of research into the prevention and cure of such dangerous ailments as cancer and heart disease. The Public Health Service also administers payments to the States for the support of their health services and for urgently needed hospital construction. The Office of Education collects, analyzes, and distributes to school administrators throughout the country information relating to the organization and management of educational systems. Among its other functions is the provision of financial help to school districts burdened by activities of the United States Government. State assistance to the aged, the blind, the totally disabled, and dependent children is heavily supported by grants-in-aid administered through the Social Security Administration. The old-age and survivors insurance system and child development and welfare programs are additional responsibilities of that Administration. Other offices of the Federal Security Agency are responsible for the conduct of Federal vocational rehabilitation programs and for the enforcement of food and drug laws.

There should be an unremitting effort to improve those health, education, and

83rd Congress, 1st Session, *House Doc*. No. 102.

social-security programs which have proved their value. I have already recommended the expansion of the social-security system to cover persons not now protected, the continuation of assistance to school districts whose population has been greatly increased by the expansion of defense activities, and the strengthening of our food and drug laws.

But good intent and high purpose are not enough; all such programs depend for their success upon efficient, responsible administration. I have recently taken action to assure that the Federal Security Administrator's views are given proper consideration in executive councils by inviting her to attend meetings of the Cabinet. Now the establishment of the new Department provided for in Reorganization Plan No. 1 of 1953 will give the needed additional assurance that these matters will receive the full consideration they deserve in the whole operation of the Government.

This need has long been recognized. In 1923, President Harding proposed a Department of Education and Welfare, which was also to include health functions. In 1924, the Joint Committee on Reorganization recommended a new department similar to that suggested by President Harding. In 1932, one of President Hoover's reorganization proposals called for the concentration of health, education and recreational activities in a single executive department. The President's Committee on Administrative Management in 1937 recommended the placing of health, education, and social-security functions in a Department of Social Welfare. This recommendation was partially implemented in 1939 by the creation of the Federal Security Agency—by which action the Congress indicated its approval of the grouping of these functions in a single agency. A new department could not be proposed at that time because the Reorganization Act of 1939 prohibited the creation of additional executive departments. In 1949, the Commission on Organization of the Executive Branch of the Government proposed the creation of a department for social security and education.

The present plan will make it possible to give the officials directing the Department titles indicative of their responsibilities and salaries comparable to those received by their counterparts in other executive departments. As the Under Secretary of an executive department, the Secretary's principal assistant will be better equipped to give leadership in the Department's organization and management activities, for which he will be primarily responsible. The plan opens the way to further administrative improvement by authorizing the Secretary to centralize services and activities common to the several agencies of the Department. . . .

Dwight D. Eisenhower.

3. Report of the President's Task Force on Government Reorganization ("Price Report," 1964)

Introduction

The primary issue of organization, as we see it during your next term, is how to focus the efforts of the Government, and the attention of the country, on the purpose of building the Great Society. This must be done in a way which also assures that the public will receive full value for its tax dollars.

During the past two decades, we concentrated our national attention on problems of defense and international affairs. As we did so, we learned four big lessons in Government administration, which we may now apply to the domestic problems of the Nation:

(1) Government need no longer maintain a distant relationship with private institutions and corporations; it may enlist them in full cooperation, while taking care to maintain responsible control of policy and programs.

(2) Research and education are likely to be the key to new policy developments and new domestic policy opportunities.

(3) Most important programs require the cooperation of two or more departments and agencies and such teamwork requires, among other things, (a) the use of Presidential staff agencies, and (b) a system for higher personnel that assures responsiveness to new policy and program objectives.

(4) Effective, economical, and responsible Executive organization depends on the full cooperation of the Congress; internal Congressional organization and procedures can support or frustrate Presidential responsibility.

In order to apply these lessons to the organization of domestic programs, it is not necessary to set up another so-called Hoover Commission. In fact, that would be a mistake. The unhappy experience of the Eisenhower Administration with the second Hoover Commission shows that the planning of organization should be done in close relation to the determination of your policy goals. This has to be done within the circle of your responsible advisers—especially in the Bureau of the Budget and the rest of the Executive Office.

Unpublished document available in the Lyndon B. Johnson Papers at the University of Texas, Austin, Texas. Appendixes as well as other supplementary material omitted.

I. *Reorganization of Executive Departments and Agencies*

Reorganization is needed from time to time as the pace of economic, social, and technological progress leads to the adoption of new action programs for which the old structure is poorly suited. The new programs already recommended by the President, and those that you may recommend as a result of the other Task Forces' recommendations, will represent our national striving toward a society that will further the highest values of humane ideals on the basis of the most effective use of our intellectual and material resources.

New patterns of organization will be needed to symbolize the President's new policies; to mobilize institutional resources more effectively in their support; and to enable you to make more effective use of your political subordinates in seeing that the administrative system helps us reach our national goals.

For these purposes, we should maintain a reasonably clear distinction between the Executive Departments and other operating agencies, on the one hand, and the Executive Office of the President on the other.

The Executive Departments should be the major permanent operating subdivisions of the Executive Branch, set up to work toward broad public purposes involving major policy considerations. Other operating agencies, no matter how large and important, are likely each to be confined to somewhat restricted purposes or to temporary missions. The Secretaries of Departments should not only be the operating heads of these Departments, and to some extent their advocates, but they should also represent the general purposes of the President in contrast to the inevitably specialized interests of their career subordinates. Indeed, as members of the Cabinet, they should be concerned with the policies and political interests of the Administration as a whole. But it should be recognized that Department and agency heads (either individually or collectively) can not be expected invariably to look at their problems from a national or Presidential perspective.

Both Executive Departments and operating agencies are responsible to the President, but should also be accountable to the Congress for the discharge of functions vested directly in them by law.

The Executive Office of the President should contain those staff agencies which the President uses to help in formulating his policies and programs, and in supervising their execution. Their number should be kept to a minimum and, to the extent possible, their heads should be appointed without Senate confirmation. They should, however, be freely available to testify before the Congress. They should, nevertheless, not be accountable to the Congress in the same way (or at least to the same degree) as the operating Departments, since generally they do not administer programs which are assigned to them by law.

The main function of the Executive Office is to help the President manage the Executive Branch. He alone is the "General Manager." The Task Force emphatically rejects all proposals which would set up by statute another official as General

Manager or Assistant General Manager, e.g., the "Administrative Vice President," "Executive Vice President," and "First Secretary" proposals. Most such proposals are based on the hope that freeing the President from "administration" will permit him to concentrate on "policy." They miss the point that inability to control administration destroys control of policy, and they would therefore result in diluting the President's power to control the Executive Branch and would tend to encroach on his constitutional powers and duties.

On the other hand, the President may find it desirable to use the Vice President, and other high officers of the Executive Branch, to help him coordinate programs, or deal with special problems, in ways that go beyond their formal Constitutional or statutory duties. As long as such arrangements are not prescribed by statute, and therefore remain flexibly within the President's control, they can be extremely useful.

The recommendations that follow deal mainly with domestic activities. This is not because we think the international and military programs are now perfect. But their main problems are, we think, not of a kind that organization and reorganization can solve. Moreover, our main attention has been devoted for two decades to improving our national security programs, and in those fields Congress has granted the Executive a much higher degree of discretion than in the domestic programs, which now represent the main challenge to our political leadership.

We have not made recommendations for the sake of mere tidiness or conformity to logical distinctions, but only where we see a chance to advance in a practical way a major policy purpose. By our definition, for example, the Post Office Department should be not a Department but an agency without Cabinet status. But we think too little would be gained by a change to make it worth the President's trouble.

A. *New Major Purpose Executive Departments*

We recommend the creation of five new Executive Departments, each of which would make a significant contribution to the attainment of our national goals.

1. *DEPARTMENT OF TRANSPORTATION; AND A TRANSPORTATION REGU-LATORY COMMISSION:* A healthy economy in a private enterprise system requires an effective system of transportation, in which all elements develop in balance, each taking full advantage of technological progress. We have not developed such a system in part because the Federal Government, by dealing with various forms of transportation through separate agencies, has made it difficult to develop a coherent policy or a rational balance. To achieve a measure of "decontrol," with less regulation and less subsidy, we need unity of policy and more consistency in our various methods of regulation.

We therefore recommend

- (a) a new Department of Transportation, administering all functions (other than economic regulation) relating to the major forms of land, sea, and air transportation:
    - (1) the agencies or functions concerned with promotion, subsidy, service, and safety regulation; i.e., the Bureau of Public Roads, the Maritime Administration, the Coast Guard, and the Federal Aviation Agency, the safety and car service activities of the ICC, and the subsidy functions of the CAB; and whatever may be needed in the way of policy or planning staff to deal with problems relating to railroads.
    - (2) other agencies and functions, e.g., the Alaska Railroad, the Panama Canal Company (and the Canal Zone Government), the St. Lawrence Seaway Development Corporation, and the Great Lakes Pilotage Administration.
- (b) a new Transportation Regulatory Commission, to include the economic regulation functions of
    - (1) the Interstate Commerce Commission,
    - (2) the Federal Maritime Commission, and
    - (3) the Civil Aeronautics Board.

The Department should also be empowered to give policy direction on civil navigation projects to the Corps of Engineers, if the construction function is left with the Corps.

The Department of Transportation, by amalgamating the staffs for economic planning and for technological research from its component parts, should be able to deal in a more balanced way with all forms of transportation and with their interrelations. Thus it should be able to develop for the President a genuinely national transportation policy that could serve as a basis for regulatory decisions of the Transportation Regulatory Commission.

2. *DEPARTMENT OF EDUCATION:* The advancement of education and of the basic research programs that are carried on primarily in educational institutions is the keystone of our future progress. The Federal Government has become a major supporter of these purposes, but without having a comprehensive organization that could help the President develop a policy for them. We believe that the President will wish to develop a policy calling for a sharp increase in Federal support for education and research and a better balance among various elements of the program. Our recommendation of a Department of Education is based on that assumption.

Because the schools have been afraid of Federal domination, the Government has never had a comprehensive policy for the advancement of education and research. But it is unrealistic to think we can protect the freedom of education by pretending to ignore it. We need to organize in a manner that will simultaneously

—facilitate our understanding of the effect of Federal actions on the educational and research institutions of the Nation;

—help distinguish between broad policy decisions regarding financial support, which must be controlled by responsible Federal officials and by law, and subordinate decisions regarding the educational or scientific merit of projects, institutions, or individuals. (The latter decisions can and should be made with the participation of educational and research leaders in such a way that everyone will know that the Federal Government is not intruding politically on academic freedom.)

Our present excessive dispersion of organization has helped to bring about an unsound balance between

(a) higher education and elementary and secondary education: leadership of the universities has not accepted its responsibility for helping to raise the intellectual standards of elementary and secondary schools;

(b) the sciences and other areas of learning: our emphasis on research project grants for military and space purposes has led to disproportionate emphasis on technology by comparison with the humanities and the social sciences;

(c) research and teaching: we are flooding the university laboratories with money, while neglecting, by comparison, the teaching side of education at all levels.

We therefore recommend the creation of a Department of Education. We do not believe that it should be the only channel by which aid is given to educational and research institutions. Every major agency will need to have its own programs of research and education, and many will need to support basic research. But a Department is warranted in order to help deal with the fundamental policies of aid to State and private institutions and to the general advancement of knowledge as the basis of national progress.

The proposed Department should not include the agencies devoted mainly to big operational programs depending on applied technology (like AEC and NASA); nor should it include their subsidiary programs of basic research or fellowships. The Office of Science and Technology will still be required, just as much as at present, to help coordinate these programs with those of the Department of Education.

The Department should include

(a) the Office of Education, whose removal would leave a Department to be known as the Department of Health and Welfare;

(b) any program that can be adopted for the support of the humanities;

(c) the National Science Foundation;

(d) the education and basic research programs of the National Institutes of Health, which have become the largest supporter of basic research in our universities; (This would include most of the grant-making programs and some of the "in-house" research; the Public Health Service should retain the applied research specifically directed toward its requirements, including some grant-supported projects as well as "in-house research. The division could be made by the Bureau of the Budget with the advice of the Director of OST.)

(e) certain bureaus or agencies, or constituents thereof, whose programs of education or basic research are not undertaken in specific support of an operating agency's mission: the National Bureau of Standards and the Smithsonian Institution (including its artistic and cultural subdivisions, such as the John F. Kennedy Center for the Performing Arts, as well as its scientific programs);

(f) the National Council on the Arts;

(g) certain minor educational responsibilities of HEW, e.g., with respect to Howard University, Gallaudet College, and educational television.

The present Board of the National Science Foundation, and the statutory Advisory Councils of the NIH, should be abolished. The Secretary should continue to use independent panels of outside advisors, like those that in both NSF and NIH make judgments of scientific or institutional merit in allocating grants.

With respect to the formulation of recommendations regarding the balance of different aspects of the total program, and the emphasis to be put on one level of education, or one field of knowledge, or one method of support, as compared with others, the Secretary should make use of less formal and less officially representative advisory groups, as well as the staff resources of the Federal Government.

3. DEPARTMENT OF HOUSING AND COMMUNITY DEVELOPMENT: The Nation is now too heavily urbanized to put all Federal programs affecting cities in a single department. However, a Department of Housing and Community Development should be constituted under which would be administered major programs relating to the physical development of our towns and cities, especially in metropolitan areas, and other programs for raising the quality and quantity of our housing.

Cabinet-level leadership is necessary to give these programs unified direction and coordinated administration. The establishment of a Department of Housing and Community Development would also serve to emphasize the importance of a healthy urban environment to the welfare of the people.

The proposed department would include the following programs and functions:

(a) All those now in HHFA (including housing, urban renewal, and other community development functions).

(b) The functions of the Federal Home Loan Bank Board (including direction of the Federal Savings and Loan Insurance Corporation), but only if it is feasible to replace the present Board with a single administrator appointed by the Secretary or to make the Secretary Chairman of the Board.

(c) The housing loan and guarantee functions of the Veterans' Administration.

(d) Home loans, loans for housing for the elderly, and loans for the construction of community water supply systems from the Farmers' Home Administration.

(e) Grants for the construction of waste treatment facilities from the Department of Health, Education, and Welfare.

4. *DEPARTMENT OF ECONOMIC DEVELOPMENT:* To develop our economy and spread prosperity more widely, the Government must be organized so as

—to further the initiative and the responsibilities of private business and of state and local institutions;

—to make use of education and research to enable the Nation, and all its citizens, to develop to their highest potential, and to offset the tendency of automation to increase unemployment;

—to insure that areas of the country with special problems such as:
economic depression
high unemployment rates
pockets of poverty
widespread natural disaster
receive assistance designed to remedy such conditions.

Such a program will require extensive collaboration among various Departments and agencies, but it should be led by the principal Executive Department that is concerned with the general economic development of the Nation.

For this reason, we recommend the creation of a Department of Economic Development, to comprise

(a) The Office of Economic Opportunity, which should carry with it responsibility for arranging and monitoring (with the support of the Executive Office) the cooperation of other departments and agencies in various aspects of the broad economic opportunity and anti-poverty program, especially those now carried on in HEW, Labor, and Agriculture.

(b) The Department of Commerce, on the assumption that its transportation components will have been transferred to the proposed Department of Transportation. Thus the new Department would include not only the older programs of Commerce relating to the general encouragement of business and industry, but also the new programs designed to further specific types of economic development:

    (1) the Area Redevelopment Administration;

    (2) the Public Works Acceleration program;

    (3) the Appalachian Regional Development program, if enacted; and

    (4) The Alaska Reconstruction and Development program.

(c) The Small Business Administration.

If the creation of such a Department is not immediately feasible, for either political or administrative reasons, we recommend the creation of an Agency for Economic Development, into which would be incorporated

(a) the Office of Economic Opportunity;

(b) the four economic development programs in the Department of Commerce, listed above;

(c) the Small Business Administration.

We would then recommend the subsequent merger of this Agency with the Department of Commerce, under the title Department of Economic Development.

At some later date, we believe that it would be desirable to merge the present Department of Labor with the proposed Department of Economic Development. The separation of the Commerce and Labor Departments, originally established as one, has been justified by the conflict between management and labor, and the need to give each a Department to represent it. That concept is obsolete in theory, and has been growing more obsolete in practice.

A minority on our Task Force believes that the Housing and Community Development activities should also be incorporated in the proposed Department of Economic Development. The majority disagreed, but all concurred that the relation of specific community development programs to the broader economic development activities requires special attention, and special procedures to guarantee coordination, and that the question of a possible merger should be reconsidered at some future date.

5. *DEPARTMENT OF NATURAL RESOURCES:* The unique American system of agricultural education and research, plus the conservation and development of our land and water resources, have helped to make the Nation highly productive.

But this productivity has been accompanied by the wasteful use of resources, by continuing rural poverty, by the pollution of our water and atmosphere, and by the destruction of natural beauty.

We need a more rational program to conserve and utilize our resources, to diffuse the benefits of scientific progress, and to protect the heritage of natural beauty. Such a program will require a consolidation of competing organizations.

We therefore recommend the creation of a Department of Natural Resources, which would be a merger of parts of Agriculture and Interior, together with the aspects of the civil functions of the Army Engineers that pertain to resource development.

This proposal is one that, in various forms, has been considered by Presidents for several decades, and always considered politically unfeasible. We recognize the difficulties and while unanimous in presenting the above recommendation, we have not been unanimous in our ideas about the detailed way in which it might be carried out. We have agreed, however, on three ideas that may serve as guides in considering the problem.

(a) The distinction between the rural and the urban areas of the Nation is becoming less clear, and future technological developments will make it even less clear in the future. We therefore do not believe that the distinction between rural and urban affairs will in the long run be a useful basis for organizing Government programs or Departments.

(b) The programs for the development of natural resources ought to be in a single Department.

(c) In the long run, the other functions of the present Agriculture and Interior Departments might better be assigned to various other Departments with related functions.

The difficulties with respect to deciding how those functions should be selected and distributed led our Task Force to propose two alternative solutions to the creation of a Department of Natural Resources.

ALTERNATIVE 1:   to merge the Departments of Agriculture and the Interior. Such a merger would make it possible to

(a) relate the various agencies planning water resources development more effectively to those planning land resources development;

(b) relate such physical plans to economic and social considerations; e.g., the crop support and marketing programs;

(c) relate both technical and economic purposes to those of maintaining natural beauty and recreational opportunity, and strengthen efforts to prevent the pollution of the environment;

(d) to make better use of the scientific and educational resources of the land-grant colleges, which have nearly worked themselves out of an agricultural job, on new aspects of our broad problems of natural resources and rural life.

ALTERNATIVE 2: to leave the Department of Agriculture in existence and convert the Department of the Interior into a Department of Natural Resources by transferring to it from Agriculture the water resources functions of the Soil Conservation Service, and the Forest Service.

Either alternative should include the transfer

—from the Federal Power Commission, of functions related to water resources which are not integral parts of its regulatory functions.

—from the Army Engineers, those aspects of their civil functions that pertain to resource development. To this latter end, we would prefer the outright transfer of the statutory responsibility for the planning and construction of public works relating to rivers and harbors, flood control, navigation, water power, and irrigation. Another possible course would be to leave the work of detailed engineering design and contracting for construction with the Corps of Engineers, but to transfer to the new Department responsibility for the economic analysis of competing opportunities, the control over policies, the decisions on the location and type of works to be built, their funding, and the actual management of completed projects.

Economic and technical trends are clearly forcing a reduction in our rural population. To this end, in the long run, programs of a welfare, housing, or business nature should not be in the Department of Natural Resources, as envisaged in Alternative 1, above, which would have a vested interest in impeding the movement of population. Instead they should be transferred gradually to the Departments of Health and Welfare, of Housing and Community Development, and of Economic Development.

The determination of the specific functions which should be left in the proposed Department should be made after further study by the Bureau of the Budget.

As for the present Interior Department, the following of its present activities should be transferred from the proposed Department of Natural Resources:

—to the Department of Health and Welfare, the Bureau of Indian Affairs and the Office of Territories;

—to the proposed Department of Transportation, the Alaska Railroad.

B. *Other Reorganization Measures*

Two other reorganizations and the transfer or abolition of certain independent agencies are also recommended.

1. *ATOMIC ENERGY COMMISSION:*   This is the only major agency organized to deal with a field of technology rather than to carry out a major purpose. As a result, the AEC has been exceptionally effective in pushing that field aggressively, with the encouragement and support of the Joint Committee on Atomic Energy.

As a means of dealing with an unknown and terrifying new field, this system of management was justified. But it is impossible to judge this aspect of technology in fair competition with other technological means toward various purposes—whether in the fields of weapons, of power, or of international technical assistance.

At some future time—surely in the long run, perhaps in the near future—it may be desirable to abolish the AEC and to transfer its various functions to the Departments and agencies with related functions (e.g., Defense, Interior or its successor, Federal Power Commission, etc.). In the immediate future, the AEC should be changed to an agency headed by a single administrator instead of a Commission, as most of its own members have been convinced in recent years.

2. *BANK SUPERVISION:*   The present system in which three Federal agencies examine and supervise banks has led to intolerable conflict and confusion, and to a disposition on the part of the banks to play one set of examiners off against the other. We recommend the creation of a single Federal organization for bank supervision under a new Assistant Secretary of the Treasury for Bank Supervision through:

(a) Abolition of the Office of the Comptroller of the Currency and assignment of its functions to the Assistant Secretary;

(b) Transfer to the Secretary of the Treasury and delegation to the Assistant Secretary of the bank examining and supervision functions of the Federal Reserve Board; and

(c) Replacement of the Board of Directors of the FDIC by a General Manager who would be the Assistant Secretary.

3. *TRANSFER OR ABOLITION OF AGENCIES:*   A large number of independent agencies presently report to the President without, apparently, presenting him with serious burdens or organizational difficulties. However, it is both unnecessary and unrealistic to hold the President responsible for overseeing the operation of almost 70 executive departments and agencies. Accordingly, reconsideration of the separate status of such agencies from time to time is desirable. Where they could logically be fitted into an executive department or other independent agency, both agencies would benefit. The program of the independent agency could be developed with greater regard for related policies and programs of its new agency. It would also gain more effective access to the President through the head of the agency. Moreover, a sharp reduction in the number of agencies—with consequent savings in overhead and other costs—would significantly aid the President in

demonstrating to the Congress and the public that he means to administer a lean and tidy Government. Most important of all, the President's leadership position would be enhanced if his formal supervisory responsibilities were narrowed to those which he can realistically discharge.

We recommend that serious consideration be given to the transfer of ten agencies to other departments and agencies, or to their abolition:

(a) Transfers

    (1) American Battle Monuments Commission (to Veterans' Administration)

    (2) Farm Credit Administration (to supervision of the Secretary of Agriculture)

    (3) Federal Mediation and Conciliation Service (to Labor)

    (4) National Mediation Board (to Labor)

    (5) National Capital Housing Authority (to D. C. Government)

    (6) Railroad Retirement Board (to HEW)

    (7) Veterans' Administration (to HEW)

(b) Abolition

    (1) National Capital Transportation Agency (abolish)

    (2) Subversive Activities Control Board (abolish)

    (3) Virgin Islands Corporation (abolish)

4.a.   The Commission on Intergovernmental Relations ("Kestnbaum Report," June 1955)

The United States has made a major contribution to the art of government by its successful operation of a federal system. This success has been especially noteworthy in view of the enormous strains on the system caused by military and economic emergencies of the sort that have occurred during the past quarter-century, and by the cumulative effect of the more gradual changes brought about by a dynamic and expanding economy.

In recent years, the almost continuous presence of a crisis, either economic or military, has accounted for vast expansions of National activities. Many of these programs have been of an emergency nature; a great many others, however, have lastingly influenced the division of governmental responsibilities between the National Government and the States.

Profound as their impact has been, war and economic crisis have not been the only major causes of the growing pressure for National action. Equally insistent pressures have been brought about by intensified industrialization and population shifts from rural to urban areas; new advances in transportation and communications; and, flowing from these developments, greatly accelerated mobility of people and interchange of ideas.

These changes have been reflected in part in a growing governmental concern with the economic and social welfare of the individual. And many individuals who once looked no further than their city hall or State capitol now turn toward Washington when problems arise. We are doing today as a Nation many things that we once did as individuals, as local communities, or as States.

The extensive readjustment of National and State responsibilities in recent decades was bound to stir questioning of the continued vitality of our federal system. Candor would probably compel many thoughtful Americans to admit having experienced some fear or occasional doubt on this score, at one stage or another of this momentous period.

To many, the expanding powers of the National Government seemed destined to reduce the States to mere administrative provinces. This prospect was sharpened by Supreme Court decisions which appeared to have the effect of removing almost all significant constitutional limitations on the expansion of National activities. It

The Commission on Intergovernmental Relations (Washington, D.C.: U.S. Government Printing Office, June 1955). Material quoted from the introduction to the Kestnbaum Report, pp. 1–6, as well as selections from chapter 3, pp. 59–89.

was often aggravated by the conviction that many of the newer activities constituted invasions of individual freedom and ought not to be undertaken by any level of government. Thus the fear of usurpation of State rights was frequently combined with the fear of undue paternalism.

On the other hand, many who had welcomed the expansion of National authority began to wonder if our system of federalism had become an obstacle to effective government. Their fear was that our form of government would prove too slow-moving and cumbersome to deal with the intricate social and economic problems of an increasingly interdependent society and to cope with authoritarian regimes of the Fascist, Nazi, and Communist varieties. Our governmental system must be remodeled, many thought, if it is to be adjusted properly to 20th century conditions.

The Commission views both positions as extremes. The National Government and the States should be regarded not as competitors for authority but as two levels of government cooperating with or complementing each other in meeting the growing demands on both. Chiefly because of war and the recurring threat of war, the expenditures of the National Government have grown much larger than those of the States and localities. But State and local activities also continue to expand. Equally significant is the increased interest in and recognition of the importance of State and local governments as essential elements in an effective federal structure.

The continuing vitality of State and local government affords the most solid evidence that our federal system is still an asset and not a liability. To be sure, it is not a neat system, and not an easy one to operate. It makes large demands on our sense of responsibility, our patience, our self-restraint. It requires toleration of diversity with respect to taxes, roads, schools, law enforcement, and many other important matters. Those who have a passion for streamlining can easily point to awkward features.

Nevertheless, the federal principle, along with the principle of checks and balances, remains one of the great institutional embodiments of our traditional distrust of too much concentrated authority in government or, to state it positively, of our traditional belief in distribution of authority among relatively independent governing bodies. Experience has demonstrated the wisdom of the view of the Founding Fathers that individual freedom is best preserved in a system in which authority is divided and in which diverse opinions are reconciled through the processes of representative government.

Living in an age of peril, we could perhaps not afford the extra margin of individual freedom which our federal system makes possible if the price were the weakening of national security. We should not think of government only in terms of the scope it leaves for the individual; we must think equally of its capacity to govern. Individual freedom depends on preserving representative government. If division of authority between the National Government and the States should impede our efforts to preserve our Nation and the rest of the free world, it would jeopardize the freedom of the individual.

But experience amply justifies the view that our federal system, with the degree of flexibility that it permits, can be adapted to crises of the present and future as successfully as it has been to those of the past. As an instrument of positive government, it possesses—at least for a nation as large and diverse as ours—a clear advantage over a strongly centralized government. In helping to bolster the principle of consent; in facilitating wide participation in government; in furnishing training grounds for leaders; in maintaining the habit of local initiative; in providing laboratories for research and experimentation in the art of government; in fostering competition among lower levels of government; in serving as outlets for local grievances and for political aspirations—in all these and many other ways, the existence of many relatively independent and responsible governments strengthens rather than weakens our capacity for government. On the whole, therefore, the enduring values of our federal system fully warrant every effort to preserve and strengthen its essence.

Out of the trying events of this past quarter-century, and out of the accompanying doubts and fears, has come a deeper understanding of what is required to maintain a proper division of activities between the National Government and the States. As with all governmental institutions in our society, the basic purpose of the division of powers is to provide a climate that favors growth of the individual's material and spiritual potential. Power will not long rest with any government that cannot or will not make proper use of it for that end. Our system of federal government can be in proper balance, therefore, only when each level is effective and responsible.

Responsibility implies restraint as well as action. The States have responsibilities not only to do efficiently what lies within their competence, but also to refrain from action injurious to the Nation; the National Government has responsibilities not only to perform, within the limits of its constitutional authority, those public functions the States cannot perform, but also to refrain from doing those things the States and their subdivisions are willing and able to do.

People in the United States, as elsewhere, have looked more and more to government for assistance in solving their social and economic problems. The National Government has sometimes responded more readily than have the State and local governments. The Commission does not deal with the issue of whether or not governments rather than individuals should satisfy these needs. What it faces is the fact that the National Government has gradually undertaken some new activities which are susceptible of a larger measure of State and local handling. The Commission does not essay a judgment as to whether unreadiness on the part of the States and localities or overzealousness on the part of the National Government, or both, may have caused the existing division of activities. It merely emphasizes the fact that the more effectively our State and local governmental structures, procedures, and policies can be adapted to present-day governmental objectives, the less occasion there will be for bypassing State action in the future.

Far from weakening the National Government, the strengthening of State and local government would increase its effectiveness. The responsibilities that unavoidably must fall on the National Government are formidable. The fullest possible utilization of the resources of the State and local governments is desirable both to supplement National action where National action is necessary, and to relieve the National Government of having to divert its resources and energies to activities that could be handled as well or better by the States and their subdivisions.

The National Government has therefore an interest, as well as a responsibility, in scrutinizing with the greatest care the degree of National participation in existing or proposed programs. It is not enough to ascertain that the contemplated activity is within the constitutional competence of the National Government and that there is a national interest in having the activity performed. In the light of recent Supreme Court decisions, and in our present highly interdependent society, there are few activities of government indeed in which there is not some degree of national interest, and in which the National Government is without constitutional authority to participate in some manner.

The degree and limits of National participation must therefore be determined by the exercise of balanced judgment. In addition to appraising carefully in each instance the need for National participation, the National Government should hold essential participation to the minimum required for attaining its objective. In all of its actions the National Government should be concerned with their effects on State and local governments.

The preservation and strengthening of our federal system depend in the last analysis on the self-restraint and responsibility, as well as the wisdom, of our actions as citizens. If we are not willing to leave some room for diversity of policy, to tolerate some lack of uniformity in standards, even in many matters which are of national concern and about which we may feel strongly, the essence of federalism, even if not the legal fiction, will have been lost. We must also realize that it can be lost, or its vitality sapped, by nonuse of State and local initiative as well as by overuse of National authority. We have therefore as citizens a responsibility to see to it that those legitimate needs of society that could be met by timely State and local action do not by default have to be met by the National Government.

Precise divisions of governmental activities need always to be considered in the light of varied and shifting circumstances; they need also to be viewed in the light of principles rooted in our history. Assuming efficient and responsible government at all levels—National, State, and local—we should seek to divide our civic responsibilities so that we:

Leave to private initiative all the functions that citizens can perform privately; use the level of government closest to the community for all public functions it can handle; utilize cooperative intergovernmental arrangements where appropriate to attain economical performance and popular approval; reserve National action for residual participation where State and local governments are not fully adequate, and for the continuing responsibilities that only the National Government can undertake.

. . . .

National Responsibilities and Cooperative Relations

The maintenance of a healthy federal system has two aspects. The States must be alert to meet the legitimate needs of their citizens, lest more and more of the business of government fall upon the National Government. At the same time, the National Government must refrain from taking over activities that the States and their subdivisions are performing with reasonable competence, lest the vitality of State and local institutions be undermined.

The division of responsibilities between Nation and States is not and cannot be set by any authority over and above both, apart from the Constitution itself and the people. The organs of the National Government determine what the Constitution permits the National Government to do and what it does not, subject to the ultimate consent of the people. And under present judicial interpretations of the Constitution, especially of the spending power and the commerce clause, the boundaries of possible National action are more and more subject to determination by legislative action. In brief, the policymaking authorities of the National Government are for most purposes the arbiters of the federal system.

The National Government has therefore a double duty: to protect and promote the national interest by adopting such substantive policies as are necessary and proper under the powers delegated to the National Government; and to protect and promote the national interest in the preservation of the federal system. The proper discharge of this dual responsibility calls for vigorous and effective National action where National action is required and, along with this, a discriminating sense of when not to act.

There are several major aspects of the responsibility of the National Government to preserve and strengthen the federal system.

1. The Constitution sets only maximum limits to National action and these are conjectural. The National Government need not do everything that it can do. It needs some sort of guidelines marking out the conditions and circumstances calling for National action. Much attention has always been given to speculation and debate about the constitutional limits of National action; too little attention has been paid to the development of a general theory or a set of principles to assist in deciding what the National Government ought and ought not to do as a matter of policy. The Commission recognizes that no set of principles can eliminate the necessity for the exercise of sound judgment in deciding particular matters. It will be helpful, however, to formulate a general concept of the types of conditions and

circumstances that warrant National action. The Commission advances a few such concepts as guides.

2. Where National action is desirable, greater attention should be given to minimizing its extent and to leaving room for and facilitating cooperative or independent State action. In this chapter, the Commission discusses the choice between direct National performance and administration through the States; the need for more care in drafting National regulatory laws to indicate selectively the boundaries of National and State control; the kind of State action, if any, that is appropriate in connection with different types of National regulatory laws; administrative cooperation in regulatory activity; the use of State facilities in carrying out National laws; and National legislative and other support of State and local law-enforcement. The discussion will show at how many points it is desirable to employ a strategy that will preserve State initiative and release the full resources of the federal system.

3. The organization of the National Government does not at present afford adequate recognition of the national interest in State and local government. Each administrative agency and legislative committee is primarily concerned with protecting and furthering the national interest in the functional area over which it has jurisdiction. This in itself is quite proper. However, some machinery is needed that will help to provide more conscious, continuous, and overall attention to the relation of National action to State and local government.

. . . .

Activities Appropriate for the National Government

It is of the essence of the federal system of the United States that public powers are divided by the Constitution between two levels of government—the National Government and the States. The powers of the National Government are delegated and enumerated; the powers of the States are reserved. Each level works within the context of what the other does and can do. Consequently, extensive as some of the powers of the National Government are, they are usually incomplete in themselves except in the fields of foreign affairs, defense, and a few others such as currency and the postal service. Outside of these fields, National action is exceptional in nature; frequently the National Government is a participant rather than the sole performer. When it acts coercively, it relies on relatively restricted grants of authority, especially the power to regulate interstate commerce, which is an element in a multitude of things but is hardly the whole of anything. The power to dispose of property and the power to spend money for the common defense and general welfare are more extensive. Here, however, the National Government's coercive power is limited.

The question of the proper scope of National action can be approached in three ways: (1) in terms of subject-matter fields of primary National responsibility; (2) in terms of conditions that justify direct National action; (3) in terms of needs that justify National participation in functions where it does not have primary responsibility. These approaches are not mutually exclusive.

Field of Primary Responsibility

The main fields of primary National responsibility are obvious. Foremost is management of foreign relations in peace and war. The international dealings of the United States have taken cautious account of the limitations inherent in the federal structure—as illustrated by the unwillingness to enter into conventions on commercial law and in the guarded policy on international labor standards. But today the country's international position has far-reaching consequences both in foreign commitments and in defense and internal security. The peacetime range of the war power is shown by central control of atomic energy.

The National Government is the natural manager of the monetary and credit system. Equally obvious is the duty of protecting freedom of trade and facilitating movement and communication within the market place. Leadership in counter-cyclical fiscal policies must come from Washington, and so must regulation of certain business structures that lie beyond the reach of any one State or even any group of States. This type of need was signalized by the declaration in the Holding Company Act that the activities of these companies "extending over many States are not susceptible of effective control by any State and make difficult, if not impossible, effective State regulation of public-utility companies." Even when the regulated activities are localized but widespread it may be not only inconvenient but also unfair to apply controls without some degree of uniformity. In the sensitive medium of a wholesomely competitive private enterprise economy, minimum elements of uniform treatment are a measure of justice to business as well as a protection to the States themselves.

At bottom much of the need for National action stems from some kind of movement, not necessarily physical, which carries the effects of local activity or inactivity beyond the local or State borders. These extraterritorial consequences are increased by the mobility of modern industrial society.

Conditions Justifying National Action

The Commission believes that, in situations warranting action by some level of government, the following conditions justify National action within the National Government's delegated powers, when the lower levels of government cannot or will not act:

(*a*) When the National Government is the only agency that can summon the resources needed for an activity. For this reason the Constitution entrusts defense to the National Government. Similarly, primary responsibility for governmental action in maintaining economic stability is given to the National Government because it alone can command the main resources for the task.

(b) When the activity cannot be handled within the geographic and jurisdictional limits of smaller governmental units, including those that could be created by compact. Regulation of radio and television is an extreme example.

(c) When the activity requires a nationwide uniformity of policy that cannot be achieved by interstate action. Sometimes there must be an undeviating standard and hence an exclusively National policy, as in immigration and naturalization, the currency, and foreign relations.

(d) When a State through action or inaction does injury to the people of other States. One of the main purposes of the commerce clause was to eliminate State practices that hindered the flow of goods across State lines. On this ground also, National action is justified to prevent unrestrained exploitation of an essential natural resource.

(e) When States fail to respect or to protect basic political and civil rights that apply throughout the United States.

Informational and Financial Support

Two kinds of reasons make it proper for the National Government to play a limited role as a participant in various service and regulatory functions that rest primarily with the States.

(a) Some of the underlying reasons for National participation flow from the simple fact that some types of information may not be available or usable at all unless gathered at a central point. A simple example is a fingerprint file. Other related reasons for National participation result from the way in which ideas are generated and diffused in the development of policy. Good ideas are likely to be discovered locally, on the firing line of practice, but they do not reach fruition unless means exist to clear them centrally and spread them. In addition, much creative thinking is possible only at levels where comparison is feasible or the wider range of relationships is visible.

Finally, certain technical resources, including special equipment and men with specialized training, can sometimes be made generally available only by the National Government. Some of the smaller units are not able to afford or obtain them, and in any case their provision by many units separately would entail costly duplication.

(b) Money is the focus of another set of reasons for National participation in certain fields of service where a strong national interest is identified. The most inclusive areas of government may properly take account of the uneven distribution of local resources when the desirability of universal minimum levels of service is established.

. . . .

Continuing Attention to Interlevel Relations

The proper functioning of the federal system requires that concerted attention be given to interlevel relationships. The Commission finds, however, that many governmental decisions are made without adequate consideration of these relationships. This occurs partly because the legislative and executive branches are both organized primarily along functional lines.

The Commission believes, therefore, that provision should be made for a permanent center for overall attention to the problems of interlevel relationships. This conclusion is supported by a considerable number of findings set forth in this and other chapters in this Report. The proposed center should be in the nature of a staff agency, located in the executive branch of the National Government, but charged with the responsibility for maintaining effective contact with both legislative and administrative agencies at the National level and with responsible officials in the States.

An appropriate staff agency at the National level should facilitate the further development of the kind of guidelines for determining the conditions and circumstances justifying National action that are outlined in this Report. It should also help policymakers in confining National commitments within the limits of clearly conceived National purposes and assist administrators in harmonizing their decisions and working relationships with the requirements of responsible general government at each level.

Linked to other agencies of overall planning, such a staff agency would supplement, not replace, existing highly useful arrangements for departmental and congressional committee planning. Its primary responsibility would be to advance a strategic sense of federal relations in the formative stages of many types of legislation and administrative action. It only emphasizes the importance of this objective to observe that some complications in planning and carrying out interlevel activities (as in the field of land and water resources) reflect organizational difficulties which call for some general improvement in the structure of the National Government.

The Commission believes that whatever agency is created should be conceived modestly. It will be good only if it is simple enough to fit in practical operations. It will be helpful only if it is used. To say that it should be simple, however, does not belittle its importance.

In this spirit the Commission suggests:

(1) There should be a Special Assistant in the Executive Office of the President to serve with a small staff as the President's chief aide and adviser on State and

local relationships. He should give his exclusive attention to these matters throughout the government. He would be the coordinating center.

(2) An Advisory Board on Intergovernmental Relations would be appointed by the President after such consultation as he deemed appropriate with associations that represent various levels. In addition to calling regular and special meetings of this board, the Special Assistant would act for the President in convening meetings of governors, mayors, and others. He would collaborate with the Treasury Department in arranging conferences for the overall consideration of National-State-local fiscal adjustments.

(3) The existence of the Special Assistant in the Executive Office would not preclude the creation of interlevel coordinating machinery for particular fields where a number of National agencies are involved in State relations which are partly interdependent and potentially conflicting. The complex realm of land and water resources is an outstanding instance of such a field.

(4) The Bureau of the Budget could profitably intensify its concern with overall fiscal aspects of National-State-local relations, and also maintain cooperative relations with the National Association of State Budget Officers.

(5) In certain of the departments, at least, Assistant Secretaries should be designated to deal with broad questions of National-State-local adjustments arising in the department's work. This arrangement is already in effect in several departments.

(6) To promote sharper attention to problems of intergovernmental relations in the drafting of statutes, the Special Assistant (aided by the Legislative Reference Division of the Bureau of the Budget) would maintain appropriate contacts throughout the government, including the Office of Legal Counsel in the Department of Justice, as well as with drafting groups at the State level.

(7) The Special Assistant in the Executive Office and the Advisory Board should be prepared to cooperate in appropriate ways with other agencies, private as well as public, that may be studying special problems or focal points of intergovernmental relationships, such as are found in metropolitan areas.

(8) Congress is urged to provide the funds necessary to accomplish these objectives. It is hoped that Congress, even more than in the past, will give attention to the overall aspects of intergovernmental relations when considering particular measures, and will systematically invite representatives of State and local levels to participate in all relevant hearings. It may be helpful to maintain active subcommittees on intergovernmental relations in the Committees on Government Operations.

4.b.　An Act to Establish an Advisory Commission on Intergovernmental Relations (1959)

Be it enacted by the Senate and House of Representatives of the United States of America in Congress assembled,

ADVISORY COMMISSION ON INTERGOVERNMENTAL RELATIONS

Section 1. There is hereby established a permanent bipartisan commission to be known as the Advisory Commission on Intergovernmental Relations, hereinafter referred to as the "Commission".

DECLARATION OF PURPOSE

Sec. 2. Because the complexity of modern life intensifies the need in a federal form of government for the fullest cooperation and coordination of activities between the levels of government, and because population growth and scientific developments portend an increasingly complex society in future years, it is essential that an appropriate agency be established to give continuing attention to intergovernmental problems.

It is intended that the Commission, in the performance of its duties, will—

(1) bring together representatives of the Federal, State, and local governments for the consideration of common problems;

(2) provide a forum for discussing the administration and coordination of Federal grant and other programs requiring intergovernmental cooperation;

(3) give critical attention to the conditions and controls involved in the administration of Federal grant programs;

(4) make available technical assistance to the executive and legislative branches of the Federal Government in the review of proposed legislation to determine its overall effect on the Federal system;

Public Law 86–380 (September 24, 1959). Sections 6, 7, and 8 were deleted since they contain technical details about the ACIR administration, compensation and appropriations.

(5) encourage discussion and study at an early stage of emerging public problems that are likely to require intergovernmental cooperation;

(6) recommend, within the framework of the Constitution, the most desirable allocation of governmental functions, responsibilities, and revenues among the several levels of government; and

(7) recommend methods of coordinating and simplifying tax laws and administrative practices to achieve a more orderly and less competitive fiscal relationship between the levels of government and to reduce the burden of compliance for taxpayers.

MEMBERSHIP OF THE COMMISSION

Sec. 3. (a) The Commission shall be composed of twenty-six members, as follows:

(1) Six appointed by the President of the United States, three of whom shall be officers of the executive branch of the Government, and three private citizens, all of whom shall have had experience or familiarity with relations between the levels of government;

(2) Three appointed by the President of the Senate, who shall be Members of the Senate;

(3) Three appointed by the Speaker of the House of Representatives, who shall be Members of the House;

(4) Four appointed by the President from a panel of at least eight Governors submitted by the Governors' Conference;

(5) Three appointed by the President from a panel of at least six members of State legislative bodies submitted by the board of managers of the Council of State Governments;

(6) Four appointed by the President from a panel of at least eight mayors submitted jointly by the American Municipal Association and the United States Conference of Mayors;

(7) Three appointed by the President from a panel of at least six elected county officers submitted by the National Association of County Officials.

(b) The members appointed from private life under paragraph (1) of subsection (a) shall be appointed without regard to political affiliation; of each class of members enumerated in paragraphs (2) and (3) of subsection (a), two shall be from the majority party of the respective houses; of each class of members enumerated in paragraphs (4), (5), (6), and (7) of subsection (a), not more than two shall be from any one political party; of each class of members enumerated in paragraphs (5), (6) and (7) of subsection (a), not more than one shall be from any one State; at least two of the appointees under paragraph (6) of subsection (a) shall be from cities under five hundred thousand population.

(c) The term of office of each member of the Commission shall be two years, but members shall be eligible for reappointment.

ORGANIZATION OF THE COMMISSION

Sec. 4. (a) The President shall convene the Commission within ninety days following enactment of this Act at such time and place as he may designate for the Commission's initial meeting.

(b) The President shall designate a Chairman and a Vice Chairman from among members of the Commission.

(c) Any vacancy in the membership of the Commission shall be filled in the same manner in which the original appointment was made; except that where the number of vacancies is fewer than the number of members specified in paragraphs (4), (5), (6), and (7) of section 3(a), each panel of names submitted in accordance with the aforementioned paragraphs shall contain at least two names for each vacancy.

(d) Where any member ceases to serve in the official position from which originally appointed under section 3(a), his place on the Commission shall be deemed to be vacant.

(e) Thirteen members of the Commission shall constitute a quorum, but two or more members shall constitute a quorum for the purpose of conducting hearings.

DUTIES OF THE COMMISSION

Sec. 5. It shall be the duty of the Commission—

(1) to engage in such activities and to make such studies and investigations as are necessary or desirable in the accomplishment of the purposes set forth in section 2 of this Act;

(2) to consider, on its own initiative, ways and means for fostering better relations between the levels of government;

(3) to submit an annual report to the President and the Congress on or before January 31 of each year. The Commission may also submit such additional reports to the President, to the Congress or any committee of the Congress, and to any unit of government or organization as the Commission may deem appropriate.

Approved September 24, 1958

4.c. Washington Metropolitan Region Development (1960)

§ 1–1301. Congressional declaration—Coordination in development of Washington metropolitan region.

The Congress hereby declares that, because the District which is the seat of the Government of the United States and has now become the urban center of a rapidly expanding Washington metropolitan region, the necessity for the continued and effective performance of the functions of the Government of the United States at the seat of said Government in the District of Columbia, the general welfare of the District of Columbia and the health and living standards of the people residing or working therein and the conduct of industry, trade, and commerce therein require that the development of the District of Columbia and the management of its public affairs shall, to the fullest extent practicable be coordinated with the development of the other areas of the Washington metropolitan region and with the management of the public affairs of such other areas, and that the activities of all of the departments, agencies, and instrumentalities of the Federal Government which may be carried out in, or in relation to, the other areas of the Washington metropolitan region shall, to the fullest extent practicable, be coordinated with the development of such other areas and with the management of their public affairs; all toward the end that, with the cooperation and assistance of the other areas of the Washington metropolitan region, all of the areas therein shall be so developed and the public affairs thereof shall be so managed as to contribute effectively toward the solution of the community development problems of the Washington metropolitan region on a unified metropolitan basis. (June 27, 1960, 74 Stat. 223, Pub. L. 86–527, § 2.)

§ 1–1302. Policy—Exercise of functions of all governmental authorities to be coordinated.

The Congress further declares that the policy to be followed for the attainment of the objective established by section 1–1301, and for the more effective exercise by the Congress, the executive branch of the Federal Government and the Commissioner of the District of Columbia and all other officers and agencies and in-

74 Stat. 223, Public Law 86–527 (June 27, 1960).

strumentalities of the District of Columbia of their respective functions, powers, and duties in respect of the Washington metropolitan region, shall be that all such functions, powers, and duties shall be exercised and carried out in such manner as (with proper recognition of the sovereignty of the State of Maryland and the Commonwealth of Virginia in respect to those areas of the Washington metropolitan region as are situated within their respective jurisdictions) will best facilitate the attainment of such objective of the coordinated development of the areas of the Washington metropolitan region and coordinated management of their public affairs so as to contribute effectively to the solution of the community development problems of the Washington metropolitan region on a unified metropolitan basis. (June 27, 1960, 74 Stat. 223, Pub. L. 86–527, § 3.)

§ 1–1303. Priority projects.

The Congress further declares that, in carrying out the policy pursuant to section 1–1302 for the attainment of the objective established by section 1–1301, priority should be given to the solution, on a unified metropolitan basis, of the problems of water supply, sewage disposal, and water pollution and transportation. (June 27, 1960, 74 Stat. 223, Pub. L. 86–527, § 4.)

§ 1–1304. All agencies of federal, district and regional governments are invited to make intensive study of final report of Joint Committee on Washington Metropolitan Problems.

The Congress further declares that the officers, departments, agencies, and instrumentalities of the executive branch of the Federal Government and the Commissioner of the District of Columbia and the other officers, agencies, and instrumentalities of the District of Columbia, and other agencies of government within the Washington metropolitan region are invited and encouraged to engage in an intensive study of the final report and recommendation of the Joint Committee on Washington Metropolitan Problems with a view to submitting to the Congress the specific recommendations of each of the agencies of government specified. (June 27, 1960, 74 Stat. 223, Pub. L. 86–527, § 5.)

§ 1–1305. "Washington metropolitan region" defined.

As used in sections 1–1301 to 1–1305, the term "Washington metropolitan region" includes the District of Columbia, the counties of Montgomery and Prince Georges in the State of Maryland, the counties of Arlington and Fairfax and the cities of Alexandria and Falls Church in the Commonwealth of Virginia. (June 27, 1960, 74 Stat. 224, Pub. L. 86–527, § 6.)

5. Bureau of the Budget Circular No. A–95 (1969)

To the Heads of Executive Departments and Establishments

SUBJECT: Evaluation, review, and coordination of Federal assistance programs and projects

1. *PURPOSE*. This Circular furnishes guidance to Federal agencies for added cooperation with States and local governments in the evaluation, review, and coordination of Federal assistance programs and projects. The circular promulgates regulations which provide, in part, for:

    a. Encouraging the establishment of a project notification and review system to facilitate coordinated development planning on an intergovernmental basis for certain Federal assistance programs in furtherance of section 204 of the Demonstration Cities and Metropolitan Development Act of 1966, and Title IV of the Intergovernmental Cooperation Act of 1968.

    b. Notification, upon request, of Governors and State legislatures of grants-in-aid made under Federal programs in each State pursuant to section 201 of the Intergovernmental Cooperation Act of 1968 (Attachment B).

    c. Coordination of Federal development programs and projects with State, regional, and local development planning pursuant to Title IV of the Intergovernmental Cooperation Act of 1968.

2. *BASIS*. This Circular has been prepared pursuant to:

    a. Section 401(a) of the Intergovernmental Cooperation Act of 1968 which provides, in part, that

> "The President shall . . . establish rules and regulations governing the formulation, evaluation, and review of Federal programs and projects having a significant impact on area and community development. . . ."

and the President's Memorandum of November 8, 1969, to the Director of the

Bureau of the Budget Circular No. A-95 (July 24, 1969), issued from Executive Office of the President, Bureau of the Budget, Washington, D. C. Parts 3 and 4 deleted and only Attachment "A" included.

Bureau of the Budget ("Federal Register," Vol. 33, No. 221, November 13, 1968) which provides:

> "By virtue of the authority vested in me by section 301 of title 3 of the United States Code and section 401(a) of the Intergovernmental Cooperation Act of 1968 (Public Law 90–577), I hereby delegate to you the authority vested in the President to establish the rules and regulations provided for in that section governing the formulation, evaluation, and review of Federal programs and projects having a significant impact on area and community development, including programs providing Federal assistance to the States and localities, to the end that they shall most effectively serve these basic objectives.
>
> "In addition, I expect the Bureau of the Budget to generally coordinate the actions of the departments and agencies in exercising the new authorizations provided by the Intergovernmental Cooperation Act, with the objective of consistent and uniform action by the Federal Government."

b. Title IV, section 403, of the Intergovernmental Cooperation Act of 1968 provides that:

> "The Bureau of the Budget, or such other agency as may be designated by the President, shall prescribe such rules and regulations as are deemed appropriate for the effective administration of this title."

c. Section 204(c) of the Demonstration Cities and Metropolitan Development Act of 1966 which provides that:

> "The Bureau of the Budget, or such other agency as may be designated by the President, shall prescribe such rules and regulations as are deemed appropriate for the effective administration of this section."

. . . .

ATTACHMENT A
CIRCULAR NO. A–95

REGULATIONS UNDER SECTION 204 OF THE DEMONSTRATION CITIES AND METROPOLITAN DEVELOPMENT ACT OF 1966 AND SECTION 201 AND TITLE IV OF THE INTERGOVERNMENTAL COOPERATION ACT OF 1968

Part I: Project Notification and Review System

1. *PURPOSE*. The purpose of this Part is to:

a. Further the policies and directives of Title IV of the Intergovernmental Cooperation Act of 1968 by encouraging the establishment of a network of State, regional, and metropolitan planning and development clearinghouses which will aid in the coordination of Federal or federally assisted social, economic, and physical development projects and programs with State, regional, and local planning for orderly growth and development;

b. Implement the requirements of section 204 of the Demonstration Cities and Metropolitan Development Act of 1966 for metropolitan areas within that network; and

c. Encourage, by means of early contact between applicants for Federal assistance and State and local governments and agencies, an expeditious process of coordination and review of proposed projects.

2. *NOTIFICATION*.

a. After September 30, 1969, any agency of State or local government or any organization or individual undertaking to apply for assistance to a project under a Federal program listed in Attachment D will be required to notify the planning and development clearinghouse of the State (or States) and the region, if there is one, or of the metropolitan area in which the project is to be located, of its intent to apply for assistance. Notifications will be accompanied by a summary description of the project for which assistance will be sought. The summary description will contain the following information:

(1) Identity of the applicant, agency, organization, or individual.

49

(2) The geographic location of the project to be assisted.

(3) A brief description of the proposed project by type, purpose, general size or scale, estimated cost, beneficiaries, or other characteristics which will enable the clearinghouses to identify agencies of State or local government having plans, programs, or projects that might be affected by the proposed project.

(4) The Federal program and agency under which assistance will be sought.

(5) The estimated date by which time the applicant expects to formally file an application.

b. Such notifications should be sent at the earliest feasible time in order to assure maximum time for effective coordination and so as not to delay the timely submission of the application, when completed, to the Federal agency.

3. *CLEARINGHOUSE FUNCTIONS.*   Clearinghouse functions include:

a. Reception and dissemination of project notifications to appropriate State agencies in the case of the State clearinghouse and to appropriate local governments and agencies in the case of regional or metropolitan clearinghouses.

b. Coordination and liaison between applicants for Federal assistance and State agencies or local governments and agencies in conferring or commenting upon projects for which Federal assistance is sought.

c. Liaison between Federal agencies contemplating Federal development projects in any area and the appropriate agencies of State and local government in that area.

d. Evaluation of the State, regional, or metropolitan significance of Federal or federally assisted projects.

4. *CONSULTATION AND COMMENT.*

a. A State clearinghouse will have 30 days after receipt of a project notification to inform appropriate State agencies and to arrange to confer and consult with the applicant on the interest of the State, if any, in the project. The State clearinghouse, in addition, will have the 30-day period prior to the date on which the application is expected to be filed to submit any comments of the State to accompany the application, where the clearinghouse has notified the applicant of the intent of the State to do so.

b. A regional or metropolitan clearinghouse will have 30 days after receipt of a project notification to inform appropriate local governments and other regional or subregional agencies in the area and to arrange to confer and consult with the applicant on regional and local interest, if any, in the project. In addition, the clearinghouse will have the 30-day period prior to the date on which the application is expected to be filed to submit any comments of its own or transmit the comments of any affected local government or other regional or subregional agencies in the area, where the clearinghouse has notified the applicant of its intent to do so. In the case of an application made by a special purpose unit of government, the metropolitan or regional clearinghouse will assure that the unit or units of general local government, within the jurisdiction(s) of which the project is to be located, have opportunity to confer, consult, and comment upon the project and the application.

c. In the case of a project of a type covered under section 204 of the Demonstration Cities and Metropolitan Development Act of 1966 (as indicated in Attachment D), which is to be located in a metropolitan area, the metropolitan clearinghouse will be given 60 days to comment on any application, unless the metropolitan clearinghouse formally notifies the applicant that it does not desire to comment or that it does not require 60 days in which to do so.

d. Applicants will include with the application:

(1) Any comments made by or through clearinghouses, along with a statement that such comments have been considered prior to submission of the application; or

(2) A statement that the procedures outlined in this section have been followed and that no comments have been received.

e. Where regions or metropolitan areas are contiguous, coordinative arrangements should be established between the clearinghouses in such abutting areas to assure that projects in one region which may have an impact on the development of the adjoining region are jointly studied. Any comments made by or through a clearinghouse in one region on a project in a contiguous region will accompany the application for assistance to that project.

5. *SUBJECT MATTER OF COMMENTS.* Comments made by or through clearinghouses with respect to any project for which assistance is being sought under a program listed in Attachment D are for the purpose of assisting the Federal agency (or State agency, in the case of projects for which the State under a Federal formula grant has final project approval) administering such a program in determining whether the project is in accord with Federal law governing that program. Comments will, as appropriate, address themselves to or include information about:

a. The extent to which the project is consistent with or contributes to the fulfillment of comprehensive planning for the State, region, metropolitan area, or locality.

b. The extent to which the project contributes to the achievement of State, regional, metropolitan, and local objectives as specified in section 401(a) of the Intergovernmental Cooperation Act of 1968.

c. In the case of a project for which assistance is being sought by a special purpose unit of government, whether the unit of general local government within the jurisdiction of which the project is to be located has applied, or plans to apply for assistance for the same or similar type project, in order to enable the Federal (or State) agency to make the judgments required under section 402 of the Intergovernmental Cooperation Act of 1968.

6. *FEDERAL AGENCY PROCEDURES*.   Federal agencies having programs covered under this Part will develop appropriate procedures for:

a. Informing potential applicants for assistance under such programs of the requirements of this Part (1) in program information materials, (2) in response to inquiries respecting application procedures, (3) in preapplication conferences, or (4) by other means which will assure earliest contact between applicant and clearinghouses.

b. Notifying clearinghouses on the disposition of applications.

c. Assuring, in the case of an application submitted by a special purpose unit of government, where accompanying comments indicate that the unit of general local government within the jurisdiction of which the project is to be located has submitted or plans to submit an application for assistance to the same or similar type project, that appropriate considerations and preferences as specified in section 402 of the Intergovernmental Cooperation Act of 1968, are accorded the unit of general local government. Where such preference cannot be so accorded, the agency shall supply, in writing, to the unit of general local government and the Bureau of the Budget its reasons therefor.

7. *STATE PLANS REQUIRED BY FEDERAL PROGRAMS*.   To the extent not presently required by statute or administrative regulation, Federal agencies administering programs requiring a State plan as a condition of assistance under such program will require that the Governor be given the opportunity to comment on the relationship of such State plan (or amendments thereto and projections or other periodic reports thereon required under the program) to comprehensive and other State plans and programs. Governors will be afforded a period of forty-five days in which to make such comments, and any such comments will be transmitted with the plan.

8. *COORDINATION OF DIRECT FEDERAL DEVELOPMENT PROJECTS WITH STATE, REGIONAL, AND LOCAL DEVELOPMENT*.

a. Federal agencies having responsibility for the construction of Federal buildings and installations or other Federal public works or for the acquisition, use, and disposal of Federal land and real property will establish procedures for:

(1) Consulting with Governors, regional and metropolitan comprehensive planning agencies, and local elected officials at the earliest practicable stage in project planning on the relationship of any project to the development plans and programs of the State, region, or localities in which the project is to be located.

(2) Assuring that any such Federal project is consistent or compatible with State, regional, and local development plans and programs. Exceptions will be made only where there is clear justification.

b. The State, regional, and metropolitan planning and development clearinghouses established pursuant to this Part should be utilized, to the greatest extent practicable, to effectuate the requirements of paragraph 7.

6. Reorganization Plan No. 2 of 1970

MESSAGE FROM
THE PRESIDENT OF THE UNITED STATES
TRANSMITTING REORGANIZATION PLAN NO. 2
OF 1970

To the Congress of the United States:

We in government often are quick to call for reform in other institutions, but slow to reform ourselves. Yet nowhere today is modern management more needed than in government itself.

In 1939, President Franklin D. Roosevelt proposed and the Congress accepted a reorganization plan that laid the groundwork for providing managerial assistance for a modern Presidency.

The plan placed the Bureau of the Budget within the Executive Office of the President. It made available to the President direct access to important new management instruments. The purpose of the plan was to improve the administration of the Government—to ensure that the Government could perform "promptly, effectively, without waste or lost motion."

Fulfilling that purpose today is far more difficult—and more important—than it was 30 years ago.

Last April, I created a President's Advisory Council on Executive Organization and named to it a distinguished group of outstanding experts headed by Roy L. Ash. I gave the Council a broad charter to examine ways in which the Executive Branch could be better organized. I asked it to recommend specific organizational changes that would make the Executive Branch a more vigorous and more effective instrument for creating and carrying out the programs that are needed today. The Council quickly concluded that the place to begin was in the Executive Office of the President itself. I agree.

The past 30 years have seen enormous changes in the size, structure and functions of the Federal Government. The budget has grown from less than $10 billion to $200 billion. The number of civilian employees has risen from one million to more than two and a half million. Four new Cabinet departments have been created, along with more than a score of independent agencies. Domestic policy issues have become increasingly complex. The interrelationships among

Reorganization Plan No. 2 of 1970, 84 Stat. 2085, 5 USC, Appendix.

Government programs have become more intricate. Yet the organization of the President's policy and management arms has not kept pace.

Over three decades, the Executive Office of the President has mushroomed but not by conscious design. In many areas it does not provide the kind of staff assistance and support the President needs in order to deal with the problems of government in the 1970s. We confront the 1970s with a staff organization geared in large measure to the tasks of the 1940s and 1950s.

One result, over the years, has been a tendency to enlarge the immediate White House staff—that is, the President's personal staff, as distinct from the institutional structure—to assist with management functions for which the President is responsible. This has blurred the distinction between personal staff and management institutions; it has left key management functions to be performed only intermittently and some not at all. It has perpetuated outdated structures.

Another result has been, paradoxically, to inhibit the delegation of authority to Departments and agencies.

A President whose programs are carefully coordinated, whose information system keeps him adequately informed, and whose organizational assignments are plainly set out, can delegate authority with security and confidence. A President whose office is deficient in these respects will be inclined, instead, to retain close control of operating responsibilities which he cannot and should not handle.

Improving the management processes of the President's own office, therefore, is a key element in improving the management of the entire Executive Branch, and in strengthening the authority of its Departments and agencies. By providing the tools that are needed to reduce duplication, to monitor performance and to promote greater efficiency throughout the Executive Branch, this also will enable us to give the country not only more effective but also more economical government—which it deserves.

To provide the management tools and policy mechanisms needed for the 1970s, I am today transmitting to the Congress Reorganization Plan No. 2 of 1970, prepared in accordance with Chapter 9 of Title 5 of the United States Code.

This plan draws not only on the work of the Ash Council itself, but also on the work of others that preceded—including the pioneering Brownlow Committee of 1936, the two Hoover Commissions, the Rockefeller Committee, and other Presidential task forces.

Essentially, the plan recognizes that two closely connected but basically separate functions both center in the President's office: policy determination and executive management. This involves (1) what government should do, and (2) how it goes about doing it.

My proposed reorganization creates a new entity to deal with each of these functions:

—It establishes a Domestic Council, to coordinate policy formulation in the domestic area. This Cabinet group would be provided with an institutional staff, and to a considerable degree would be a domestic counterpart to the National Security Council.

—It establishes an Office of Management and Budget, which would be the President's principal arm for the exercise of his managerial functions.

The Domestic Council will be primarily concerned with *what* we do; the Office of Management and Budget will be primarily concerned with *how* we do it, and *how well* we do it.

DOMESTIC COUNCIL

The past year's experience with the Council for Urban Affairs has shown how immensely valuable a Cabinet-level council can be as a forum for both discussion and action on policy matters that cut across departmental jurisdictions.

The Domestic Council will be chaired by the President. Under the plan, its membership will include the Vice President, and the Secretaries of the Treasury, Interior, Agriculture, Commerce, Labor, Health, Education and Welfare, Housing and Urban Development, and Transportation, and the Attorney General. I also intend to designate as members the Director of the Office of Economic Opportunity and, while he remains a member of the Cabinet, the Postmaster General. (Although I continue to hope that the Congress will adopt my proposal to create, in place of the Post Office Department, a self-sufficient postal authority.) The President could add other Executive Branch officials at his discretion.

The Council will be supported by a staff under an Executive Director who will also be one of the President's assistants. Like the National Security Council staff, this staff will work in close coordination with the President's personal staff but will have its own institutional identity. By being established on a permanent, institutional basis, it will be designed to develop and employ the "institutional memory" so essential if continuity is to be maintained, and if experience is to play its proper role in the policy-making process.

There does not now exist an organized, institutionally-staffed group charged with advising the President on the total range of domestic policy. The Domestic Council will fill that need. Under the President's direction, it will also be charged with integrating the various aspects of domestic policy into a consistent whole.

Among the specific policy functions in which I intend the Domestic Council to take the lead are these:

—Assessing national needs, collecting information and developing forecasts, for the purpose of defining national goals and objectives.

—Identifying alternative ways of achieving these objectives, and recommending consistent, integrated sets of policy choices.

—Providing rapid response to Presidential needs for policy advice on pressing domestic issues.

—Coordinating the establishment of national priorities for the allocation of available resources.

—Maintaining a continuous review of the conduct of ongoing programs from a policy standpoint, and proposing reforms as needed.

Much of the Council's work will be accomplished by temporary, ad hoc project committees. These might take a variety of forms, such as task forces, planning groups or advisory bodies. They can be established with varying degrees of formality, and can be set up to deal either with broad program areas or with specific problems. The committees will draw for staff support on Department and agency experts, supplemented by the Council's own staff and that of the Office of Management and Budget.

Establishment of the Domestic Council draws on the experience gained during the past year with the Council for Urban Affairs, the Cabinet Committee on the Environment and the Council for Rural Affairs. The principal key to the operation of these Councils has been the effective functioning of their various subcommittees. The Councils themselves will be consolidated into the Domestic Council; Urban, Rural and Environment subcommittees of the Domestic Council will be strengthened, using access to the Domestic Council staff.

Overall, the Domestic Council will provide the President with a streamlined, consolidated domestic policy arm, adequately staffed, and highly flexible in its operation. It also will provide a structure through which departmental initiatives can be more fully considered, and expert advice from the Departments and agencies more fully utilized.

OFFICE OF MANAGEMENT AND BUDGET

Under the reorganization plan, the technical and formal means by which the Office of management and budget is created is by re-designating the Bureau of the Budget as the Office of Management and Budget. The functions currently vested by law in the Bureau, or in its director, are transferred to the President, with the provision that he can then re-delegate them.

As soon as the reorganization plan takes effect, I intend to delegate those statutory functions to the Director of the new Office of Management and Budget, including those under section 212 of the Budget and Accounting Act, 1921.

However, creation of the Office of Management and Budget represents far more than a mere change of name for the Bureau of the Budget. It represents a basic change in concept and emphasis, reflecting the broader management needs of the Office of the President.

The new Office will still perform the key function of assisting the President in the preparation of the annual Federal budget and overseeing its execution. It will draw upon the skills and experience of the extraordinarily able and dedicated career staff developed by the Bureau of the Budget. But preparation of the budget as such will no longer be its dominant, overriding concern.

While the budget function remains a vital tool of management, it will be strengthened by the greater emphasis the new office will place on fiscal analysis. The budget function is only one of several important management tools that the President must now have. He must also have a substantially enhanced institutional staff capability in other areas of executive management—particularly in program evaluation and coordination, improvement of Executive Branch organization, information and management systems, and development of executive talent. Under this plan, strengthened capability in these areas will be provided partly through internal reorganization, and it will also require additional staff resources.

The new Office of Management and Budget will place much greater emphasis on the evaluation of program performance: on assessing the extent to which programs are actually achieving their intended results, and delivering the intended services to the intended recipients. This is needed on a continuing basis, not as a one-time effort. Program evaluation will remain a function of the individual agencies as it is today. However, a single agency cannot fairly be expected to judge overall effectiveness in programs that cross agency lines—and the difference between agency and Presidential perspectives requires a capacity in the Executive Office to evaluate program performance whenever appropriate.

The new Office will expand efforts to improve interagency cooperation in the field. Washington-based coordinators will help work out interagency problems at the operating level, and assist in developing efficient coordinating mechanisms throughout the country. The success of these efforts depends on the experience, persuasion, and understanding of an Office which will be an expediter and catalyst. The Office will also respond to requests from State and local governments for assistance on intergovernmental programs. It will work closely with the Vice President and the Office of Intergovernmental Relations.

Improvement of Government organization, information and management systems will be a major function of the Office of management and Budget. It will maintain a continuous review of the organizational structures and management processes of the Executive Branch, and recommend needed changes. It will take the lead in developing new information systems to provide the President with the performance and other data that he needs but does not now get. When new programs are launched, it will seek to ensure that they are not simply forced into or grafted onto existing organizational structures that may not be appropriate. Resistance to organizational change is one of the chief obstacles to effective government; the new Office will seek to ensure that organization keeps abreast of program needs.

The new Office will also take the lead in devising programs for the development of career executive talent throughout the Government. Not the least of the President's needs as Chief Executive is direct capability in the Executive Office for insuring that talented executives are used to the full extent of their abilities.

Effective, coordinated efforts for executive manpower development have been hampered by the lack of a system for forecasting the needs for executive talent and
appraising leadership potential. Both are crucial to the success of an enterprise—
whether private or public.

The Office of Management and Budget will be charged with advising the President on the development of new programs to recruit, train, motivate, deploy, and
evaluate the men and women who make up the top ranks of the civil service, in the
broadest sense of that term. It will not deal with individuals, but will rely on the
talented professionals of the Civil Service Commission and the Departments and
agencies themselves to administer these programs. Under the leadership of the
Office of Management and Budget there will be joint efforts to see to it that all
executive talent is well utilized wherever it may be needed throughout the Executive Branch, and to assure that executive training and motivation meet not only
today's needs but those of the years ahead.

Finally, the new Office will continue the Legislative Reference functions now
performed by the Bureau of the Budget, drawing together agency reactions on all
proposed legislation, and helping develop legislation to carry out the President's
program. It also will continue the Bureau's work of improving and coordinating
Federal statistical services.

SIGNIFICANCE OF THE CHANGES

The people deserve a more responsive and more effective Government. The
times require it. These changes will help provide it.

Each reorganization included in the plan which accompanies this message is
necessary to accomplish one or more of the purposes set forth in Section 901(a) of
Title 5 of the United States Code. In particular, the plan is responsive to Section
901(a)(1), "to promote the better execution of the laws, the more effective management of the Executive Branch and of its agencies and functions, and the expeditious administration of the public business;" and Section 901(a)(3), "to increase
the efficiency of the operations of the Government to the fullest extent practicable."

The reorganizations provided for in this plan make necessary the appointment
and compensation of new officers as specified in Section 102(c) of the plan. The
rates of compensation fixed for these officers are comparable to those fixed for other
officers in the Executive Branch who have similar responsibilities.

While this plan will result in a modest increase in direct expenditures, its
strengthening of the Executive Office of the President will bring significant indirect
savings, and at the same time will help ensure that people actually receive the
return they deserve for every dollar the Government spends. The savings will result
from the improved efficiency these changes will provide throughout the Executive
Branch—and also from curtailing the waste that results when programs simply fail

to achieve their objectives. It is not practical, however, to itemize or aggregate these indirect expenditure reductions which will result from the reorganization.

I expect to follow with other reorganization plans, quite possibly including ones that will affect other activities of the Executive Office of the President. Our studies are continuing. But this by itself is a reorganization of major significance, and a key to the more effective functioning of the entire Executive Branch.

These changes would provide an improved system of policy making and coordination, a strengthened capacity to perform those functions that are now the central concerns of the Bureau of the Budget, and a more effective set of management tools for the performance of other functions that have been rapidly increasing in importance.

The reorganization will not only improve the staff resources available to the President, but will also strengthen the advisory roles of those members of the Cabinet principally concerned with domestic affairs. By providing a means of formulating integrated and systematic recommendations on major domestic policy issues, the plan serves not only the needs of the President but also the interests of the Congress.

This reorganization plan is of major importance to the functioning of modern government. The national interest requires it. I urge that the Congress allow it to become effective.

Richard Nixon.

The White House, *March 12, 1970*.

REORGANIZATION PLAN NO. 2 OF 1970

Prepared by the President and transmitted to the Senate and the House of Representatives in Congress assembled, March 12, 1970, pursuant to the provisions of chapter 9 of title 5 of the United States Code.

Part I. Office of Management and Budget. Section 101. *Transfer of functions to the President.*—There are hereby transferred to the President of the United States all functions vested by law (including reorganization plan) in the Bureau of the Budget or the Director of the Bureau of the Budget.

Sec. 102. *Office of Management and Budget.*—(a) The Bureau of the Budget in the Executive Office of the President is hereby designated as the Office of Management and Budget.

(b) the offices of Director of the Bureau of the Budget and Deputy Director of the Bureau of the Budget, and the offices of Assistant Directors of the Bureau of the Budget which are established by statute (31 U.S.C. 16a and 16c), are hereby designated Director of the Office of Management and Budget, Deputy Director of the Office of Management and Budget, respectively.

(c) There shall be within the office of Management and Budget not more than six additional officers, as determined from time to time by the Director of the Office of Management and Budget (hereinafter referred to as the Director). Each such officer shall be appointed by the Director, subject to the approval of the President, under the classified civil service, shall have such title as the Director shall from time to time determine, and shall receive compensation at the rate now or hereafter prescribed for offices and positions at Level V of the Executive Schedule (5 U.S.C. 5316).

(d) The Office of Management and Budget and the Director shall perform such functions as the President may from time to time delegate or assign thereto. The Director, under the direction of the President, shall supervise and direct the administration of the Office of Management and Budget.

(e) The Deputy Director of the Office of Management and Budget, the Assistant Directors of the Office of Management and Budget designated by this reorganization plan, and the officers provided for in subsection (c) of this section shall perform such functions as the Director may from time to time direct.

(f) The Deputy Director (or during the absence or disability of the Deputy Director or in the event of a vacancy in the office of Deputy Director, such other officials of the Office of Management and Budget in such order as the President may from time to time designate) shall act as Director during the absence or disability of the Director or in the event of a vacancy in the office of Director.

Sec. 103. *Records, property, personnel, and funds.* —The records, property, personnel, and unexpended balances, available or to be made available, of appropriations, allocations, and other funds of the Bureau of the Budget shall, upon the taking effect of the provisions of this reorganization plan, become records, property, personnel, and unexpended balances of the Office of Management and Budget.

Part II. Domestic Council.   Sec. 201. *Establishment of the Council.*—(a) There is hereby established in the Executive Office of the President a Domestic Council, hereinafter referred to as the Council.

(b) The Council shall be composed of the following:

> The President of the United States
> The Vice President of the United States
> The Attorney General
> Secretary of Agriculture
> Secretary of Commerce
> Secretary of Health, Education, and Welfare
> Secretary of Housing and Urban Development
> Secretary of the Interior

Secretary of Labor

Secretary of Transportation

Secretary of the Treasury

and such other officers of the Executive Branch as the President may from time to time direct.

(c) The President of the United States shall preside over meetings of the Council: *Provided,* That, in the event of his absence, he may designate a member of the Council to preside.

Sec. 202. *Functions of the Council*—The Council shall perform such functions as the President may from time to time delegate or assign thereto.

Sec. 203. *Executive Director*—The staff of the Council shall be headed by an Executive Director who shall be an assistant to the President designated by the President. The Executive Director shall perform such functions as the President may from time to time direct.

Part III. Taking Effect. Sec. 301. *Effective date.*—The provisions of this reorganization plan shall take effect as provided by section 906(a) of title 5 of the United States Code, or on July 1, 1970, whichever is later.

7. The Organization and Management of Great Society Programs

A FINAL REPORT BY THE PRESIDENT'S TASK FORCE ON GOVERNMENT ORGANIZATION

("Heineman Report," June 1967)

Many domestic social programs are under severe attack. Some criticism is political. It comes from those who oppose the goals of these national programs. Some criticism stems from deflated hopes, with current funding levels well below ultimate need and demand.

Some criticism arises because of alleged organizational and managerial weaknesses. After several months of study, we believe that organizational criticism is merited.

We would define and summarize the organizational problem as follows:

(1) The target problems—poverty, discrimination, urban blight, dirty air and water—are not the sole concern of any one Federal department; they will not yield to a series of isolated program efforts.

(2) In spite of the obvious need for program integration, Federal social programs remain badly coordinated, in Washington and in the field. In some cases departments war over jurisdiction, and program managers compete rather than cooperate. In other cases related programs fail to mesh at the target area at all.

(3) Social problems are in the field, but administration of Federal domestic programs is centralized excessively in Washington—centralized in autonomous bureaus and administrations below the Presidential and departmental level.

CAUSES OF ORGANIZATIONAL WEAKNESS

To address the organizational problem, five present managerial and organizational deficiencies must be corrected:

Unpublished document available in the Lyndon B. Johnson Papers at the University of Texas, Austin, Texas. Only Executive Summary Section of *Report* is cited here.

(1) The President lacks institutional staff[1] and machinery:

—to anticipate, surface, assess, and settle wasteful program and jurisdictional conflicts between peer Federal departments in Washington;

—to control and pull together the related programs of Federal departments in Washington and in the field;

—to mediate problems and disputes between Federal departments in the field;

—to reflect the Presidential perspective in program areas requiring cooperation between Federal agencies and between the Federal, State and local governments.

(2) The President does not now have institutional staff whose sole responsibility is:

—to plan ahead;

—to take the measure of complex social problems;

—to review the effectiveness of existing government programs;

—to support the President as he develops a long-term domestic strategy and a coordinated annual legislative program for domestic affairs.

(3) Channels for consultation and cooperation between the White House, Governors and Mayors and their staffs are haphazard and insufficient, heavily dominated by crises and relatively inattentive to longer term program, organization and political relationships and problems.

(4) Key domestic department heads do not have full control of their various program responsibilities because of their failure to command, develop and use Secretarial-level staff to dominate the vital managerial levers of planning, evaluation, program budgeting, and intradepartmental program coordination.

(5) The field structure of domestic departments is powerless and fragmented. It is poorly staffed, in quality and quantity, from the top down. Field officials are expected to cooperate in managing interdepartmental programs even though they do not have operational authority over programs within their own departments. This is a hopeless administrative formula.

SUMMARY OF RECOMMENDATIONS

Organizational strength must be built in Washington and in the Federal field structure. It must be built both in the Executive Office of the President and in Cabinet departments.

1. Our entire analysis distinguishes between the President's personal staff—White House counsel, special assistants, and their aides—whose day-to-day work must necessarily be shaped by the president's personal and immediate requests, and institutional staff support for presidential-level issues and problems that are continuing, regular and routine in character.

In some cases existing institutions must be changed and modernized. In others organizational gaps will have to be filled through the creation of new institutions.

Executive Office of the President

To strengthen the Presidency we recommend:

(1) Establishing a new Office of Program Coordination for domestic affairs parallel to, but outside, the Bureau of the Budget[2]

　　—to mediate and settle interagency arguments;

　　—to spur and insure cooperation between Federal agencies;

　　—to provide a focal point in the President's Office for Governors, Mayors and other key executives on domestic program issues.

(2) Providing the Office of Program Coordination with a permanent field force

　　—to reflect the President's perspective, concerns, and desires in program areas requiring cooperation between two or more Federal agencies, and State and local governments;

　　—to mediate and resolve program problems or disputes between Federal agencies in the field, referring problems to Washington that will yield only to Presidential arbitration;

　　—to provide the President and his Executive Office staffs with an independent flow of intelligence on program operations and problems;

　　—to increase field liaison between the President and State and local political executives and key officials.

(3) Creating a new Office for Program Development with clear responsibility to develop a domestic social program for the President as a part of a reorganized Bureau of the Budget.

Executive Departments

To improve the management of domestic programs we recommend that the President:

(1) Require Cabinet Secretaries to expand, develop, and use high-calibre staff assistance for the tasks of program planning, review, budgeting and coordinated field management to enable department heads to unify and to discharge their program management responsibilities effectively.

2. While the majority of the Task Force recommends creation of a new, independent staff office outside the Budget Bureau, Messrs. Heineman, McNamara, and Schultze would locate the proposed Office of Program Coordination in a completely reorganized and reoriented Budget Bureau. Members of the Task Force unanimously view the need for creation of this Office as far more important than its precise location in the Executive Office.

(2) Continue efforts to reduce—through merger and realignment—the number of departments substantially in the grip of parochial interests (Labor, Commerce, Interior, and Agriculture), and resist proposals to create additional departments likely to be dominated by narrow, specialized interests or professional clienteles (Health or Education).

(3) Direct Cabinet Secretaries to unify operations in the field under strengthened departmental regional executives of higher rank and calibre who owe clear allegiance to department heads and the President.

(4) Direct Cabinet Secretaries to decentralize maximum authority for program operations and specific grant decisions to these strengthened regional executives and hold them responsible directly to the Office of the Secretary.

(5) Direct the Secretaries of HEW, HUD, Labor and the Director of OEO to agree on a plan and begin as quickly as possible to colocate field offices in common regional cities serving common geographical areas. (We have attached one example of a reasonable plan to accomplish this urgently needed consolidation of Federal departmental regions and headquarters.)

(6) Consolidate, through transfer, the manpower development, training, and work experience programs now in Labor and OEO in a unified Manpower Administration in the Department of HEW.

8.   Economic Opportunity Act of 1964
An Act to Mobilize the Human and Financial
Resources of the Nation to Combat Poverty in
the United States

Be it enacted by the Senate and House of Representatives of the United States of America in Congress assembled, That this Act may be cited as the "Economic Opportunity Act of 1964."

. . . .

FINDINGS AND DECLARATION OF PURPOSE

Sec. 2. Although the economic well-being and prosperity of the United States have progressed to a level surpassing any achieved in world history, and although these benefits are widely shared throughout the Nation, poverty continues to be the lot of a substantial number of our people. The United States can achieve its full economic and social potential as a nation only if every individual has the opportunity to contribute to the full extent of his capabilities and to participate in the workings of our society. It is, therefore, the policy of the United States to eliminate the paradox of poverty in the midst of plenty in this Nation by opening to everyone the opportunity for education and training, the opportunity to work, and the opportunity to live in decency and dignity. It is the purpose of this Act to strengthen, supplement, and coordinate efforts in furtherance of that policy.

TITLE II—URBAN AND RURAL COMMUNITY ACTION PROGRAMS

Part A—General Community Action Programs

STATEMENT OF PURPOSE

Sec. 201. The purpose of this part is to provide stimulation and incentive for urban and rural communities to mobilize their resources to combat poverty through community action programs.

(Title II) Urban and Rural Community Action Program, Public Law 88–452, (August 20, 1964). Title I and introductory material has been omitted as well as Part B of Title II pertaining to Adult Educational Programs.

Sec. 202. (a) The term "community action program" means a program—

(1) which mobilizes and utilizes resources, public or private, of any urban or rural, or combined urban and rural, geographical area (referred to in this part as a "community"), including but not limited to a State, metropolitan area, county, city, town, multicity unit, or multicounty unit in an attack on poverty;

(2) which provides services, assistance, and other activities of sufficient scope and size to give promise of progress toward elimination of poverty or a cause or causes of poverty through developing employment opportunities, improving human performance, motivation, and productivity, or bettering the conditions under which people live, learn, and work;

(3) which is developed, conducted, and administered with the maximum feasible participation of residents of the areas and members of the groups served; and

(4) which is conducted, administered, or coordinated by a public or private nonprofit agency (other than a political party), or a combination thereof.

(b) The Director is authorized to prescribe such additional criteria for programs carried on under this part as he shall deem appropriate.

ALLOTMENTS TO STATES

Sec. 203. (a) From the sums appropriated to carry out this title for a fiscal year, the Director shall reserve the amount needed for carrying out sections 204 and 205. Not to exceed 2 per centum of the amount so reserved shall be allotted by the Director among Puerto Rico, Guam, American Samoa, the Trust Territory of the Pacific Islands, and the Virgin Islands according to their respective needs for assistance under this part. Twenty per centum of the amount so reserved shall be allotted among the States as the Director shall determine. The remainder of the sums so reserved shall be allotted among the States as provided in subsection (b).

(b) Of the sums being allotted under this subsection—

(1) one-third shall be allotted by the Director among the States so that the allotment to each State under this clause will be an amount which bears the same ratio to such one-third as the number of public assistance recipients in such State bears to the total number of public assistance recipients in all the States;

(2) one-third shall be allotted by him among the States so that the allotment to each State under this clause will be an amount which bears the same ratio to such one-third as the annual average number of persons unemployed in such State bears to the annual average of persons unemployed in all the States; and

(3) the remaining one-third shall be allotted by him among the States so that

the allotment to each State under this clause will be an amount which bears the same ratio to such one-third as the number of related children under 18 years of age living in families with incomes of less than $1,000 in such State bears to the number of related children under 18 years of age living in families with incomes of less than $1,000 in all the States.

(c) The portion of any State's allottment under subsection (a) for a fiscal year which the Director determines will not be required for such fiscal year for carrying out this part shall be available for reallotment from time to time, on such dates during such year as the Director may fix, to other States in proportion to their original allotments for such year, but with such proportionate amount for any of such other States being reduced to the extent it exceeds the sum which the Director estimates such State needs and will be able to use for such year for carrying out this part; and the total of such reductions shall be similarly reallotted among the States whose proportionate amounts are not so reduced. Any amount reallotted to a State under this subsection during a year shall be deemed part of its allotment under subsection (a) for such year.

(d) For the purposes of this section, the term "State" does not include Puerto Rico, Guam, American Samoa, the Trust Territory of the Pacific Islands, and the Virgin Islands.

FINANCIAL ASSISTANCE FOR DEVELOPMENT OF COMMUNITY ACTION PROGRAMS

Sec. 204. The Director is authorized to make grants to, or to contract with, appropriate public or private nonprofit agencies, or combinations thereof, to pay part or all of the costs of development of community action programs.

FINANCIAL ASSISTANCE FOR CONDUCT AND ADMINISTRATION OF COMMUNITY ACTION PROGRAMS

Sec. 205. (a) The Director is authorized to make grants to, or to contract with, public or private nonprofit agencies, or combinations thereof, to pay part or all of the costs of community action programs which have been approved by him pursuant to this part, including the cost of carrying out programs which are components of a community action program and which are designed to achieve the purposes of this part. Such component programs shall be focused upon the needs of low-income individuals and families and shall provide expanded and improved services, assistance, and other activities, and facilities necessary in connection therewith. Such programs shall be conducted in those fields which fall within the purposes of this part including employment, job training and counseling, health, vocational rehabilitation, housing, home management, welfare, and special remedial and other noncurricular educational assistance for the benefit of low-income individuals and families.

(b) No grant or contract authorized under this part may provide for general aid to elementary or secondary education in any school or school system.

(c) In determining whether to extend assistance under this section the Director shall consider among other relevant factors the incidence of poverty within the community and within the areas or groups to be affected by the specific program or programs, and the extent to which the applicant is in a position to utilize efficiently and expeditiously the assistance for which application is made. In determining the incidence of poverty the Director shall consider information available with respect to such factors as: the concentration of low-income families, particularly those with children; the extent of persistent unemployment and underemployment; the number and proportion of persons receiving cash or other assistance on a needs basis from public agencies or private organizations; the number of migrant or transient low-income families; school dropout rates, military service rejection rates, and other evidences of low educational attainment; the incidence of disease, disability, and infant mortality; housing conditions; adequacy of community facilities and services; and the incidence of crime and juvenile delinquency.

(d) In extending assistance under this section the Director shall give special consideration to programs which give promise of effecting a permanent increase in the capacity of individuals, groups, and communities to deal with their problems without further assistance.

TECHNICAL ASSISTANCE

Sec. 206. The Director is authorized to provide, either directly or through grants or other arrangements, (1) technical assistance to communities in developing, conducting, and administering community action programs, and (2) training for specialized personnel needed to develop, conduct, or administer such programs or to provide services or other assistance thereunder.

RESEARCH, TRAINING, AND DEMONSTRATIONS

Sec. 207. The Director is authorized to conduct, or to make grants to or enter into contracts with institutions of higher education or other appropriate public agencies or private organizations for the conduct of, research, training, and demonstrations pertaining to the purposes of this part. Expenditures under this section in any fiscal year shall not exceed 15 per centum of the sums appropriated or allocated for such year to carry out the purposes of this part.

LIMITATIONS ON FEDERAL ASSISTANCE

Sec. 208. (a). Assistance pursuant to sections 204 and 205 paid for the period ending two years after the date of enactment of this Act, or June 30, 1966, whichever is later, shall not exceed 90 per centum of the costs referred to in those sections, respectively, and thereafter shall not exceed 50 per centum of such costs, unless the Director determines, pursuant to regulations adopted and promulgated by him establishing objective criteria for such determinations, that assistance in excess of such percentages is required in furtherance of the purposes of this part. Non-Federal contributions may be in cash or in kind, fairly evaluated, including but not limited to plant, equipment, and services.

(b) The expenditures or contributions made from non-Federal sources for a community action program or component thereof shall be in addition to the aggregate expenditures or contributions from non-Federal sources which were being made for similar purposes prior to the extension of Federal assistance.

PARTICIPATION OF STATE AGENCIES

Sec. 209. (a) The Director shall establish procedures which will facilitate effective participation of the States in community action programs.

(b) The Director is authorized to make grants to, or to contract with, appropriate State agencies for the payment of the expenses of such agencies in providing technical assistance to communities in developing, conducting, and administering community action programs.

(c) In carrying out the provisions of title I and title II of this Act, no contract, agreement, grant, loan, or other assistance shall be made with, or provided to, any State or local public agency or any private institution or organization for the purpose of carrying out any program, project, or other activity within a State unless a plan setting forth such proposed contract, agreement, grant, loan, or other assistance has been submitted to the Governor of the State, and such plan has not been disapproved by him within thirty days of such submission: *Provided, however,* That this section shall not apply to contracts, agreements, grants, loans, or other assistance to any institution of higher education in existence on the date of the approval of this Act.

(d) No private institution or organization shall be eligible for participation under this part unless it (1) is itself an institution or organization which has, prior to its consideration for such participation, had a concern with problems of poverty, or (2) is sponsored by one or more such institutions or organizations or by a public agency, or (3) is an institution of higher education (as defined by section 401(f) of the Higher Education Facilities Act of 1963).

EQUITABLE DISTRIBUTION OF ASSISTANCE

Sec. 210. The Director shall establish criteria designed to achieve an equitable distribution of assistance under this part within the States between urban and rural areas. In developing such criteria, he shall consider the relative numbers in the States or areas therein of: (1) low-income families, particularly those with children;

(2) unemployed persons; (3) persons receiving cash or other assistance on a needs basis from public agencies or private organizations; (4) school dropouts; (5) adults with less than an eighth-grade education; (6) persons rejected for military service; and (7) persons living in urban places compared to the number living in rural places as determined by the Bureau of the Census for the 1960 census.

PREFERENCE FOR COMPONENTS OF APPROVED PROGRAMS

Sec. 211. In determining whether to extend assistance under this Act, the Director shall, to the extent feasible, give preference to programs and projects which are components of a community action program pursuant to this part.

PART II

The Quest for Improved Public Personnel Systems: Key Values in Conflict

The Quest for Improved
Public Personnel Systems: Key Values
in Conflict

Postwar developments in the public personnel field must first and foremost be viewed within the context of the preceding half-century's "civil service movement" to eradicate the perniciousness of "spoils" from all aspects of government employment. The Civil Service Act of 1883 (Pendleton Act) marked the apogee of a moral crusade to end the more destructive influences of patronage in the public service and establish a "neutral" system, emulating the British experience, of an independent civil service selected through open, competitive examinations.[1] "Merit" should replace "politics," according to the visions of the civil service reformers, as the central criterion for employment in government.

The battle for a neutral civil service, based on "merit," though, only began with the passage of the Pendleton Act. The new law covered at the outset only approximately 10 percent of those in the federal service. Thereafter, for more than fifty years presidential election campaigns were at least partially fought over such questions as will the number and extent of public service jobs covered under civil service shrink or grow with the selection of a new president. There were at times setbacks for the reformers, but on the whole the cause of "merit" advanced steadily in pre-World War II America—at the federal as well as the state and local levels. Also especially important in pre-World War II America for fostering the values of a neutral, efficient, merit-based civil service were the Classification Act of 1923, which established the concept of "equal pay for equal work" and provided for institutional means at the federal level to implement this concept; the growth of the council-manager plan after the turn of the century, which extended the ideals of merit to many local governments; and the Hatch Acts (1939, 1940), which further tightened the neutrality concept for civil servants working at all levels of government by means of precise, strict statutory language.[2]

1. The best single-volume history of this subject is still Paul P. Van Riper, *History of the United States Civil Service* (New York: Harper & Row, 1958); though shorter but still useful is Frederick C. Mosher, *Democracy and the Public Service* (New York: Oxford University Press, 1968).

2. See Frederick C. Mosher, *Basic Documents of American Public Administration: 1776–1950* (New York: Holmes & Meier, 1976), pp. 108–109.

By contrast, the basic documents contained in Part II of this volume indicate a pronounced shift away from the values of neutrality, efficiency, and merit as the overriding ideals of postwar personnel administration. Instead, twin, often contradictory, values emerge as being of preeminent importance: that is, "group representation" and "executive leadership." That is not to say that "merit" as a key value "evaporated" entirely from the personnel field. Indeed fostering merit principles remains even today a strong and vital concern within the public personnel field. But, by and large, the critical public documents of the postwar era indicate the innovative drive of the personnel field shifted elsewhere: that is, to enhancing "group interests" and "executive leadership."

On one hand, postwar documents reflect a new commitment to "group representation" inside the public sector, particularly for "targeted" groups in society that many believed, for a variety of reasons, should be given special preference in public employment. The best example of this new emphasis is certainly reflected in the Veterans Preference Act of 1944 (see Frederick C. Mosher's *Basic Documents of American Public Administration, 1776–1950*). Some would argue the Veteran Act is *the* critical document "impacting" on today's public personnel policy. The 1944 act gave veterans special advantages in examination, appointments, certification and appeals process by virtue of the dates of their active duty service in the U.S. Armed Forces.

In a different manner, though aimed at achieving fundamentally similar results in advancing a particular organized group's interests in terms of public employment, President Kennedy's Executive Orders 10987 and 10988 (1962) established for the first time a federalwide policy to permit public employee organizations to play an important, ongoing part in the development of public personnel policies. Similarly, the concern for minorities, women, and the disadvantaged resulted in President Johnson's Executive Order 11246 (1965), which sought to eliminate official discrimination and create more opportunity for advancement within the public service by means of "affirmative action" measures. Ultimately, the 1972 Equal Employment Opportunity Act Amendments to the 1964 Civil Rights Act brought all levels of government employment under the national commitment of promoting affirmative action for those who many viewed as having in the past been deprived of these employment opportunities.

On the other hand, several of the documents contained in Part II place significant emphasis upon strengthening of "executive leadership" within the public service, that is, documents that serve to enhance executive capacities for oversight, direction, discretion, and control of personnel management by chief executives—as opposed to either enhancing particular "group interests" or "neutral expertise" of the civil service. Much of the new post-World War II stress upon executive leadership came from both the scholars and practitioners who argued that independence for the civil service had been extended too far and that public executives were being hamstrung by personnel rules and procedures. The belief expressed by many writers was that public executives were unable to manage their programs effectively, if at all. In the apt phrase of one noted public personnel expert, Wallace Sayre, the personnel field had become "the triumph of technique over purpose."[3] And many observers, inside and outside government, largely agreed. Thus, one finds important documents contained in Part II promoting executive managerial capabilities such as the Second Hoover Commission proposal for "Senior Civil Service" with its provisions for greater "horizontal public executive mobility" within the federal public service. The Intergovernmental Personnel Act of 1970, on the other hand, sought more effective management through wider "vertical mobility" for civil servants *between* levels of government. The Civil Service Reform Act of 1978, especially in terms of its creation of both the Office of Personnel Management and the Senior Executive Service, instituted important new devices for making public managers more responsive and accountable to presidential leadership. Granted, certain parts of the 1978 Reform Act tried to protect merit principles (that is, the Merit Protection Board). Nevertheless, the central emphasis of this Reform Act, as well as many other postwar documents, clearly placed a premium upon broader leadership discretion for chief executives vis-à-vis the public personnel system in order to allow managers to manage public service programs more effectively. In some documents, enhancing executive discretion came because of less worthy reasons in postwar America. For instance, the "Malek Manual" outlined techniques to extend presidential control of federal workers for highly questionable purposes—a particular president's personal political aspirations.

1. U.S. Commission on Organization of the Executive Branch of Government, "Senior Civil Service Proposal" (Second Hoover Commission, 1955)

The Second Hoover Commission's operational design, structure, and selection of members followed much the same pattern as the First Hoover Commission with its task force emphasis, significant business representation and close and careful overall direction by former President Herbert Hoover. Also there was continuity of fundamental "classical orthodox" value perspectives from the First to Second Hoover Reports due to the fact that five of the Second Hoover's members were alumni of the First Hoover Commission.

While Second Hoover's overall recommendations were largely more technical,

---

3. Wallace S. Sayre, "Triumph of Technique over Purpose" *Public Administration Review*, vol. 8, no. 1 (Spring 1948), pp. 134–137.

more specialized, and generally less exciting by comparison to the First Hoover Commission, one highly innovative proposal was offered in the Task Force Report on Personnel and Civil Service, namely "The Senior Civil Service Concept." This proposal to develop a mobile pool of highly qualified top managers within the federal government was first formulated by Professor Leonard White, of the University of Chicago, in the 1930s. In many respects his idea emulated the British personnel practice of an "administrative class" composed of a top group of British civil servants, politically neutral, highly competent, and with managerial expertise capable of serving any political party in power.[1] Although the Senior Civil Service proposal was not adopted in 1955, it was widely discussed at the time, and later, in a revised form, became one of the centerpieces of the Civil Service Reform Act of 1978, with the creation of the Senior Executive Service (SES). The Senior Civil Service idea, like the later SES, aimed to improve overall federal management effectiveness.

2. President John Kennedy's Executive Orders 10987 and 10988 (1962)

The right of federal employees to join or refrain from joining labor unions was first affirmed by the Lloyd-LaFollette Act of 1912. Nevertheless, unionization in the public sector grew in fits and starts in various areas of skilled, unskilled, and professional groups of public servants. By 1960 some federal employees like those in the Post Office Department were more than 90 percent unionized. However, many areas of government operated without unions, and labor-management policies throughout the federal government were set haphazardly by individual departments and agencies. Federal policies in this field were thus developed unevenly in design, procedure, and application.

Federal labor-management reforms were initiated largely through the efforts of President John Kennedy's new Secretary of Labor, Arthur Goldberg. His report on the subject early in his term (curiously presented to the president in the form of a personal letter) resulted in President Kennedy's Executive Orders 10987 and 10988. Both executive orders promulgated for the first time federal-wide labor-management policies and opened "a new era" of growth of union representation in government. Many state and local governments soon followed the federal example. The Kennedy executive orders were revised in 1969 and amended in 1971 and ultimately written into law as part of the Civil Service Reform Act of 1978. Ironically, one should note in reading both Kennedy executive orders that they contain more prohibitions on unions than actual positive statements about their new roles, prerogatives, and rights.

---

4. For an excellent discussion of this subject, read Frederick C. Mosher, *Democracy and the Public Service* (New York: Oxford University Press, 1968). pp. 87–88.

3. a. *President Lyndon Johnson's Executive Order 11246 (1965)*

b. *President Richard Nixon's Executive Order 11478 (1969)*

c. *Title VII of the Civil Rights Act of 1964 as amended by the Equal Employment Opportunity Act of 1972.*

Throughout the 1960s and early 1970s, primarily in response to the civil rights movement, a new emphasis within the federal government was placed upon eliminating discriminatory practices and promoting equal opportunities for both minorities and women. Certainly, there had been a substantial history of this effort at the federal level dating back to the 1940s, even 1930s (for example, racial integration of the armed forces occurred in the 1940s).[5] However, the 1960s saw something new with the concept of affirmative action as developed by President Johnson's Executive Order 11246 (1965), and later, strengthened by Richard Nixon's Executive Order 11478 (1969), and still later written into statute by Title VII of the Civil Rights Act of 1964 as amended by the Equal Employment Opportunity Act of 1972. Affirmative action as defined by these and other writings in the personnel field generally meant "positive" emphasis to enhance public service job opportunities for women and minorities through special efforts in recruitment, promotions, job redesign, skill training, and information methods. Clearly affirmative action was and still remains a complex issue because it raises basic questions about the traditional "color blind" neutrality of the civil service. Debate over the purposes, effectiveness, and results of affirmative action programs continues today, particularly in terms of recent court decisions.

4. *Intergovernmental Personnel Act of 1970*

The Intergovernmental Personnel Act of 1970 (commonly referred to as IPA) represented an important "first" in federal cooperation with states and localities relative to strengthening personnel management capabilities and resources throughout all levels of government. Enacted after many years of work by Senator Edmund Muskie (Maine, Democrat) and others in the personnel and intergovernmental field, IPA sought to improve the public service through several strategies: grants to states and localities for personnel management training and improvement, government service fellowships, technical assistance programs, talent sharing programs, access of municipalities to federal training programs, promotion of coopera-

---

5. Richard J. Stillman II, *Integration of the Negro in the U.S. Armed Forces* (New York: Praeger Publishers, 1968).

tive training, recruiting, and examining efforts. Some personnel specialists, like
O. Glenn Stahl, argue that IPA's opening Declaration of Policy (section 2) is still
today one of the best and clearest statements of the merit principles ever written
into the law books.[6]

5. Excerpts from the Federal Political Personnel Manual ("Malek Manual")

To be certain, there had been abuses, some very major ones, of civil service
rules by prior administrations, but most observers agree that more blatant ones
occurred in the Nixon years. The Federal Political Personnel Manual, prepared
prior to President Nixon's 1972 reelection campaign under the direction of Fred
Malek, an associate director in the Office of Management and Budget, summarized
in written form the very worst of these abusive personnel practices for flagrantly
partisan purposes. Prepared ostensibly for the new Nixon political appointees from
the business world in order to familiarize them with unique aspects of the government personnel system, the Malek Manual's contents were hardly new ideas to
anyone knowledgeable in the personnel field at that time. Yet, its publication by
the Ervin Committee investigating the problems associated with the Watergate
Affair brought sharp public reaction and demand for reform of existing civil service
procedures and practices.

6. a. President's Reorganization Project, Personnel Management, Introduction to the Final Staff Report ("Ink Report," 1977)

b. The Civil Service Reform Act of 1978

Unquestionably, the most profound change in the federal civil service system
since its inception in 1883 occurred with the enactment of the Civil Service Reform
Act of 1978. The 1978 Reform Act was a product of an overall federal reorganization project initiated by President Jimmy Carter shortly after he assumed office in
1977. Specifically, the Final Staff Report on Personnel Management, chaired by
Dwight Ink, compiled a set of recommendations (based on findings of nine task
forces). Many of these recommendations of the Ink Report served as the basis for
the Civil Service Reform Act of 1978. The popular sentiment favoring civil service
reform, President Carter's campaign commitment to this reform, coupled with the
skillful political tactics of Civil Service Director Alan K. Campbell and Congressman Morris ("Mo") Udall (Arizona, Democrat), who chaired a key House commit-

---

6. For a discussion of the idea of merit, refer to chapter 3 of O. Glenn Stahl, *Public Personnel
Administration,* 7th ed. (New York: Harper & Row, 1976).

tee at the time—all combined to allow for the enactment of the Reform Act. Among the important new elements contained in the Reform Act were (1) the elimination of the independent Civil Service Commission and the establishment of the Office of Personnel Management as the key personnel staff arm of the president; (2) development of the Senior Executive Service to provide greater management flexibility in using talented top federal executives throughout government; (3) establishment of an independent Merit Protection Board to insure stronger protection of "merit" within the civil service; (4) creation of the merit pay concept, based upon experience of business firms, that permits rewarding outstanding public managerial performance; (5) initiation of a broad scale of research and development programs relative to federal management and personnel practices, and (6) statutory provisions for strengthening federal labor-management policy as well as existing affirmative action programs. Selections that outline these important new features, as well as the opening statement by Dwight Ink outlining the basic justifications and central perspectives of the report that led to the Civil Service Reform Act of 1978, are included in Part II.

1. The Second Hoover Commission Report (1955)

THE SENIOR CIVIL SERVICE PROPOSAL

In the pages which follow it is the purpose of the task force to outline improved means of providing within the civil service system a highly competent group of professional administrators, neutral in politics, who will work under the direction of political executives in operating the machinery of the national administration and who will aid the political executives to meet their responsibilities. This "Senior Civil Service," as it is called in this report, would consist of career men at the highest levels who have capacity for managerial work and for important staff responsibilities, and it would be carefully selected from the entire body of Federal employees. It would be open to all solely on the basis of merit demonstrated within the Federal civil service.

The system of personnel administration which now exists in the Government of the United States has several serious defects when it comes to supplying competent civil servants for the most important managerial and staff positions.

Although the Government is the largest employer with the greatest continuing need for managerial competence, it has no system by which it identifies men and women of great capacity within the Government. It has no means of officially recognizing competence even after it is demonstrated. The personnel system as such does not place major emphasis on affording incentives for those who would devote outstanding talents to a career within the civil service, although the Government is dependent upon men who will make national administration their life work. The civil service system emphasizes positions, not people. Jobs are classified, ranked, rated, and paid on the bland assumption that they can always be filled like so many jugs, merely by turning the tap. The Government as an employer does not systematically develop the talents of its employees. There is no positive governmentwide program to supply managerial talent at any level, and especially the highest level. There is insufficient official recognition in laws, regulations, policies, or procedures that the Government as an employer ought to try to meet its management needs by systematic measures. There is also very little flexibility in

Task Force Report "Personnel and Civil Service" by Task Force on Personnel and Civil Service for U.S. Commission on Organization of the Executive Branch of the Government, February 1955, pp. 49–59. Only the section of the report pertaining to the Senior Civil Service proposal is included in this excerpt.

the use of managerial manpower at high levels within the civil service system. The main features of the civil service system as it has evolved have to be circumvented in many cases by escape clauses, exceptions, interpretations, and a certain amount of judicious disregard to make it workable in dealing with the more responsible administrative posts—a source of embarrassment to all concerned. In the aggregate, this combination of improvisation, manipulation, and rationalization is a long way from a reasonable or practical means of meeting the Government's great and continued need for high administrative talent.

The civil service law and the civil service system, which have been built upon the law, are designed primarily for other purposes. Originating as a reaction against the spoils system, and adapted to the large-scale employment problem of 20th century government, the present civil service has not been well designed to provide professional administrators at the higher levels. The extension to higher posts of concepts and procedures which were designed for large numbers of standardized positions at lower levels has been awkward for both political executives and career administrators, because they disregard so completely both the personalities and the careers of individual men. Some new concepts, policies, and procedures are needed which are designed specifically to supply career administrators at the higher levels. The Senior Civil Service and the executive development program proposed by the task force are an effort to meet this need.

The Proposed Senior Civil Service Defined

The Senior Civil Service should consist of a group of professional administrators carefully selected from all parts of the civil service and from all departments and agencies solely on the basis of demonstrated competence. They should be given an appointment resembling that of a commissioned officer in the Armed Forces in that they would have status, rank, and salary as individuals, and could be employed flexibly in a number of authorized positions calling for high administrative talents. The rules governing senior civil servants should require them to keep clear of all "political" activity, to preserve their neutrality in matters of politics, and to serve each Chief Executive faithfully. These rules should be respected in the assignments given to senior civil servants as well as in the way that they handle their assignments.

The primary objective is to have always at hand in the Government a designated group of highly qualified administrators whose competence, integrity, and faithfulness cannot reasonably be questioned; who will make it easier for political executives to discharge their responsibilities; and who will add to the smoothness, the effectiveness, and the economy of governmental operations. A secondary but related purpose is to make the civil service more attractive as a career to able men and women.

Principal Features of the Proposed Senior Civil Service

The task force believes that a Senior Civil Service of highly competent career administrators should be established along the lines outlined below. It does not emphasize details of the proposal, and it is aware that the plan presented may be improved in operation. But the task force is strongly convinced that action of the general nature outlined should be taken promptly and carried through until it is firmly established in the institutional framework of the Government—a process that will require several years. There will be immediate and positive benefits from establishing a Senior Civil Service, and the benefits should increase steadily as the full effects of the plan are felt.

1. Personal-Rank Status. Congress should authorize and the President should establish a Senior Civil Service consisting of experienced civil servants who have so well demonstrated their administrative competence, integrity, and qualities of leadership that their rank, basic salary, and status should be vested in them as individual civil servants. This would differ from the traditional practice of attaching rank and salary to the job. In a sense they would be "commissioned officers" of high rank and would occupy high administrative positions subordinate to agency heads and their political associates in the political executive group. Although the process of identifying the civil servants best qualified for this personal-rank status will take some time since it must be done carefully, it is suggested that initially 1,500 men be appointed as rapidly as qualified persons can be found and that the number be increased progressively. An ultimate strength of 3,000 may be needed. The President should have authority to fix the strength of the service, within broad limits set by law.

The size should be determined by the number of positions in which senior civil servants can be used appropriately. These positions (which include administrative assistant secretaries and equivalent posts; bureau chiefs; assistant bureau chiefs; some division chiefs; heads of regional or district offices, heads of budget, personnel and other organic staff offices; deputy heads of policy staff offices, and professional aides and assistants to important political executives) now total more than 2,950 in the 47 larger agencies of the Government that have been studied by the task force. The number in all Federal agencies probably exceeds 3,000 today.

Within the Senior Civil Service two ranks or groups may be needed eventually to provide recognition for advancement and, also, in the upper group, to mark the men who are qualified for the more responsible posts. At the outset they should be constituted as a single group.

2. Flexibility. Members could be shifted from one job or assignment to another in top management without the present danger of suffering loss of pay or status. For example, a senior civil servant might be moved from a position as head of a division, in an operating bureau, to be the aide to an assistant secretary, and from there he might later be assigned to the position of director in a regional office. This transferability would recognize facts which tend to be obscured by the civil service position-classification system: at high levels where each position tends to be unique the difficulty of the job varies from time to time; and the man who fills it may make the job, not the job the man.

3. Obligation To Serve. The corollary of personal-rank status is an obligation upon the part of the senior civil servant to serve where needed most. Subject to a rule of reason and, of course, with a right to have his views considered in the decisions, he could be expected to fill an appropriate position in Washington, in the field service, or abroad, as needed. The men commissioned as senior civil servants should have a substantial area of transferability; they should be more than narrow specialists.

4. Political Neutrality. Senior civil servants as a group should be fully prepared to serve faithfully each administration that takes office. This means that they must avoid such emotional attachment to the policies of any administration that they cannot accept change. Senior civil servants would necessarily refrain from all political activities that would affect adversely their ability to perform their official duties fairly, or that would tend to identify them with a party policy. The Hatch Act has made this obligation clear where electoral campaign activities are concerned. The obligation needs to be clarified also in other ways. It is suggested that a senior civil servant should be guided by the following principles:

(a) He should make no public or private statements to the press where there is a political executive available to do so, except of a purely factual nature. (In field offices, of course, the senior civil servant would find it necessary to deal with the press—releasing information, answering questions, and making explanations.)

(b) The senior civil servant should make no public speeches of a political character. He should avoid controversial public discussion of policies; but where it is appropriate to do so in the line of duty, he should explain and if necessary defend public policies established by law.

(c) He should not contribute to political campaign funds.

(d) The senior civil servant should avoid testimony before committees of Congress on political questions. If asked to comment on a controversial issue, he should refer the questions to his political superiors, or at most should explicitly state his department's official position. He should resolutely but courteously decline to give his personal views. On the other hand, he should be ready at all times to provide background information, relevant data, and even technical advice where such assistance can be helpful.

(e) He should avoid public identification with a political party, e.g., in rallies, fund-raising drives, and the like. But this neutrality should not impair his right to

vote, in primaries as well as final elections, and his right to be active in civic affairs. For example, service on a school board should be permitted. In this group of 1,500 to 3,000 men and women, however, great care to avoid political involvement is needed. When there is doubt about the propriety of such activities as public speaking or participating in the affairs of local governments, the approval of the Senior Civil Service Board should be sought, as described below.

The political neutrality of senior civil servants must be recognized and respected also by the political executives who are their superiors, by Members of Congress, and by the public.

Senior civil servants should be paid adequately. As has been explained above, salaries of political executives should be increased to reduce the discrepancy between Government pay and compensation for comparable positions in private life. This would require an adjustment to bring the pay of assistant secretaries to $25,000 a year, and the salaries of under secretaries and secretaries to points above that figure. The compensation of senior civil servants should be adjusted to keep pace with these changes in the political executives' pay scale. Their salaries should range from the equivalent of GS–15 (presently $10,800 to $11,800) at entrance into the Senior Civil Service, upward to a figure equivalent to that of under secretaries (presently $17,500). The latter salary would be attained by men of long service with outstanding records.

Increases in pay above the entrance rate should be awarded in recognition of continued growth and satisfactory performance of the senior civil servant.

Retirement annuities of senior civil servants should also be increased at least to a point where they would be on a par with other commissioned groups such as the Foreign Service.

The Machinery of Administration

Authority and responsibility for setting up and operating the Senior Civil Service should be vested in a bipartisan Senior Civil Service Board of five members, which should consist of three distinguished citizens (not Federal officials) appointed by the President; the chairman of the Civil Service Commission or his designated deputy; and the Director of the Bureau of the Budget or his designated deputy.

The chairman of the Board should be designated by the president from among the lay members, and the Board should be served by an executive secretary and appropriate staff selected by it. The autonomy of the Senior Civil Service Board is useful in its early years to make sure that it has an opportunity to view its problems freshly and to develop appropriate policies and procedures without being restricted by traditional civil service attitudes and conventions. Representatives on the Board from the Civil Service Commission and the Bureau of the Budget will serve to keep it in touch with personnel experts of the Government and with general management considerations. The Board's autonomy is also important at the outset to emphasize its responsibility for launching the Senior Civil Service and for getting it established.

When the Senior Civil Service has been well established, however, an autonomous Senior Civil Service Board should be less necessary. At some later stage the administration of the Senior Civil Service program might appropriately be taken over by the Civil Service Commission. In the meantime, the Board might be associated with the Commission for the provision of administrative services. It is suggested that the overhead organization should be reconsidered at the end of 10 years.

The Selection of Senior Civil Servants

Persons should be appointed or commissioned as senior civil servants by the Senior Civil Service Board only after their qualifications have been fully established according to the procedures set up by the Board. Nominations should be made to the Board by the Executive departments and agencies, which should be responsible for making the initial selection and for preparing the supporting documents.

Men and women recommended to the Senior Civil Service Board should be outstanding civil servants. In examining the nominees the Board should look for qualities of leadership, judgment, adaptability, skill in working with people, and capacity for continued growth. It should look for professional or technical competence at least of the quality now expected at the GS–15 level, and it should require a minimum of 5 years' Federal service.

Other desirable qualifications, which could not be insisted upon at the outset but which could be attained after the proposed executive development program is well under way, are: experience in more than one agency, experience in both staff and line (operating) work, and experience in both the departmental and field services.

The evaluation of qualifications should be based on full consideration of the documents and data submitted as may be specified by the Senior Civil Service Board, examinations of the nominee's record, and normally a personal interview (except when waived by the board). The Board should have full authority to obtain information judged to be relevant to an evaluation, but political endorsements of any sort should be rigidly excluded. The Senior Civil Service Board should take great pains to make sure that all nominees are considered on their merits, and that influence is not a factor.

Appropriate procedures should be established by the Senior Civil Service Board (perhaps through selection and evaluation committees of persons drawn from both private life and the Government) to determine fitness for the Senior Civil Service, and to review the status of senior civil servants periodically. The Senior Civil

Service Board itself should then consider the case of each senior civil servant to determine whether he should be advanced in pay or "selected out" of the Senior Civil Service.

Appointments to the Senior Civil Service and promotions within it by the Board should be effective when approved by the President. Members of the Senior Civil Service should have the prestige which goes with this recognition.

Executive departments would have a stake in establishing the Senior Civil Service. It would offer a superior status for their top civil servants so that a department's success in getting nominees accepted would increase its attractiveness as a place to work. The flexibility in assignment would also be an advantage, for emergencies could be met more easily; and as managerial problems changed, faster adjustments could be made to get the right man in each job. Mistakes in placement should be less likely and could be corrected more easily. The disadvantage of losing people to other departments would be more than offset by the possibility of later recapture and by the opportunity to enrich a departmental staff with outstanding men developed in other agencies.

The Senior Civil Service also offers clear advantages to the employee—improved career tenure instead of merely job tenure, better pay, more probable full utilization of abilities, fewer dead-ends, prospect of steadier promotion growing out of the broadened career opportunities and above all official recognition of his function and of his value to the Nation.

The general Government's gains from the Senior Civil Service are also clear— immediately improved utilization, and ultimately a strengthened corps of management talent. Tested career administrators would be known and available. The top administrative personnel would be a broadened group. They would know each other better and the Government better. They would be better equipped and more inclined to work out the problems of horizontal coordination which are so important in the Government. They could be moved to positions where needed most in emergencies without disruption of the civil service. The Government would have a known group of experienced administrators to draw upon.

The Senior Civil Service in Operation

With the Senior Civil Service in existence, a department or agency head might appoint a senior civil servant to any approved position. The selection of an individual from among the members of the Senior Civil Service and his assignment to a particular position in any department or agency would be the function of the department or agency head. The approval of positions suitable for senior civil servants would be a function of the Senior Civil Service Board, and each agency's list of approved positions would, in effect, amount to a quota—the measure of its normal claim upon the Senior Civil Service.

The agency's quota should not be so rigid as to preclude appointment of senior civil servants to additional temporary assignments, or so hard and fast as to interfere with reasonable flexibility in assignment. The President also should have authority to make use of senior civil servants for special assignments or temporary appointments, e.g., serving as secretary to a presidential committee, or making special studies for the Chief Executive. These special assignments, however, should be in keeping with the basic principle that senior civil servants must keep out of "politics."

Senior civil servants should be paid from the funds of the agency in which employed, at their basic rate as fixed by the Senior Civil Service Board.

In practice, the placement of senior civil servants in positions would rest largely with agency heads who would make the final decisions; but the Senior Civil Service Board with its records and extensive knowledge of the Service would naturally contribute substantially to the placement decisions. It would be natural for an employing agency to consult the Board when it needed additional manpower, or when it wanted to make changes. Senior civil servants, also, would probably consult the Board's executive secretary informally if interested in a change of assignment. The Board and its staff could fill a gap in the existing machinery of personnel administration by making the Senior Civil Service a pool of known and available talent for high level assignments, and by advising and counseling both agency heads and senior civil servants.

If a member of the Senior Civil Service should for any reason be temporarily unassigned, for example during a change of administrations, he would continue to draw his basic salary for a time. During such periods, senior civil servants should be utilized in temporary assignments. If no assignment had been worked out at the end of 6 months, the Board should have authority to continue the senior civil servant at full salary for an additional 6 months, to put him on half salary for a 6 months' period, or to retire him.

It should be the policy of the Board to develop the full usefulness of members of the Senior Civil Service and at the same time to preserve the professional character of the Service as a body of faithful and impartial employees. To these ends, the Board well might encourage movement between Washington and field positions, between staff and line work, and among agencies. While giving due consideration to the immediate needs and wishes of both employer and employees, the Board also must have in view the longer range interests of the employer, the employee, and the Government. For example, senior civil servants doubtless will be assigned at times as special assistants to political executives. These assignments are useful to all concerned. But although it may be highly convenient to continue a particular senior civil servant as an aide, it may be unwise generally to do so beyond a period of a few years. Exceptions to this principle may be necessary; but they should be made with due regard for the danger that the aide may be identified with his principal in such a way as to involve the aide in "politics" and to tag him as a partisan. Such "hot" assignments can be very valuable, but they should not be too long continued. The Board by suggesting suitable replacements in time can minimize the burns.

In the formative years of the Senior Civil Service, the Board can play a very useful part in helping members of the Service, political executives, and also the public to recognize and give precedence to the mission of the Service as a continuing body of professional administrators obligated to serve the public through competent and faithful service to each administration as it comes. Although the Board will have some authority to regulate the conduct of senior civil servants, it will have to rely on diplomacy with outsiders in advocating respect for the political neutrality of the Service. For example, it may need to use its good offices with political executives to persuade them not to draw senior civil servants, who are their subordinates, into political controversies. Similarly, it will not be easy to convince press, radio, and television reporters that they normally should preserve the anonymity of the Senior Civil Service, and that it will suffer in effectiveness if its members are drawn into the limelight. Publicity in the nature of public recognition of distinguished work of individual senior civil servants should, if possible, be postponed until the time of their retirement.

The Board should periodically review the progress of every senior civil servant, and the Board's staff should keep in touch with developments on a day-to-day basis. This regular appraisal should be made with as much thoroughness as in making original appointments. Following such an evaluation, the Senior Civil Service Board might authorize an increase in pay (or a promotion if and when internal ranks are established).

If the Board's review of a senior civil servant's progress should result in an adverse judgment, it could lead to dropping the employee from the Senior Civil Service. He might be "selected out," also, under rules which the Board should prescribe, if passed over repeatedly for increase in pay. The Board should have power to drop members from the roster of the Senior Civil Service for improper conduct. It is suggested that in actions of this sort, the Board utilize a review committee if it does not itself initially review the case. Action might be initiated by the staff of the Board, by the employing agency, by a Senior Civil Service colleague, or by charges from some other person. The senior civil servant challenged should have a right to a hearing by the Board before its decision is final. Action to drop a senior civil servant, either for cause or through selection-out procedures, would vacate his position and end his status as a senior civil servant.

It is believed that if a Senior Civil Service of the sort envisaged by the task force can be established, a large part of the responsibility for discipline should be assumed by the Senior Civil Service itself through a recognized code of conduct emphasizing standards of political neutrality in official conduct, impartial judgment, and faithful service.

2.a.   Executive Order 10987 (1962) Agency Systems for Appeals from Adverse Actions

WHEREAS the public interest requires the maintenance of high standards of employee performance and integrity in the public service, prompt administrative action where such standards are not met, and safeguards to protect employees against arbitrary or unjust adverse actions; and

WHEREAS the prompt reconsideration of protested administrative decisions to take adverse actions against employees will promote the efficiency of the service, assist in maintaining a high level of employee morale, further the objective of improving employee-management relations, and insure timely correction of improper adverse actions;

NOW, THEREFORE, by virtue of the authority vested in me by the Constitution of the United States, by Section 1753 of the Revised Statutes (5 U.S.C. 631), by the Civil Service Act of 1883 (22 Stat. 403; 5 U.S.C. 632, et. seq.), and as President of the United States, it is hereby ordered as follows:

Section 1. The head of each department and agency, in accord with the provisions of this order and regulations issued thereunder by the Civil Service Commission, and to the extent specified in such regulations, shall establish within the department or agency a system for the reconsideration of administrative decisions to take adverse action against employees. Information on the system shall be brought to the attention of all employees. Within the principles established by this order and subject to the broad guidelines contained in the regulations, each department and agency is authorized to develop such agency appeals procedures as may be appropriate to its own organizational requirements.

Sec. 2. (a) The Civil Service Commission shall, not later than April 1, 1962, issue regulations to put this order into effect and shall make a continuing review of the manner in which this order is being implemented by the departments and agencies.

(b) Nothing in this order shall be deemed to enlarge or restrict the authority of the Civil Service Commission to adjudicate appeals submitted in accordance with Chapter I of Title 5 of the Code of Federal Regulations.

Sec. 3. The Civil Service Commission in issuing regulations and the depart-

Both E. O. 10987 and 10988 cited without deletions from *U.S. Code of Federal Regulations, Title 3—The President, 1959–1963, Compilation*, pp. 519–528.

ments and agencies in developing an appeals system shall be guided by the following principles:

(1) The appeals system shall be a simple, orderly method through which an employee or former employee may seek timely administrative reconsideration of a decision to take adverse action against him.

(2) Employees and representatives of employee organizations shall have an opportunity to express their views as to the formulation and operation of the appeals procedures.

(3) An appeal shall be in writing and indicate clearly the corrective action sought and the reasons therefor.

(4) The system shall provide ordinarily for one level of appeal, except that it may include further administrative review when the delegations of authority or organizational arrangements of the agency so require.

(5) An employee who has not previously had an opportunity for a hearing in connection with the agency decision to take adverse action shall, on his request, be granted one hearing, except when the holding of a hearing is impracticable by reason of unusual location or other extraordinary circumstance.

(6) The employee shall be assured freedom from restraint, interference, coercion, discrimination, or reprisal in presenting his appeal.

(7) The employee shall have the right to be accompanied, represented, and advised by a representative of his own choosing in presenting his appeal.

(8) The employee shall be assured of a reasonable amount of official time to present his appeal.

(9) An appeal shall be resolved expeditiously. To this end, both the employee and the department or agency shall proceed with an appeal without undue delay.

Sec. 4. The head of each department and agency is authorized to include provision for advisory arbitration, where appropriate, in the agency appeals system.

Sec. 5. (a) This order shall not apply to the Central Intelligence Agency, the National Security Agency, the Federal Bureau of Investigation, the Atomic Energy Commission, and the Tennessee Valley Authority.

(b) The Civil Service Commission, on the recommendation of the heads of the agencies concerned, may exclude classes of employees the nature of whose work makes the application of the provisions of this order inappropriate.

Sec. 6. This order shall become effective as to all adverse actions commenced by issuance of a notification of proposed action on or after July 1, 1962.

John F. Kennedy

The White House, *January 17, 1962*.

2.b. Executive Order 10988 (1962) Employee-Management Cooperation in the Federal Service

WHEREAS participation of employees in the formulation and implementation of personnel policies affecting them contributes to effective conduct of public business; and

WHEREAS the efficient administration of the Government and the well-being of employees require that orderly and constructive relationships be maintained between employee organizations and management officials; and

WHEREAS subject to law and the paramount requirements of the public service, employee-management relations within the Federal service should be improved by providing employees an opportunity for greater participation in the formulation and implementation of policies and procedures affecting the conditions of their employment; and

WHEREAS effective employee-management cooperation in the public service requires a clear statement of the respective rights and obligations of employee organizations and agency management:

NOW, THEREFORE, by virtue of the authority vested in me by the Constitution of the United States, by section 1753 of the Revised Statutes (5 U.S.C. 631), and as President of the United States, I hereby direct that the following policies shall govern officers and agencies of the executive branch of the Government in all dealings with Federal employees and organizations representing such employees.

Section 1. (a) Employees of the Federal Government shall have, and shall be protected in the exercise of, the right, freely and without fear of penalty or reprisal, to form, join and assist any employee organization or to refrain from any such activity. Except as hereinafter expressly provided, the freedom of such employees to assist any employee organization shall be recognized as extending to participation in the management of the organization and acting for the organization in the capacity of an organization representative, including presentation of its views to officials of the executive branch, the Congress or other appropriate authority. The head of each executive department and agency (hereinafter referred to as "agency") shall take such action, consistent with law, as may be required in order to assure that employees in the agency are apprised of the rights described in this section, and that no interference, restraint, coercion or discrimination is practiced within such agency to encourage or discourage membership in any employee organization.

(b) The rights described in this section do not extend to participation in the

93

management of an employee organization, or acting as a representative of any such organization, where such participation or activity would result in a conflict of interest or otherwise be incompatible with law or with the official duties of an employee.

Sec. 2. When used in this order, the term "employee organization" means any lawful association, labor organization, federation, council, or brotherhood having as a primary purpose the improvement of working conditions among Federal employees, or any craft, trade or industrial union whose membership includes both Federal employees and employees of private organizations; but such term shall not include any organization (1) which asserts the right to strike against the Government of the United States or any agency thereof, or to assist or participate in any such strike, or which imposes a duty or obligation to conduct, assist or participate in any such strike, or (2) which advocates the overthrow of the constitutional form of Government in the United States, or (3) which discriminates with regard to the terms or conditions of membership because of race, color, creed or national origin.

Sec. 3. (a) Agencies shall accord informal, formal or exclusive recognition to employee organizations which request such recognition in conformity with the requirements specified in sections 4, 5 and 6 of this order, except that no recognition shall be accorded to any employee organization which the head of the agency considers to be so subject to corrupt influences or influences opposed to basic democratic principles that recognition would be inconsistent with the objectives of this order.

(b) Recognition of an employee organization shall continue so long as such organization satisfies the criteria of this order applicable to such recognition; but nothing in this section shall require any agency to determine whether an organization should become or continue to be recognized as exclusive representative of the employees in any unit within 12 months after a prior determination of exclusive status with respect to such unit has been made pursuant to the provisions of this order.

(c) Recognition, in whatever form accorded, shall not—

(1) preclude any employee, regardless of employee organization membership, from bringing matters of personal concern to the attention of appropriate officials in accordance with applicable law, rule, regulation, or established agency policy, or from choosing his own representative in a grievance or appellate action; or

(2) preclude or restrict consultations and dealings between an agency and any veterans organization with respect to matters of particular interest to employees with veterans preference; or

(3) preclude an agency from consulting or dealing with any religious, social, fraternal or other lawful association, not qualified as an employee organization, with repsect to matters or policies which involve individual members of the association or are of particular applicability to it or its members, when such consultations or dealings are duly limited so as not to assume the character of formal consultation

on matters of general employee-management policy or to extend to areas where recognition of the interests of one employee group may result in discrimination against or injury to the interests of other employees.

Sec. 4. (a) An agency shall accord an employee organization, which does not qualify for exclusive or formal recognition, informal recognition as representative of its member employees without regard to whether any other employee organization has been accorded formal or exclusive recognition as representative of some or all employees in any unit.

(b) When an employee organization has been informally recognized, it shall, to the extent consistent with the efficient and orderly conduct of the public business, be permitted to present to appropriate officials its views on matters of concern to its members. The agency need not, however, consult with an employee organization so recognized in the formulation of personnel or other policies with respect to such matters.

Sec. 5 (a) An agency shall accord an employee organization formal recognition as the representative of its members in a unit as defined by the agency when (1) no other employee organization is qualified for exclusive recognition as representative of employees in the unit, (2) it is determined by the agency that the employee organization has a substantial and stable membership of no less than 10 per centum of the employees in the unit, and (3) the employee organization has submitted to the agency a roster of its officers and representatives, a copy of its constitution and by-laws, and a statement of objectives. When, in the opinion of the head of an agency, an employee organization has a sufficient number of local organizations or a sufficient total membership within such agency, such organization may be accorded formal recognition at the national level, but such recognition shall not preclude the agency from dealing at the national level with any other employee organization on matters affecting its members.

(b) When an employee organization has been formally recognized, the agency, through appropriate officials, shall consult with such organization from time to time in the formulation and implementation of personnel policies and practices, and matters affecting working conditions that are of concern to its members. Any such organization shall be entitled from time to time to raise such matters for discussion with appropriate officials and at all times to present its views thereon in writing. In no case, however, shall an agency be required to consult with an employee organization which has been formally recognized with respect to any matter which, if the employee organization were one entitled to exclusive recognition, would not be included within the obligation to meet and confer, as described in section 6(b) of this order.

Sec. 6. (a) An agency shall recognize an employee organization as the exclusive representative of the employees, in an appropriate unit when such organization is eligible for formal recognition pursuant to section 5 of this order, and has been designated or selected by a majority of the employees of such unit as the representative of such employees in such unit. Units may be established on any plant or installation, craft, functional or other basis which will ensure a clear and identifiable community of interest among the employees concerned, but no unit shall be established solely on the basis of the extent to which employees in the proposed unit have organized. Except where otherwise required by established practice, prior agreement, or special circumstances, no unit shall be established for purposes of exclusive recognition which includes (1) any managerial executive, (2) any employee engaged in Federal personnel work in other than a purely clerical capacity, (3) both supervisors who officially evaluate the performance of employees and the employees whom they supervise, or (4) both professional employees and nonprofessional employees unless a majority of such professional employees vote for inclusion in such unit.

(b) When an employee organization has been recognized as the exclusive representative of employees of an appropriate unit it shall be entitled to act for and to negotiate agreements covering all employees in the unit and shall be responsible for representing the interests of all such employees without discrimination and without regard to employee organization membership. Such employee organization shall be given the opportunity to be represented at discussions between management and employees or employee representatives concerning grievances, personnel policies and practices, or other matters affecting general working conditions of employees in the unit. The agency and such employee organization, through appropriate officials and representatives, shall meet at reasonable times and confer with respect to personnel policy and practices and matters affecting working conditions, so far as may be appropriate subject to law and policy requirements. This extends to the negotiation of an agreement, or any question arising thereunder, the determination of appropriate techniques, consistent with the terms and purposes of this order, to assist in such negotiation, and the execution of a written memorandum of agreement or understanding incorporating any agreement reached by the parties. In exercising authority to make rules and regulations relating to personnel policies and practices and working conditions, agencies shall have due regard for the obligation imposed by this section, but such obligation shall not be construed to extend to such areas of discretion and policy as the mission of an agency, its budget, its organization and the assignment of its personnel, or the technology of performing its work.

Sec. 7. Any basic or initial agreement entered into with an employee organization as the exclusive representative of employees in a unit must be approved by the head of the agency or an official designated by him. All agreements with such employee organizations shall also be subject to the following requirements, which shall be expressly stated in the initial or basic agreement and shall be applicable to all supplemental, implementing, subsidiary or informal agreements between the agency and the organization:

(1) In the administration of all matters covered by the agreement officials and

employees are governed by the provisions of any existing or future laws and regulations, including policies set forth in the Federal Personnel Manual and agency regulations, which may be applicable, and the agreement shall at all times be applied subject to such laws, regulations and policies;

(2) Management officials of the agency retain the right, in accordance with applicable laws and regulations, (a) to direct employees of the agency, (b) to hire, promote, transfer, assign, and retain employees in positions within the agency, and to suspend, demote, discharge, or take other disciplinary action against employees, (c) to relieve employees from duties because of lack of work or for other legitimate reasons, (d) to maintain the efficiency of the Government operations entrusted to them, (e) to determine the methods, means and personnel by which such operations are to be conducted; and (f) to take whatever actions may be necessary to carry out the mission of the agency in situations of emergency.

Sec. 8. (a) Agreements entered into or negotiated in accordance with this order with an employee organization which is the exclusive representative of employees in an appropriate unit may contain provisions, applicable only to employees in the unit, concerning procedures for consideration of grievances. Such procedures (1) shall conform to standards issued by the Civil Service Commission, and (2) may not in any manner diminish or impair any rights which would otherwise be available to any employee in the absence of an agreement providing for such procedures.

(b) Procedures established by an agreement which are otherwise in conformity with this section may include provisions for the arbitration of grievances. Such arbitration (1) shall be advisory in nature with any decisions or recommendations subject to the approval of the agency head; (2) shall extend only to the interpretation or application of agreements or agency policy and not to changes in or proposed changes in agreements or agency policy; and (3) shall be invoked only with the approval of the individual employee or employees concerned.

Sec. 9. Solicitation of memberships, dues, or other internal employee organization business shall be conducted during the non-duty hours of the employees concerned. Officially requested or approved consultations and meetings between management officials and representatives of recognized employee organizations shall, whenever practicable, be conducted on official time, but any agency may require that negotiations with an employee organization which has been accorded exclusive recognition be conducted during the non-duty hours of the employee organization representatives involved in such negotiations.

Sec. 10. No later than July 1, 1962, the head of each agency shall issue appropriate policies, rules and regulations for the implementation of this order, including: A clear statement of the rights of its employees under the order; policies and procedures with respect to recognition of employee organizations; procedures for determining appropriate employee units; policies and practices regarding consultation with representatives of employee organizations, other organizations and individual employees; and policies with respect to the use of agency facilities by employee organizations. Insofar as may be practicable and appropriate, agencies shall consult with representatives of employee organizations in the formulation of these policies, rules and regulations.

Sec. 11. Each agency shall be responsible for determining in accordance with this order whether a unit is appropriate for purposes of exclusive recognition and, by an election or other appropriate means, whether an employee organization represents a majority of the employees in such a unit so as to be entitled to such recognition. Upon the request of any agency, or of any employee organization which is seeking exclusive recognition and which qualifies for or has been accorded formal recognition, the Secretary of Labor, subject to such necessary rules as he may prescribe, shall nominate from the National Panel of Arbitrators maintained by the Federal Mediation and Conciliation Service one or more qualified arbitrators who will be available for employment by the agency concerned for either or both of the following purposes, as may be required: (1) to investigate the facts and issue an advisory decision as to the appropriateness of a unit for purposes of exclusive recognition and as to related issues submitted for consideration; (2) to conduct or supervise an election or otherwise determine by such means as may be appropriate, and on an advisory basis, whether an employee organization represents the majority of the employees in a unit. Consonant with law, the Secretary of Labor shall render such assistance as may be appropriate in connection with advisory decisions or determinations under this section, but the necessary costs of such assistance shall be paid by the agency to which it relates. In the event questions as to the appropriateness of a unit or the majority status of an employee organization shall arise in the Department of Labor, the duties described in this section which would otherwise be the responsibility of the Secretary of Labor shall be performed by the Civil Service Commission.

Sec. 12. The Civil Service Commission shall establish and maintain a program to assist in carrying out the objectives of this order. The Commission shall develop a program for the guidance of agencies in employee-management relations in the Federal service; provide technical advice to the agencies on employee-management programs; assist in the development of programs for training agency personnel in the principles and procedures of consultation, negotiation and the settlement of disputes in the Federal service, and for the training of management officials in the discharge of their employee-management relations responsibilities in the public interest; provide for continuous study and review of the Federal employee-management relations program and, from time to time, make recommendations to the President for its improvement.

Sec. 13. (a) The Civil Service Commission and the Department of Labor shall jointly prepare (1) proposed standards of conduct for employee organizations and (2) a proposed code of fair labor practices in employee-management relations in the Federal service appropriate to assist in securing the uniform and effective implementation of the policies, rights and responsibilities described in this order.

(b) There is hereby established the President's Temporary Committee on the Implementation of the Federal Employee-Management Relations Program. The Committee shall consist of the Secretary of Labor, who shall be chairman of the Committee, the Secretary of Defense, the Postmaster General, and the Chairman of the Civil Service Commission. In addition to such other matters relating to the implementation of this order as may be referred to it by the President, the Committee shall advise the President with respect to any problems arising out of completion of agreements pursuant to sections 6 and 7, and shall receive the proposed standards of conduct for employee organizations and proposed code of fair labor practices in the Federal service, as described in this section, and report thereon to the President with such recommendations or amendments as it may deem appropriate. Consonant with law, the departments and agencies represented on the Committee shall, as may be necessary for the effectuation of this section, furnish assistance to the Committee in accordance with section 214 of the Act of May 3, 1945, 59 Stat. 134 (31 U.S.C. 691). Unless otherwise directed by the President, the Committee shall cease to exist 30 days after the date on which it submits its report to the President pursuant to this section.

Sec. 14. The head of each agency, in accordance with the provisions of this order and regulations prescribed by the Civil Service Commission, shall extend to all employees in the competitive civil service rights identical in adverse action cases to those provided preference eligibles under section 14 of the Veterans' Preference Act of 1944, as amended. Each employee in the competitive service shall have the right to appeal to the Civil Service Commission from an adverse decision of the administrative officer so acting, such appeal to be processed in an identical manner to that provided for appeals under section 14 of the Veterans' Preference Act. Any recommendation by the Civil Service Commission submitted to the head of an agency on the basis of an appeal by an employee in the competitive service shall be complied with by the head of the agency. This section shall become effective as to all adverse actions commenced by issuance of a notification of proposed action on or after July 1, 1962.

Sec. 15. Nothing in this order shall be construed to annul or modify, or to preclude the renewal or continuation of, any lawful agreement heretofore entered into between any agency and any representative of its employees. Nor shall this order preclude any agency from continuing to consult or deal with any representative of its employees or other organization prior to the time that the status and representation rights of such representative or organization are determined in conformity with this order.

Sec. 16. This order (except section 14) shall not apply to the Federal Bureau of Investigation, the Central Intelligence Agency, or any other agency, or to any office, bureau or entity within an agency, primarily performing intelligence, investigative, or security functions if the head of the agency determines that the provisions of this order cannot be applied in a manner consistent with national security requirements and considerations. When he deems it necessary in the national interest, and subject to such conditions as he may prescribe, the head of any agency may suspend any provision of this order (except section 14) with respect to any agency installation or activity which is located outside of the United States.

Approved—January 17th, 1962.

John F. Kennedy

The White House, *January 17, 1962.*

3.a. Executive Order 11246 (1965)
Equal Employment Opportunity

Under and by virtue of the authority vested in me as President of the United States by the Constitution and statutes of the United States, it is ordered as follows:

Part I—Nondiscrimination in Government Employment

Section 101. It is the policy of the Government of the United States to provide equal opportunity in Federal employment for all qualified persons, to prohibit discrimination in employment because of race, creed, color, or national origin, and to promote the full realization of equal employment opportunity through a positive, continuing program in each executive department and agency. The policy of equal opportunity applies to every aspect of Federal employment policy and practice.

Sec. 102. The head of each executive department and agency shall establish and maintain a positive program of equal employment opportunity for all civilian employees and applicants for employment within his jurisdiction in accordance with the policy set forth in Section 101.

Sec. 103. The Civil Service Commission shall supervise and provide leadership and guidance in the conduct of equal employment opportunity programs for the civilian employees of and applications for employment within the executive departments and agencies and shall review agency program accomplishments periodically. In order to facilitate the achievement of a model program for equal employment opportunity in the Federal service, the Commission may consult from time to time with such individuals, groups, or organizations as may be of assistance in improving the Federal program and realizing the objective of this Part.

Sec. 104. The Civil Service Commission shall provide for the prompt, fair, and impartial consideration of all complaints of discrimination in Federal employment on the basis of race, creed, color, or national origin. Procedures for the consideration of complaints shall include at least one impartial review within the executive department or agency and shall provide for appeal to the Civil Service Commission.

Sec. 105. The Civil Service Commission shall issue such regulations, orders,

U.S. Code of Federal Regulations, Title 3—The President—Parts II, III and IV deleted. (U.S. Government Printing Office, Washington, D.C., 1967).

and instructions as it deems necessary and appropriate to carry out its responsibilities under this Part, and the head of each executive department and agency
shall comply with the regulations, orders, and instructions issued by the Commission under this Part.

                                                    Lyndon B. Johnson

The White House, *September 24, 1965*

3.b. Executive Order 11478 (1969) Equal Employment Opportunity in the Federal Government

It has long been the policy of the United States Government to provide equal opportunity in Federal employment on the basis of merit and fitness and without discrimination because of race, color, religion, sex, or national origin. All recent Presidents have fully supported this policy, and have directed department and agency heads to adopt measures to make it a reality.

As a result, much has been accomplished through positive agency programs to assure equality of opportunity. Additional steps, however, are called for in order to strengthen and assure fully equal employment opportunity in the Federal Government.

NOW, THEREFORE, under and by virtue of the authority vested in me as President of the United States by the Constitution and statutes of the United States, it is ordered as follows:

Section 1. It is the policy of the Government of the United States to provide equal opportunity in Federal employment for all persons, to prohibit discrimination in employment because of race, color, religion, sex, or national origin, and to promote the full realization of equal employment opportunity through a continuing affirmative program in each executive department and agency. This policy of equal opportunity applies to and must be an integral part of every aspect of personnel policy and practice in the employment, development, advancement, and treatment of civilian employees of the Federal Government.

Sec. 2. The head of each executive department and agency shall establish and maintain an affirmative program of equal employment opportunity for all civilian employees and applicants for employment within his jurisdiction in accordance with the policy set forth in section 1. It is the responsibility of each department and agency head, to the maximum extent possible, to provide sufficient resources to administer such a program in a positive and effective manner; assure that recruitment activities reach all sources of job candidates; utilize to the fullest extent the present skills of each employee; provide the maximum feasible opportunity to employees to enhance their skills so they may perform at their highest potential and advance in accordance with their abilities; provide training and advice to managers and supervisors to assure their understanding and implementation of the policy

U.S. *Code of Federal Regulations, Title 3—The President, 1966–70* (U.S. Government Printing Office, Washington, D.C., 1971).

expressed in this Order; assure participation at the local level with other employers, schools, and public or private groups in cooperative efforts to improve community conditions which affect employability; and provide for a system within the department or agency for periodically evaluating the effectiveness with which the policy of this Order is being carried out.

Sec. 3. The Civil Service Commission shall provide leadership and guidance to departments and agencies in the conduct of equal employment opportunity programs for the civilian employees of and applicants for employment within the executive departments and agencies in order to assure that personnel operations in Government departments and agencies carry out the objective of equal opportunity for all persons. The Commission shall review and evaluate agency program operations periodically, obtain such reports from departments and agencies as it deems necessary, and report to the President as appropriate on overall progress. The Commission will consult from time to time with such individuals, groups, or organizations as may be of assistance in improving the Federal program and realizing the objectives of this Order.

Sec. 4. The Civil Service Commission shall provide for the prompt, fair, and impartial consideration of all complaints of discrimination in Federal employment on the basis of race, color, religion, sex, or national origin. Agency systems shall provide access to counseling for employees who feel aggrieved and shall encourage the resolution of employee problems on an informal basis. Procedures for the consideration of complaints shall include at least one impartial review within the executive department or agency and shall provide for appeal to the Civil Service Commission.

Sec. 5. The Civil Service Commission shall issue such regulations, orders, and instructions as it deems necessary and appropriate to carry out this Order and assure that the executive branch of the Government leads the way as an equal opportunity employer, and the head of each executive department and agency shall comply with the regulations, orders, and instructions issued by the Commission under this Order.

Sec. 6. This Order applies (a) to military departments as defined in section 102 of title 5, United States Code, and executive agencies (other than the General Accounting Office) as defined in section 105 of title 5, United States Code, and to the employees thereof (including employees paid from nonappropriated funds), and (b) to those portions of the legislative and judicial branches of the Federal Government and of the Government of the District of Columbia having positions in the competitive service and to the employees in those positions. This Order does not apply to aliens employed outside the limits of the United States.

Sec. 7. Part I of Executive Order No. 11246 of September 24, 1965, and those parts of Executive Order No. 11375 of October 13, 1967, which apply to Federal employment, are hereby superseded.

Richard Nixon

The White House, *August 8, 1969.*

3.c.   Title VII of the Civil Rights Act of 1964 as Amended by The Equal Employment Opportunity Act of 1972 U.S. Congress

An Act

To enforce the constitutional right to vote, to confer jurisdiction upon the district courts of the United States to provide injunctive relief against discrimination in public accommodations, to authorize the Attorney General to institute suits to protect constitutional rights in public facilities and public education, to extend the Commission on Civil Rights, to prevent discrimination in federally assisted programs, to establish a Commission on Equal Employment Opportunity, and for other purposes.

. . . .

Nondiscrimination in Federal Government Employment

Section 717. *(a) All personnel actions affecting employees or applicants for employment (except with regard to aliens employed outside the limits of the United States) in military departments as defined in section 102 of title 5, United States Code, in executive agencies (other than the General Accounting Office) as defined in section 105 of title 5, United States Code (including employees and applicants for employment who are paid from nonappropriated funds), in the United States Postal Service and the Postal Rate Commission, in those units of the Government of the District of Columbia having positions in the competitive service, and in those units of the legislative and judicial branches of the Federal Government having positions in the competitive service, and in the Library of Congress shall be made free from any discrimination based on race, color, religion, sex, or national origin.*

(b) Except as otherwise provided in this subsection, the Civil Service Commission shall have authority to enforce the provisions of subsection (a) through appropriate remedies, including reinstatement or hiring of employees with or without back pay,

Source: Subcommittee on Labor of the Committee on Labor and Public Welfare, U.S. Senate (Washington: U.S. Government Printing Office, 1972). Amendments made by the EEO Act of 1972 (P.L. 92–261) are printed in italics. Sections 701–716 deleted.

105

as will effectuate the policies of this section, and shall issue such rules, regulations, orders, and instructions as it deems necessary and appropriate to carry out its responsibilities under this section. The Civil Service Commission shall—

    (1) be responsible for the annual review and approval of a national and regional equal employment opportunity plan which each department and agency and each appropriate unit referred to in subsection (a) of this section shall submit in order to maintain an affirmative program of equal employment opportunity for all such employees and applicants for employment;

    (2) be responsible for the review and evaluation of the operation of all agency equal employment opportunity programs, periodically obtaining and publishing (on at least a semiannual basis) progress reports from each such department, agency or unit; and

    (3) consult with and solicit the recommendation of interested individuals, groups, and organizations relating to equal employment opportunity.

The head of each such department, agency or unit shall comply with such rules, regulations, orders, and instructions which shall include a provision that an employee or applicant for employment shall be notified of any final action taken on any complaint of discrimination filed by him thereunder. The plan submitted by each department, agency, and unit shall include, but not be limited to—

    (1) provision for the establishment of training and education programs designed to provide a maximum opportunity for employees to advance so as to perform at their highest potential; and

    (2) a description of the qualifications in terms of training and experience relating to equal employment opportunity for the principal and operating officials of each such department, agency, or unit responsible for carrying out the equal employment opportunity program and of the allocation of personnel and resources proposed by such department, agency, or unit to carry out its equal employment opportunity program.

With respect to employment in the Library of Congress, authorities granted in this subsection to the Civil Service Commission shall be exercised by the Librarian of Congress.

    (c) Within thirty days of receipt of notice of final action taken by a department, agency, or unit referred to in subsection 717(a), or by the Civil Service Commission upon an appeal from a decision or order of such department, agency, or unit on a complaint of discrimination based on race, color, religion, sex, or national origin, brought pursuant to subsection (a) of this section, Executive Order 11478 or any succeeding Executive orders, or after one hundred and eighty days from the filing of the initial charge with the department, agency, or unit or with the Civil Service

Commission on appeal from a decision or order of such department, agency, or unit until such time as final action may be taken by a department, agency, or unit, an employee or applicant for employment, if aggrieved by the final disposition of his complaint, or by the failure to take final action on his complaint, may file a civil action as provided in section 706, in which civil action the head of the department, agency, or unit, as appropriate, shall be the defendant.

(d) The provisions of section 706(f) through (k), as applicable, shall govern civil actions brought hereunder.

(e) Nothing contained in this Act shall relieve any Government agency or official of its or his primary responsibility to assure nondiscrimination in employment as required by the Constitution and statutes or of its or his responsibilities under Executive Order 11478 relating to equal employment opportunity in the Federal Government.

4. Intergovernmental Personnel Act of 1970

An Act

To reinforce the federal system by strengthening the personnel resources of State and local governments, to improve intergovernmental cooperation in the administration of grant-in-aid programs, to provide grants for improvement of State and local personnel administration, to authorize Federal assistance in training State and local employees, to provide grants to State and local governments for training of their employees, to authorize interstate compacts for personnel and training activities, to facilitate the temporary assignment of personnel between the Federal Government, and State and local governments, and for other purposes.

Be it enacted by the Senate and House of Representatives of the United States of America in Congress assembled, That this Act may be cited as the "Intergovernmental Personnel Act of 1970".

DECLARATION OF POLICY

Sec. 2. The Congress hereby finds and declares—

That effective State and local governmental institutions are essential in the maintenance and development of the Federal system in an increasingly complex and interdependent society.

That, since numerous governmental activities administered by the State and local governments are related to national purpose and are financed in part by Federal funds, a national interest exists in a high caliber of public service in State and local governments.

That the quality of public service at all levels of government can be improved by the development of systems of personnel administration consistent with such merit principles as—

(1) recruiting, selecting, and advancing employees on the basis of their relative ability, knowledge, and skills, including open consideration of qualified applicants for initial appointment;

(2) providing equitable and adequate compensation;

(3) training employees, as needed, to assure high-quality performance;

P.L. 91–648, (January 5, 1971). The more technical aspects of this law have been omitted in each of the four titles cited here as well as all of Title V involving "General Provisions."

(4) retaining employees on the basis of the adequacy of their performance, correcting inadequate performance, and separating employees whose inadequate performance cannot be corrected;

(5) assuring fair treatment of applicants and employees in all aspects of personnel administration without regard to political affiliation, race, color, national origin, sex, or religious creed and with proper regard for their privacy and constitutional rights as citizens; and

(6) assuring that employees are protected against coercion for partisan political purposes and are prohibited from using their official authority for the purpose of interfering with or affecting the result of an election or a nomination for office.

That Federal financial and technical assistance to State and local governments for strengthening their personnel administration in a manner consistent with these principles is in the national interest.

Sec. 3. The authorities provided by this Act shall be administered in such manner as (1) to recognize fully the rights, powers, and responsibilities of State and local governments, and (2) to encourage innovation and allow for diversity on the part of State and local governments in the design, execution, and management of their own systems of personnel administration.

TITLE I—DEVELOPMENT OF POLICIES AND STANDARDS

DECLARATION OF PURPOSE

Sec. 101. The purpose of this title is to provide for intergovernmental cooperation in the development of policies and standards for the administration of programs authorized by this Act.

ADVISORY COUNCIL

Sec. 102. (a) Within one hundred and eighty days following the date of enactment of this Act, the President shall appoint, without regard to the provisions of title 5, United States Code, governing appointments in the competitive service, an advisory council on intergovernmental personnel policy. The President may terminate the council at any time after the expiration of three years following its establishment.

(b) The advisory council of not to exceed fifteen members, shall be composed primarily of officials of the Federal Government and State and local governments, but shall also include members selected from educational and training institutions or organizations, public employee organizations, and the general public. At least half of the governmental members shall be officials of State and local governments. The President shall designate a Chairman and a Vice Chairman from among the members of the advisory council.

(c) It shall be the duty of the advisory council to study and make recommendations regarding personnel policies and programs for the purpose of—

(1) improving the quality of public administration at State and local levels of government, particularly in connection with programs that are financed in whole or in part from Federal funds;

(2) strengthening the capacity of State and local governments to deal with complex problems confronting them;

(3) aiding State and local governments in training their professional, administrative, and technical employees and officials;

(4) aiding State and local governments in developing systems of personnel administration that are responsive to the goals and needs of their programs and effective in attracting and retaining capable employees; and

(5) facilitating temporary assignments of personnel between the Federal Government and State and local governments and institutions of higher education.

(d) Members of the advisory council who are not regular full-time employees of the United States, while serving on the business of the council, including travel time, may receive compensation at rates not exceeding the daily rate for GS-18; and while so serving away from their homes or regular places of business, all members may be allowed travel expenses, including per diem in lieu of subsistence, as authorized by section 5703 of title 5, United States Code, for individuals in the Government service employed intermittently.

REPORTS OF ADVISORY COUNCIL

Sec. 103. (a) The advisory council on intergovernmental personnel policy shall from time to time report to the President and to the Congress its findings and recommendations.

(b) Not later than eighteen months after its establishment, the advisory council shall submit an initial report on its activities, which shall include its views and recommendations on—

(1) the feasibility and desirability of extending merit policies and standards to additional Federal-State grant-in-aid programs;

(2) the feasibility and desirability of extending merit policies and standards to grant-in-aid programs of a Federal-local character;

(3) appropriate standards for merit personnel administration, where applicable, including those established by regulations with respect to existing Federal grant-in-aid programs; and

(4) the feasibility and desirability of financial and other incentives to encourage State and local governments in the development of comprehensive systems of personnel administration based on merit principles.

(c) In transmitting to the Congress reports of the advisory council, the President shall submit to the Congress proposals of legislation which he deems desirable to carry out the recommendations of the advisory council.

TITLE II—STRENGTHENING STATE AND LOCAL PERSONNEL ADMINISTRATION

Declaration of Purpose

Sec. 201. The purpose of this title is to assist State and local governments to strengthen their staffs by improving their personnel administration.

STATE GOVERNMENT AND STATEWIDE PROGRAMS AND GRANTS

Sec. 202. (a) The United States Civil Service Commission (hereinafter referred to as the "Commission") is authorized to make grants to a State for up to 75 per centum (or, with respect to fiscal years commencing after the expiration of three years following the effective date of the grant provisions of this Act, for up to 50 per centum) of the costs of developing and carrying out programs or projects, on the certification of the Governor of that State that the programs or projects contained within the State's application are consistent with the applicable principles set forth in clauses (1)–(6) of the third paragraph of section 2 of this Act, to strengthen personnel administration in that State government or in local governments of that State. The authority provided by this section shall be employed in such a manner as to encourage innovation and allow for diversity on the part of State and local governments in the design, execution, and management of their own systems of personnel administration.

(b) An application for a grant shall be made at such time or times, and contain such information, as the Commission may prescribe. The Commission may make a grant under subsection (a) of this section only if the application therefor—

(1) provides for designation, by the Governor or chief executive authority, of the State office that will have primary authority and responsibility for the

development and administration of the approved program or project at the State level;

(2) provides for the establishment of merit personnel administration where appropriate and the further improvement of existing systems based on merit principles;

(3) provides for specific personnel administration improvement needs of the State government and, to the extent appropriate, of the local governments in that State, including State personnel administration services for local governments;

(4) provides assurance that the making of a Federal Government grant will not result in a reduction in relevant State or local government expenditures or the substitution of Federal funds for State or local funds previously made available for these purposes; and

(5) sets forth clear and practicable actions for the improvement of particular aspects of personnel administration such as—

(A) establishment of statewide personnel systems of general or special functional coverage to meet the needs of urban, suburban, or rural governmental jurisdictions that are not able to provide sound career services, opportunities for advancement, adequate retirement and leave systems, and other career inducements to well-qualified professional, administrative, and technical personnel;

(B) making State grants to local governments to strengthen their staffs by improving their personnel administration;

(C) assessment of State and local government needs for professional, administrative, and technical manpower, and the initiation of timely and appropriate action to meet such needs;

(D) strengthening one or more major areas of personnel administration, such as recruitment and selection, training and development, and pay administration;

(E) undertaking research and demonstration projects to develop and apply better personnel administration techniques, including both projects conducted by State and local government staffs and projects conducted by colleges or universities or other appropriate nonprofit organizations under grants or contracts;

(F) strengthening the recruitment, selection, assignment, and development of handicapped persons, women, and members of disadvantaged groups whose capacities are not being utilized fully;

(G) training programs related directly to upgrading within the agency for nonprofessional employees who show promise of developing a capacity for assuming professional responsibility;

(H) achieving the most effective use of scarce professional, administrative, and technical manpower; and

(I) increasing intergovernmental cooperation in personnel administration, with respect to such matters as recruiting, examining, pay studies, training, education, personnel interchange, manpower utilization, and fringe benefits.

LOCAL GOVERNMENT PROGRAMS AND GRANTS

Sec. 203. (a) The Commission is authorized to make grants to a general local government, or a combination of general local governments, that serve a population of fifty thousand or more, for up to 75 per centum (or, with respect to fiscal years commencing after the expiration of three years following the effective date of the grant provisions of this Act, for up to 50 per centum) of the costs of developing and carrying out programs or projects, on the certification of the mayor(s), or chief executive officer(s), of the general local government or combination of local governments that the programs or projects are consistent with the applicable principles set forth in clauses (1)–(6) of the third paragraph of section 2 of this Act, to strengthen the personnel administration of such governments. Such a grant may not be made—

(1) if, at the time of submission of an application, the State concerned has an approved plan which, with the agreement of the particular local government concerned, provides for strengthening one or more aspects of personnel administration in that local government, unless the local government concerned has problems which are not met by the previously approved plan and for which, with the agreement of the State government concerned with respect to those aspects of personnel administration covered in the approved plan, it is submitting an application; or

(2) after the State concerned has a statewide plan which has been developed by an appropriate State agency designated or established pursuant to State law which provides such agency with adequate authority, administrative organization, and staffing to develop and administer such a statewide plan, and to provide technical assistance and other appropriate support in carrying out the local components of the plan, and which provides procedures insuring adequate involvement of officials of affected local governments in the development and administration of such a statewide plan, unless the local government concerned has special, unique, or urgent problems which are not met by the approved statewide plan and for which it submits an application for funds to be distributed under section 506(a).

Upon the request of a Governor or chief executive authority, a grant to a general local government or combination of such governments in that State may not be made during a period not to exceed ninety days commencing with the date provided in section 513, or the date on which official regulations for this Act are promulgated, whichever date is later: *Provided,* That the request of the Governor or chief executive authority indicates that he is developing a plan under (1) above, or during a period not to exceed one hundred and eighty days commencing with the date provided in section 513, or the date on which official regulations for this Act are promulgated, whichever date is later, provided the request of the Governor or chief executive authority indicates that he is developing a statewide plan under (2) above.

. . . .

INTERGOVERNMENTAL COOPERATION IN RECRUITING AND EXAMINING

Sec. 204. (a) The Commission may join, on a shared-cost basis, with State and local governments in cooperative recruiting and examining activities under such procedures and regulations as may jointly be agreed upon.

(b) The Commission also may, on the written request of a State or local government and under such procedures as may be jointly agreed upon, certify to such governments from appropriate Federal registers the names of potential employees. The State or local government making the request shall pay the Commission for the costs, as determined by the Commission, of performing the service, and such payments shall be credited to the appropriation or fund from which the expenses were or are to be paid.

TECHNICAL ASSISTANCE

Sec. 205. The Commission may furnish technical advice and assistance, on request, to State and general local governments seeking to improve their systems of personnel administration. The Commission may waive, in whole or in part, payments from such governments for the costs of furnishing such assistance. All such payments shall be credited to the appropriation or fund from which the expenses were or are to be paid.

COORDINATION OF FEDERAL PROGRAMS

Sec. 206. The Commission, after consultation with other agencies concerned, shall—

(1) coordinate the personnel administration support and technical assistance given to State and local governments and the support given State pro-

grams or projects to strengthen local government personnel administration, including the furnishing of needed personnel administration services and technical assistance, under authority of this Act with any such support given under other Federal programs; and

(2) make such arrangements, including the collection, maintenance, and dissemination of data on grants for strengthening State and local government personnel administration and on grants to States for furnishing needed personnel administration services and technical assistance to local governments, as needed to avoid duplication and insure consistent administration of related Federal activities.

TITLE III—TRAINING AND DEVELOPING STATE AND LOCAL EMPLOYEES

DECLARATION OF PURPOSE

Sec. 301. The purpose of this title is to strengthen the training and development of State and local government employees and officials, particularly in professional, administrative, and technical fields.

ADMISSION TO FEDERAL EMPLOYEE TRAINING PROGRAMS

Sec. 302. (a) In accordance with such conditions as may be prescribed by the head of the Federal agency concerned, a Federal agency may admit State and local government employees and officials to agency training programs established for Federal professional, administrative, or technical personnel.

(b) Federal agencies may waive, in whole or in part, payments from, or on behalf of, State and local governments for the costs of training provided under this section. Payments received by the Federal agency concerned for training under this section shall be credited to the appropriation or fund used for paying the training costs.

(c) The Commission may use appropriations authorized by this Act to pay the initial additional development or overhead costs that are incurred by reason of admittance of State and local government employees to Federal training courses and to reimburse other Federal agencies for such costs.

GRANTS TO STATE AND LOCAL GOVERNMENTS FOR TRAINING

Sec. 303. (a) If in its judgment training is not adequately provided for under grant-in-aid or other statutes, the Commission is authorized to make grants to State and general local governments for up to 75 per centum (or, with respect to fiscal years commencing after the expiration of three years following the effective date of the grant provisions of this Act, for up to 50 per centum) of the costs of developing and carrying out programs, on the certification of the Governor of that State, or the mayor or chief executive officer of the general local government, that the programs are consistent with the applicable principles set forth in clauses (1)–(6) of the third paragraph of section 2 of this Act, to train and educate their professional, administrative, and technical employees and officials. Such grants may not be used to cover costs of full-time graduate study, provided for in section 305 of this Act, or the costs of the construction or acquisition of training facilities. The State and local government share of the cost of developing and carrying out training and education plans and programs may include, but shall not consist solely of, the reasonable value of facilities and of supervisory and other personal services made available by such governments. The authority provided by this section shall be employed in such a manner as to encourage innovation and allow for diversity on the part of State and local governments in developing and carrying out training and education programs for their personnel.

(b) An application for a grant from a State or general local government shall be made at such time or times, and shall contain such information, as the Commission may prescribe. The Commission may make a grant under subsection (a) of this section, only if the application therefor meets requirements established by this subsection unless any requirement is specifically waived by the Commission. Such grant to a State, or to a general local government under subsection (c) of this section, may cover the costs of developing the program covered by the application. The program covered by the application shall—

(1) provide for designation, by the Governor or chief executive authority, of the State office that will have primary authority and responsibility for the development and administration of the program at the State level;

(2) provide, to the extent feasible, for coordination with relevant training available under or supported by other Federal Government programs or grants;

(3) provide for training needs of the State government and of local governments in that State;

(4) provide, to the extent feasible, for intergovernmental cooperation in employee training matters, especially within metropolitan or regional areas; and

(5) provide assurance that the making of a Federal Government grant will not result in a reduction in relevant State or local government expenditures or the substitution of Federal funds for State or local funds previously made available for these purposes.

(c) A grant authorized by subsection (a) of this section may be made to a general local government, or a combination of such governments, that serve a population of fifty thousand or more, for up to 75 per centum (or, with respect to fiscal years commencing after the expiration of three years following the effective date of the grant provisions of this Act, for up to 50 per centum) of the costs of developing and carrying out programs or projects, on the certification of the mayor(s), or chief executive officer(s), of the general local government or combination of local governments that the programs or projects are consistent with the applicable principles set forth in clauses (1)–(6) of the third paragraph of section 2 of this Act, to train and educate their professional, administrative, and technical employees and officials. Such a grant may not be made—

(1) if, at the time of submission of an application, the State concerned has an approved plan which, with the agreement of the particular local government concerned, provides for strengthening one or more aspects of training in that local government, unless the local government concerned has problems which are not met by the previously approved plan and for which, with the agreement of the State government concerned with respect to those aspects of training covered in the approved plan, it is submitting an application; or

(2) after the State concerned has a statewide plan which has been developed by an appropriate State agency designated or established pursuant to State law which provides such agency with adequate authority, administrative organization, and staffing to develop and administer such a statewide plan, and to provide technical assistance and other appropriate support in carrying out the local components of the plan, and which provides procedures insuring adequate involvement of officials of affected local governments in the development and administration of such a statewide plan, unless the local government concerned has special, unique, or urgent problems which are not met by the approved statewide plan and for which it submits an application for funds to be distributed under section 506(a).

Upon the request of a Governor or chief executive authority, a grant to a general local government or combination of such governments in that State may not be made during a period not to exceed ninety days commencing with the date provided in section 513, or the date on which official regulations for this Act are promulgated, whichever date is later: *Provided,* That the request of the Governor or chief executive authority indicates that he is developing a plan under (1) above, or during a period not to exceed one hundred and eighty days commencing with the date provided in section 513, or the date on which official regulations for this Act are promulgated, whichever date is later, provided the request of the Governor or chief executive authority indicates that he is developing a statewide plan under (2) above. To be approved, an application for a grant under this subsection must meet requirements similar to those established in subsection (b) of this section for State applications, unless any such requirement is specifically waived by the Commission, and the requirements of subsection (d) of this section. The Commission may make grants to general local governments, or combinations of such governments that serve a population of less than fifty thousand if it finds that such grants will help meet essential needs in programs or projects of national interest and will assist general local governments experiencing special needs for personnel training and education related to such programs or projects.

(d) An application to be submitted to the Commission under subsection (c) of this section shall first be submitted by the general local government or combination of such governments to the Governor for review, comments, and recommendations. The Governor may refer the application to the State office designated under section 303(b)(1) of this Act for review. Comments and recommendations (if any) made as a result of the review and a statement by the general local government or combination of such governments that it has considered the comments and recommendations of the Governor shall accompany the application to the Commission. The application need not be accompanied by the comments and recommendations of the Governor if the general local government or combination of such governments certifies to the Commission that the application has been before the Governor for review and comment for a period of sixty days without comment by the Governor. An explanation in writing shall be sent to the Governor of a State by the Commission whenever the Commission does not concur with recommendations of the Governor in approving any local government applications.

GRANTS TO OTHER ORGANIZATIONS

Sec. 304. (a) The Commission is authorized to make grants to other organizations to pay up to 75 per centum (or, with respect to fiscal years commencing after the expiration of three years following the effective date of the grant provisions of this Act, up to 50 per centum) of the costs of providing training to professional, administrative, or technical employees and officials of State or local governments if the Commission—

(1) finds that State or local governments needs the specific proposed program;

(2) determines that the capability to provide such training does not exist, or is not readily available, within the Federal or the State or local governments requesting such program or within associations of State or local governments, or if such capability does exist that such government or association is not disposed to provide such training; and

(3) approves the program as meeting such requirements as may be prescribed by the Commission in its regulations pursuant to this Act.

(b) For the purpose of this section "other organization" means—

(1) a national, regional, statewide, areawide, or metropolitan organization, representing member State or local governments;

(2) an association of State or local public officials; or

(3) a nonprofit organization one of whose principal functions is to offer professional advisory, research, development, educational or related services to governments.

GOVERNMENT SERVICE FELLOWSHIPS

Sec. 305. (a) The Commission is authorized to make grants to State and general local governments to support programs approved by the Commission for providing Government Service Fellowships for State and local government personnel. The grants may cover—

(1) the necessary costs of the fellowship recipient's books, travel, and transportation, and such related expenses as may be authorized by the Commission;

(2) reimbursement to the State or local government for not to exceed one-fourth of the salary of each fellow during the period of the fellowship; and

(3) payment to the educational institutions involved of such amounts as the Commission determines to be consistent with prevailing practices under comparable federally supported programs for each fellow, less any amount charged the fellow for tuition and nonrefundable fees and deposits.

(b) Fellowships awarded under this section may not exceed two years of full-time graduate-level study for professional, administrative, and technical employees. The regulations of the Commission shall include eligibility criteria for the selection of fellowship recipients by State and local governments.

(c) The State or local government concerned shall—

(1) select the individual recipients of the fellowships;

(2) during the period of the fellowship, continue the full salary of the recipient and normal employment benefits such as credit for seniority, leave accrual, retirement, and insurance; and

(3) make appropriate plans for the utilization and continuation in public service of employees completing fellowships and outline such plans in the application for the grant.

COORDINATION OF FEDERAL PROGRAMS

Sec. 306. The Commission, after consultation with other agencies concerned, shall—

(1) prescribe regulations concerning administration of training for employees and officials of State and local governments provided for in this title, including requirements for coordination of and reasonable consistency in such training programs;

(2) coordinate the training support given to State and local governments under authority of this Act with training support given such governments under other Federal programs; and

(3) make such arrangements, including the collection and maintenance of data on training grants and programs, as may be necessary to avoid duplication of programs providing for training and to insure consistent administration of related Federal training activities, with particular regard to title IX of the Higher Education Act of 1965.

TITLE IV—MOBILITY OF FEDERAL, STATE, AND LOCAL EMPLOYEES

DECLARATION OF PURPOSE

Sec. 401. The purpose of this title is to provide for the temporary assignment of personnel between the Federal Government and State and local governments and institutions of higher education.

"Subchapter VI—Assignments To and From States

"§ 3371. *Definitions*

"For the purpose of this subchapter—

"(1) 'State' means—

"(A) a State of the United States, the District of Columbia, the Commonwealth of Puerto Rico, and a territory or possession of the United States; and

"(B) an instrumentality or authority of a State or States as defined in subparagraph (A) of this paragraph (1) and a Federal-State authority or instrumentality; and

"(2) 'local government' means—

"(A) any political subdivision, instrumentality, or authority of a State or States as defined in subparagraph (A) of paragraph (1); and

"(B) any general or special purpose agency of such a political subdivision, instrumentality, or authority.

"§3372. *General Provisions*

"(a) On request from or with the concurrence of a State or local government, and with the consent of the employee concerned, the head of an executive agency may arrange for the assignment of—

　"(1) an employee of his agency to a State or local government; and

　"(2) an employee of a State or local government to his agency; for work of mutual concern to his agency and the State or local government that he determines will be beneficial to both. The period of an assignment under this subchapter may not exceed two years. However, the head of an executive agency may extend the period of assignment for not more than two additional years.

　"(b) This subchapter is authority for and applies to the assignment of—

　　"(1) an employee of an executive agency to an institution of higher education; and

　　"(2) an employee of an institution of higher education to an executive agency.

5. Excerpts from the Federal Political Personnel Manual (The "Malek Manual")

Techniques for Removal Through Organizational or Management Procedures

The Civil Service system creates many hardships in trying to remove undesirable employees from their positions. Because of the rape of the career service by the Kennedy and Johnson Administrations, as described in the Introduction, this Administration has been left a legacy of finding disloyalty and obstruction at high levels while those incumbents rest comfortably on career civil service status. Political disloyalty and insimpatico relationships with the Administration, unfortunately, are not grounds for the removal or suspension of an employee. Career employees . . . can only be dismissed or otherwise punished for direct disobedience of lawful orders, actions which are tantamount to the commission of a crime, and well documented and provable incompetence. Even if you follow the time-consuming process of documenting a case to proceed with an adverse action, the administrative and legal process is slow and lengthy and great damage can accrue to the Department prior to your successful conclusion of your case. However, there are several techniques which can be designed, carefully, to skirt around the adverse action proceedings. One must always bear in mind the following rules. The reduction of a person to a position of lower status and/or grade is considered an adverse action which necessitates formal proceedings. Secondly, an administrative or management decision cannot be based on the political background or persuasion of an individual, his race, sex, religion or national origin.

a. Individual Techniques

(a–1) Frontal Assault

You simply call an individual in and tell him he is no longer wanted, that you'll assist him in finding another job and will keep him around until such time as he finds other employment. But you do expect him to immediately relinquish his

U.S. Senate, Select Committee on Presidential Campaign Activities: Use of Incumbency-Responsiveness Program, 19, 93rd Congress, 2nd Session, pp. 8903–9017.

duties, accept reassignment to a make-shift position at his current grade and then quietly resign for the good of the service. Of course, you promise him that he will leave with honor and with the finest recommendations, a farewell luncheon, and perhaps even a Departmental award. You, naturally, point out that should he not accept such an offer, and he later is forced to resign or retire through regular process or his own volition, that his employment references from the Department and his permanent personnel record may not look the same as if he accepted your offer. There should be no witnesses in the room at the time. Caution: This technique should only be used for the timid at heart with a giant ego. This is an extremely dangerous technique and the very fact of your conversation can be used against the Department in any subsequent adverse action proceedings. It should never be used with that fervent, zealous employee committed to Democratic policies and programs, or to the bureaucracy, who might relish the opportunity to be martyred on the cross of his cause.

(a-2) Transfer Technique

By carefully researching the background of the proposed employee victim, one can always establish that geographical part of the country and/or organizational unit to which the employee would rather resign than obey and accept transfer orders. For example, if you have an employee in your Boston Regional Office, and his record shows reluctance to move far from that location (he may have family and financial commitments not easily severed), a transfer accompanied by a promotion to an existing or newly created position in Dallas, Texas might just fill the bill. It is always suggested that a transfer be accompanied with a promotion, if possible. Since a promotion is per se beneficial to the employee, it immediately forecloses any claim that the transfer is an adverse action. It also reduces the possibility of a claim that the transfer was motivated for prohibited purposes since, again, the transfer resulted in a beneficial action for the employee and the word discrimination implies some adversity to have been suffered. It is also important that you carefully check your organizational charts to insure that not only is there no reduction in grade, but no reduction in status. For instance, if a person is a Deputy Regional Director at GS14, the promotion to a position of State Director in another region (who reports to a Deputy Regional Director) even at a grade increase to GS15 will be a demotion in status and thus an adverse action. Transfers must also be presented as necessary for "the efficiency of the service." It is, therefore, necessary that the position to which the person is being transferred fits in with his current job experience or his past responsibilities. The technical assistance of your personnel office is indispensable in prosecuting such transfers. But there is no reason why they cannot artfully find, or create, the necessary position that will satisfy the transfer requirements necessary to cause the prospective transferee to be confronted with the choice of being transferred to a position he does not want or

resigning. Of course, one can sweeten the potion by privately assuring the proposed transferee, upon delivery of his transfer notification, that should he refuse
the transfer, and resign, that his resignation will be accepted without prejudice.
Further, he may remain for a period until he finds other employment and leave with
the highest honors and references.

(a-3) Special Assistant Technique (The Traveling Salesman)

This technique is especially useful for the family man and those who do not
enjoy traveling. What you do is to suddenly recognize the outstanding abilities of
your employee-victim and immediately seize upon his competence and talent to
assign him to a special research and evaluation project. This is best explained by
way of example. Let us assume that our employee is a program analyst with the
Department of Transportation. You immediately discover the high level interest
and policy requirements for creating a program to meet the transportation needs of
all U.S. cities and towns with a population of 20,000 and under. Nothing is more
revealing than first hand inspections and consultation with town officials. And so
you hand your chosen expert a promotion and his new assignment. (Again, a
promotion is desirable to diminish any possible claim of adversity.) Along with his
promotion and assignment your expert is given extensive travel orders criss-
crossing him across the country to towns (hopefully with the worst accommodations
possible) of a population of 20,000 or under. *Until his wife threatens him with
divorce unless he quits, you have him out of town and out of the way* [emphasis
added]. When he finally asks for relief you tearfully reiterate the importance of the
project and state that he must continue to obey travel orders or resign. *Failure to
obey travel orders is a grounds for immediate separation* [emphasis added].

b. The Layering Technique

The layering technique, as it full name implies, is an organizational technique to
"layer" over insubordinate subordinates, managers who are loyal and faithful. This
technique, however, requires at least the temporary need for additional slots and
may, in some cases, require supergrade authorities. Again, the best way to explain
the layering technique is to depict its application in an example. Let us assume you
have two branches whose chiefs are GS 14s and report directly to your deputy, who
is a GS 15, who in turn reports to you (you are a GS 16). The object is to remove
from critical responsibilities your deputy and the two GS 14 branch chiefs. All
three positions you find were costly frozen into the career service when you assumed your noncareer office head post.

A slot saving can be realized if you have any vacancies within your office no
matter what type of job they were previously utilized for, such as secretarial
vacancies. (Remember your ceiling does not address itself to how you are going to

use your positions. Don't ever let the bureaucrats tell you it is automatically a such-and-such slot. By budget adjustment you can use existing vacancies to create any new positions and functions you desire.) Utilizing vacant positions, or new positions, and acquiring the appropriate budget adjustment, you get your position upgraded to a GS 17 NEA. You can create a new position of Deputy Office Director, at a noncareer GS 16. Because that position is noncareer, your former deputy has no rights to it. (Note of caution: The question may be asked why you simply don't convert those positions from career to noncareer and then fire the incumbents. The Civil Service rules and regulations contain a "grandfather clause" which provides that if a position which is filled by a career incumbent is converted from career to noncareer, the incumbent still maintains his career status in the job. Operationally, therefore, the position does not become noncareer until the career incumbent vacates that position. If you convert it to noncareer before he vacates the position, you run the risk that if you take some administrative action to transfer him out of the position later he can claim political discrimination pointing to the very fact that you converted his position to excepted status as evidence.) To make sure that the reorganization does not result in a reduction of status for your former deputy, you appoint him as a GS 15 Special Assistant to yourself so that he retains both his grade and his direct reporting relationship. You then create two Staff Assistant positions for your Branch Chiefs reporting to your new Special Assistant. They also retain their GS 14 grades. You upgrade the Branch Chief positions to GS 15 and create two Deputy Branch Chief positions at GS 14. To your new deputy position, the two upgraded branch chief positions and the two new deputy branch chief positions you then effect the appointment of persons of unquestioned loyalty. You have thus layered into the organization into key positions your own people, still isolating your road-blocks into powerless make-shift positions. In all likelihood the three will probably end up resigning out of disgust and boredom. You can then return the three slots from wherever you borrowed them. If this does not occur, you can have a reduction in force which will cause certain job abolitions and thus the elimination of selected employees. As mentioned in the Introduction, this layering technique followed by a reduction in force, after a respectable waiting period, was the technique used extensively by Lyndon Johnson's Administration.

A variation of the layering technique is called the Bypass Layering Technique which may be utilized in the event the two GS 14 branch chiefs should be eligible for promotion and placement in the upgraded GS 15 branch chief positions. That will frequently be the case, especially if those upgraded branch chief positions cannot be made noncareer. In that case the scenario for the creation of a new upgraded deputy to yourself remains the same. Your former deputy is likewise made a Special Assistant to yourself at GS 15 having no rights to the noncareer GS 16 position. The two GS 14 branch chiefs are promoted to GS 15 making way for the creation of two deputy branch chief positions at GS 14. You then layer in your own people to the deputy branch chief positions. From then on all business is conducted between the deputy branch chiefs, your deputy and yourself. You rudely bypass your branch chiefs on all office matters. You also totally ignore your special assistant. If all three don't at least quit in disgust, at least your have removed them from the mainstream of office operations.

c. Shifting Responsibilities and Isolation Techniques

This is a classic organizational technique first introduced by Franklin D. Roosevelt. It does involve a sizeable investment of budget and slots. Its purpose is to isolate and bypass an entire organization while is so hopeless that there is an immediate desire to deal with nobody in the organization at all. The shifting responsibilities and isolation technique entails the setting up a parallel organization to one already in existence, and giving that new organization most of the real authorities previously vested in the old organization it parallels. The alphabet agencies created by FDR to usurp existing functions of existing departments and to assume new functions that ordinarily would have gone to those existing departments is an example of the wholesale uses of the shifting functions technique. Let's use another example. Perhaps you're unhappy with your whole budget office. You inform the budget office that the tail will no longer wag the dog. From now on they will exercise what are supposed to be the functions of the budget office which are the technical accounting procedures and documenting procedures necessary for promulgating a budget. You create a new Office of Financial Policy Review which will have the responsibility for examining the proposed budgets of the component parts of your organization and then recommend the "policy decisions" necessary to put together your organization's budget. Because of the policy content, the positions in the new office will be largely noncareer and thus unavailable as a matter of right to those bureaucrats in your existing budget office. You then impose unbearable ceilings on your budget office specifically in the areas of accounting. This renders that budget office increasingly incapable of producing adequate accounting data to the new Financial Policy Review Office. As a result, the Financial Policy Review Office must of a necessity create its own accounting area (hopefully from slots you have squeezed out of the budget office. Note: It is important that you do not create career positions in the new office comparable to those in the old budget office at the same time you reduce the personnel ceilings in the old budget office creating a RIF. Whereas the civil service rules do not allow careerists being RIF'd to exercise claims to like positions in the noncareer service, they do grant careerists the right to claim placement into like career positions that are created.) Slowly but surely the new Financial Policy Review Office accrues all of the meaningful functions of the budget office isolating those bureaucrats who have not quit in disgust into meaningless technical positions out of the mainstream of the Department's operations.

d. New Activity Technique

Another organizational technique for the wholesale isolation and disposition of undesirable employee-victims is the creation of an apparently meaningful, but essentially meaningless, new activity to which they are all transferred. This technique, unlike the shifting responsibilities and isolation technique designed to immobilize a group of people in a single organizational entity, is designed to provide a single barrel into which you can dump a large number of widely located bad apples. Again let us use an example to illustrate this technique. Let us apply this to the Department of Health, Education, and Welfare. A startling new thrust to HEW's participation in the Model Cities Program might be a new research and development Model Cities Laboratory. With the concurrence of the Governor of Alabama, one might choose Alabama, or a region thereof, to be a "model state" or "model region" like we now have sections of cities designated as "model cities." For office facilities the Department of the Army might be prevailed upon to provide surplus buildings at Fort Rucker, Alabama. The Alabama State Department of Education, would, I am sure, be more than happy to provide school buses to bus HEW employees between their offices and the nearest town where they would live. Naturally, to such a high priority and high visibility project as a "model state" lab you would want to assign some of the most "qualified" employees and administrators you could find throughout the Department, both in Washington and in the field. By carefully looking at the personnel jackets of your selected employee-victims, you can easily design an organization chart for the project that would create positions to which these employee-victims can be transferred that meet the necessary job description requirements, offer promotional opportunities in grade, and by having the project report directly into the Secretary's office provide for promotions in status.

e. Additional Notes (Bureaucratic Countermeasures)

The techniques proffered above are not unknown to our loyal civil servants. Since extensive use of the layering techniques and the shifting responsibilities techniques were made by the previous Administration, between November of 1968 and January 20, 1969, tremendous reorganizations occurred within the Federal Government designed to make those techniques difficult to apply to our new Administration. With the help of the OMB, following the policies of the Revenue Expenditure Control Act, many positions not filled in the spring of 1969 were eliminated from the personnel ceilings of the Departments, or Agencies, and their funding for salaries was commensurately reduced. With the OMB continuing to reduce personnel ceilings, the availability of extra slots and salary funds for purposes of both layering and shifting responsibilities all but do not exist. Had the

OMB acted in the President's best interests to help him obtain control over his Administration, and rule rather than reign, it would have recommended an expansion of personnel ceilings and funding for salaries for the first two years. This would have enabled the Departments and Agencies to conduct the necessary layering and shifting responsibility functions during those first two years. During the last two years of the Administration, we could have enjoyed a reduction in personnel ceilings and funds and conducted a selected reduction in force. As it is, by and large, the personnel ceilings and funding policies of the OMB has only frustrated this Administration from any meaningful program for bringing in substantial numbers of loyal team members into the bureaucracy.

Likewise the OMB cooperated with the Johnson Administration during 1968 in the distribution to the Departments and Agencies of all but a few of the Executive Levels in the President's pool which were promptly filled, mostly on a career basis. This deprived this Administration of a flexible resource of Executive Level positions from which new positions for layering and shifting responsibilities at a high level could have been accomplished. The Administration was left with the alternative of seeking additional Executive Level positions from a Congress not likely to be cooperative.

Furthermore, as mentioned in the Introduction, the Departments and Agencies absorbed and filled on a career basis most of the outstanding supergrade quota allocations given to the Executive Branch by Congress. This again makes the creation of additional supergrade positions for the purposes of layering, shifting responsibilities, or setting up a new activity extremely difficult. It is to an uncooperative Congress that the Administration must look for additional supergrade quota allocations.

Further, between November 7, 1968 and January 20, 1969, most Government departments and agencies experienced a rapid increase in the classification of positions to their optimum level, followed by the promotion to and filling of those positions with those who had been loyal to that Administration. Again, this "counterlayering" activity had made it difficult for this Administration.

Conclusion

There is no substitute in the beginning of any Administration for a very active political personnel operation. Whatever investment is made in positions, salaries, sytems, training and intelligent work in this area, will yield a return ten-fold. Conversely, the failure to invest what is necessary to a political personnel program, will cost the Administration and the Department or Agency fifty-fold what they might otherwise have invested. These estimates are borne out by experience. Where Departments and Agencies, and Administrations, have failed to invest the manpower and other necessary aforementioned items into an effective political personnel program—blindly paying lip service to such a function and proceeding immediately to invest heavily in the management and program functions—they have only been plagued by such folly. The time consumed of high level Administration appointees, and the manpower and expenses involved in the creation of firefighting forces, caused by acts in attempt to frustrate the Administration's policies, program objectives and management objectives, as well as to embarrass the Administration, engaged in by unloyal employees of the Executive Branch, has far exceeded the investment a political personnel operation would have required. In those few organizations where an effective political personnel office was the forerunner of "new directions" in policy, program objectives, and management objectives, the ease and low visibility with which they were accomplished was markedly contrasted to the rest of the Administration. There is no question that the effective activities of a political personnel office will invoke a one-shot furor in the hostile press and Congress. But there is no question that these costs are far less than the costs of the frequent crescendos of bad publicity that are sure to occur frequently and indefinitely if you do not. In short, it is far better and healthier to swallow a large bitter pill in the beginning, and then run rigorously toward your objectives, than to run toward your objectives stopping so frequently for small bitter pills that you become drained of the endurance, the will and the ability to ever reach your objectives. As one of the ranking members of this Administration once put it: "You cannot hope to achieve policy, program or management control until you have achieved political control. *That is the difference between ruling and reigning*".

6.a. President's Reorganization Project

Personnel Management ("Ink Report," 1977)

The Civil Service System is a product of earlier reform. It emerged as a protest against the 19th Century "spoils system" with its widespread political patronage and mass influx of unqualified employees with each change of Administration. The new civil service concept promised a competent, continuing workforce, in which employees were selected and advanced on the basis of what they knew, rather than who they knew.

To a large extent the system has successfully achieved this goal. As the Federal Government has assumed increasing responsibilities in meeting critical needs of a dynamic society, the merit system has added many processes, but not enough major changes have emerged to adequately meet these new demands. And with the evolution and expansion of this system over almost a century, there have been frequent and determined attempts to circumvent merit principles, some of which have been painfully succesful in recent years.

To counter these assaults, there has gradually developed a bewildering array of complex protective procedures and additional checks and balances. Complexity has also been increased through procedural safeguards for various disadvantaged groups where rights have been too long ignored. The resultant time-consuming and confusing red tape undermines confidence in the merit system. Managers and personnel officers complain that it stresses form over substance, and that the procedures intended to assure merit and to protect employees from arbitrary and capricious management actions have too often become the refuge and protection of the incompetent and the problem employee.

Ironically, the entangling web of safeguards spun over the years often fails to protect against major political assaults and cronyism. With each new protective measure, there seems to have emerged new techniques to manipulate the system, as best illustrated by the so-called "Malek Manual" compiled for an earlier Administration. Further, any system which is too unwieldy to work tends to breed contempt and invites political abuse. Also, many well-intentioned managers and personnel officers who are earnestly trying to attain legitimate objectives believe that strict adherence to the procedures makes timely personnel actions very

Volume 1, Introduction to the Final Staff Report, U. S. Government Printing Office, December 1977. Only introductory "Perspectives" section is included here.

difficult if not impossible. Those who are credited with being action-oriented and successful are often those who have become skilled in short-cutting the procedures.

The Federal personnel system has grown so complicated that neither managers nor employees understand it. Both have been forced to rely on highly trained personnel technicians to interpret it for them. As a result, personnel management has frequently become divorced from the day-to-day supervisor-employee relationships. This separation hurts employees and managers alike. The system's rigid, impersonal procedures make it almost as difficult to adequately reward the outstanding employee as it is to remove the incompetent employee. Excessive delays in filling positions frustrate both the employees applying for these jobs and the managers trying to fill them. Most importantly, when incompetent and unmotivated employees are allowed to stay on the rolls, it is the dedicated and competent employees who must carry more than their share of the load in order to maintain service to the public.

The personnel officer occupies the untenable position of simultaneously trying to serve both the manager and the employee while trapped in a maze of red tape. Personnel officers are increasingly squeezed out of the mainstream of departmental management, and these positions no longer hold the attraction they once did for young men and women with imagination and outstanding talent for public service.

Confidence in the civil service system has been so low at points in the past that several large agencies with programs of high public urgency, most notably the National Aeronautics and Space Administration and the Atomic Energy Commission, were wholly or partially excepted from the system in order to provide their managers the flexibility needed to get the job done. The record in these organizations indicates that agencies can maintain sound merit principles without having to impose rigid procedural barriers.

It is the public which suffers from a system which neither permits managers to manage nor provides employees adequate assurance against political abuse. Valuable resources are lost to the public service by a system increasingly too cumbersome to compete effectively for talent. The opportunity for more effective service to the public is denied by a system so tortuous in operation that managers often regard it as almost impossible to remove those who are not performing. It is families everywhere who suffer from mismanagement of social programs caused by incompetent and inexperienced executives appointed on the basis of personal friendships rather than managerial qualifications. It is hardpressed neighborhoods and communities across the nation who are discriminated against on a massive basis by managerial decisions which divert grants elsewhere because of the influence of a mayor, governor, or member of Congress.

The staff recommendations in this report are based on the premise that jobs and programs in the Federal Government belong neither to employees nor to managers.

They belong to the people. The public has a right to have an effective Government, which is responsive to their needs as perceived by the President and Congress, but which at the same time is impartially administered.

Managers have no right to impose new spoils systems under the guise of flexibility. Neither do they have a right to mismanage public programs by hiring incompetent cronies. They must, however, be free to manage, or there will be little accountability and citizens will be deprived of the effective Government they have a right to demand. Employees have no right to place their personal gain above the ability of the Government to meet public needs. Neither should they have the right to cling to jobs in which they cannot, or will not, perform adequately. They do, however, have a right to work in a public service that is free of discrimination and partisan political influence, and they have a right to expect advancement to be determined on the basis of merit.

We are proposing a number of reforms which we believe will help restore an appropriate balance between these sometimes competing needs for flexibility and efficiency on the one hand, and adequate safeguards on the other, in order to foster effective, fair management in the Federal Government.

To be meaningful, however, their adoption must be accompanied by the assignment of a higher priority to sound and equitable personnel management by the White House, agency heads and members of Congress.

The Executive Director

6.b. Civil Service Reform Act of 1978

An Act to Reform the Civil Service Laws.

Be it enacted by the Senate and House of Representatives of the United States of America in Congress assembled,

SHORT TITLE

Section 1. This Act may be cited as the "Civil Service Reform Act of 1978".

. . . .

FINDINGS AND STATEMENT OF PURPOSE

Sec. 3. It is the policy of the United Stated that—

(1) in order to provide the people of the United States with a competent, honest, and productive Federal work force reflective of the Nation's diversity, and to improve the quality of public service, Federal personnel management should be implemented consistent with merit system principles and free from prohibited personnel practices;

(2) the merit system principles which shall govern in the competitive service and in the executive branch of the Federal Government should be expressly stated to furnish guidance to Federal agencies in carrying out their responsibilities in administering the public business, and prohibited personnel practices should be statutorily defined to enable Federal employees to avoid conduct which undermines the merit system principles and the integrity of the merit system;

(3) Federal employees should receive appropriate protection through increasing the authority and powers of the Merit Systems Protection Board in processing hearings and appeals affecting Federal employees;

(4) the authority and power of the Special Counsel should be increased so that the Special Counsel may investigate allegations involving pro-

Public Law 95–454 (October 13, 1978). Many of the more technical provisions have been omitted in each of the major sections of the act. All of Titles VI, VII, VIII and IX dealing with (1) Research, Demonstration, and other Programs (VI), (2) Federal Service Labor Management Relations (VII), (3) Grade and Pay Retention (VIII), (4) Miscellaneous (IX) were deleted.

hibited personnel practices and reprisals against Federal employees for the lawful disclosure of certain information and may file complaints against agency officials and the employees who engage in such conduct;

(5) the function of filling positions and other personnel functions in the competitive service and in the executive branch should be delegated in appropriate cases to the agencies to expedite processing appointments and other personnel actions, with the control and oversight of this delegation being maintained by the Office of Personnel Management to protect against prohibited personnel practices and the use of unsound management practices by the agencies;

(6) a Senior Executive Service should be established to provide the flexibility needed by agencies to recruit and retain the highly competent and qualified executives needed to provide more effective management of agencies and their functions, and the more expeditious administration of the public business;

(7) in appropriate instances, pay increases should be based on quality of performance rather than length of service;

(8) research programs and demonstration projects should be authorized to permit Federal agencies to experiment, subject to congressional oversight, with new and different personnel management concepts in controlled situations to achieve more efficient management of the Government's human resources and greater productivity in the delivery of service to the public;

(9) the training program of the Government should include retraining of employees for positions in other agencies to avoid separations during reductions in force and the loss to the Government of the knowledge and experience that these employees possess; and

(10) the right of Federal employees to organize, bargain collectively, and participate through labor organizations in decisions which affect them, with full regard for the public interest and the effective conduct of public business, should be specifically recognized in statute.

TITLE I—MERIT SYSTEM PRINCIPLES

MERIT SYSTEM PRINCIPLES; PROHIBITED PERSONNEL PRACTICES

Sec. 101. (a) Title 5, United States Code, is amended by inserting after chapter 21 the following new chapter:

"CHAPTER 23—MERIT SYSTEM PRINCIPLES

Sec.
2301. Merit system principles.
2302. Prohibited personnel practices.
2303. Prohibited personnel practices in the Federal Bureau of Investigation.
2304. Responsibility of the General Accounting Office.
2305. Coordination with certain other provisions of law.

2301. Merit system principles

"(a) This section shall apply to—

"(1) an Executive agency;

"(2) the Administrative Office of the United States Courts; and

"(3) the Government Printing Office.

"(b) Federal personnel management should be implemented consistent with the following merit system principles:

"(1) Recruitment should be from qualified individuals from appropriate sources in an endeavor to achieve a work force from all segments of society, and selection and advancement should be determined solely on the basis of relative ability, knowledge, and skills, after fair and open competition which assures that all receive equal opportunity.

"(2) All employees and applicants for employment should receive fair and equitable treatment in all aspects of personnel management without regard to political affiliation, race, color, religion, national origin, sex, marital status, age, or handicapping condition, and with proper regard for their privacy and constitutional rights.

"(3) Equal pay should be provided for work of equal value, with appropriate consideration of both national and local rates paid by employers in the private sector, and appropriate incentives and recognition should be provided for excellence in performance.

"(4) All employees should maintain high standards of integrity, conduct, and concern for the public interest.

"(5) The Federal work force should be used efficiently and effectively.

"(6) Employees should be retained on the basis of the adequacy of their performance, inadequate performance should be corrected, and employees should be separated who cannot or will not improve their performance to meet required standards.

"(7) Employees should be provided effective education and training in cases in which such education and training would result in better organizational and individual performance.

"(8) Employees should be—

"(A) protected against arbitrary action, personal favoritism, or coercion for partisan political purposes, and

"(B) prohibited from using their official authority or influence for the purpose of interfering with or affecting the result of an election or a nomination for election.

"(9) Employees should be protected against reprisal for the lawful disclosure of information which the employees reasonaly believe evidences—

"(A) a violation of any law, rule, or regulation, or

"(B) mismanagement, a gross waste of funds, an abuse of authority, or a substantial and specific danger to public health or safety.

"(c) In administering the provisions of this chapter—

"(1) with respect to any agency (as defined in section 2302(a)(2)(C) of this title), the President shall, pursuant to the authority otherwise available under this title, take any action, including the issuance of rules, regulations, or directives; and

"(2) with respect to any entity in the executive branch which is not such an agency or part of such an agency, the head of such entity shall, pursuant to authority otherwise available, take any action, including the issuance of rules, regulations, directives; which is consistent with the provisions of this title and which the President or the head, as the case may be, determines is necessary to ensure that personnel management is based on and embodies the merit system principles.

. . . .

TITLE II—CIVIL SERVICE FUNCTIONS; PERFORMANCE APPRAISAL; ADVERSE ACTIONS

OFFICE OF PERSONNEL MANAGEMENT

Sec. 201. (a) Chapter 11 of title 5, United States Code, is amended to read as follows:

"CHAPTER 11—OFFICE OF PERSONNEL MANAGEMENT

"§ 1101. Office of Personnel Management

"The Office of Personnel Management is an independent establishment in the executive branch. The Office shall have an official seal which shall be judicially noticed, and shall have its principal office in the District of Columbia, and may have field offices in other appropriate locations.

"§ 1102. Director; Deputy Director; Associate Directors

"(a) There is at the head of the Office of Personnel Management a Director of the Office of Personnel Management appointed by the President, by and with the advice and consent of the Senate. The term of office of any individual appointed as Director shall be 4 years.

"(b) There is in the Office a Deputy Director of the Office of Personnel Management appointed by the President, by and with the advice and consent of the Senate. The Deputy Director shall perform such functions as the Director may from time to time prescribe and shall act as Director during the absence or disability of the Director or when the office of Director is vacant.

"(c) No individual shall, while serving as Director or Deputy Director, serve in any other office or position in the Government of the United States except as otherwise provided by law or at the direction of the President. The Director and Deputy Director shall not recommend any individual for appointment to any position (other than Deputy Director of the Office) which requires the advice and consent of the Senate.

"(d) There may be within the Office of Personnel Management not more than 5 Associate Directors, as determined from time to time by the Director. Each Associate Director shall be appointed by the Director.

"§ 1103. *Functions of the Director*

"(a) The following functions are vested in the Director of the Office of Personnel Management, and shall be performed by the Director, or subject to section 1104 of this title, by such employees of the Office as the Director designates:

"(1) securing accuracy, uniformity, and justice in the functions of the Office;

"(2) appointing individuals to be employed by the Office;

"(3) directing and supervising employees of the Office, distributing business among employees and organizational units of the Office, and directing the internal management of the Office;

"(4) directing the preparation of requests for appropriations for the Office and the use and expenditure of funds by the Office;

"(5) executing, administering, and enforcing—

"(A) the civil service rules and regulations of the President and the Office and the laws governing the civil service; and

"(B) the other activities of the Office including retirement and classification activities;

except with respect to functions for which the Merit Systems Protection Board or the Special Counsel is primarily responsible;

"(6) reviewing the operations under chapter 87 of this title;

"(7) aiding the President, as the President may request, in preparing such civil service rules as the President prescribes, and otherwise advising the President on actions which may be taken to promote an efficient civil service and a systematic application of the merit system principles, including recommending policies relating to the selection, promotion, transfer, performance, pay, conditions of service, tenure, and separation of employees; and

"(8) conducting, or otherwise providing for the conduct of, studies and research under chapter 47 of this title into methods of assuring improvements in personnel management.

"(b)(1) The Director shall publish in the Federal Register general notice of any rule or regulation which is proposed by the Office and the application of which does not apply solely to the Office or its employees. Any such notice shall include the matter required under section 553(b) (1), (2), and (3) of this title.

"(2) The Director shall take steps to ensure that—

"(A) any proposed rule or regulation to which paragraph (1) of this subsection applies is posted in offices of Federal agencies maintaining copies of the Federal personnel regulations; and

"(B) to the extent the Director determines appropriate and practical, exclusive representatives of employees affected by such proposed rule or regulation and interested members of the public are notified of such proposed rule or regulation.

"(3) Paragraphs (1) and (2) of this subsection shall not apply to any proposed rule or regulation which is temporary in nature and which is necessary to be implemented expediously as a result of an emergency.

"§ 1104. Delegation of authority for personnel management

"(a) Subject to subsection (b)(3) of this section—

"(1) the President may delegate, in whole or in part, authority for personnel management functions, including authority for competitive examinstions, to the Director of the Office of Personnel Management; and

"(2) the Director may delegate, in whole or in part, any function vested in or delegated to the Director, including authority for competitive examinations (except competitive examinations for administrative law judges appointed under section 3105 of this title), to the heads of agencies in the executive branch and other agencies employing persons in the competitive service;

except that the Director may not delegate authority for competitive examinations with respect to positions that have requirements which are common to agencies in the Federal Government, other than in exceptional cases in which the interests of economy and efficiency require such delegation and in which such delegation will not weaken the application of the merit system principles.

"(b)(1) The Office shall establish standards which shall apply to the activities of the Office or any other agency under authority delegated under subsection (a) of this section.

"(2) The Office shall establish and maintain an oversight program to ensure that activities under any authority delegated under subsection (a) of this section are in accordance with the merit system principles and the standards established under paragraph (1) of this subsection.

"(3) Nothing in subsection (a) of this section shall be construed as affecting the responsibility of the Director to prescribe regulations and to ensure compliance with the civil service laws, rules, and regulations.

"(c) If the Office makes a written finding, on the basis of information obtained under the program established under subsection (b)(2) of this section or otherwise, that any action taken by an agency pursuant to authority delegated under subsection (a)(2) of this section is contrary to any law, rule, or regulation, or is contrary to any standard established under subsection (b)(1) of this section, the agency involved shall take any corrective action the Office may require.

. . . .

"CHAPTER 12—MERIT SYSTEMS PROTECTION BOARD AND SPECIAL COUNSEL

"Sec.
"1201. Appointment of members of the Merit Systems Protection Board.
"1202. Term of office; filling vacancies; removal.
"1203. Chairman; Vice Chairman.
"1204. Special Counsel; appointment and removal.
"1205. Powers and functions of the Merit Systems Protection Board and Special Counsel.
"1206. Authority and responsibilities of the Special Counsel.
"1207. Hearings and decisions on complaints filed by the Special Counsel.
"1208. Stays of certain personnel actions.
"1209. Information.

"§ 1201. *Appointment of members of the Merit Systems Protection Board (5 USC 1201.)*

"The Merit Systems Protection Board is composed of 3 members appointed by the President, by and with the advice and consent of the Senate, not more than 2 of whom may be adherents of the same political party. The Chairman and members of the Board shall be individuals who, by demonstrated ability, background, training, or experience are especially qualified to carry out the functions of the Board. No member of the Board may hold another office or position in the Government of the United States, except as otherwise provided by law or at the direction of the President. The Board shall have an official seal which shall be judicially noticed. The Board shall have its principal office in the District of Columbia and may have field offices in other appropriate locations.

"§ 1202. *Term of office, filling vacancies; removal*

"(a) The term of office of each member of the Merit Systems Protection Board is 7 years.
"(b) A member appointed to fill a vacancy occurring before the end of a term of

office of his predecessor serves for the remainder of that term. Any appointment to fill a vacancy is subject to the requirements of section 1201 of this title.

"(c) Any member appointed for a 7-year term may not be reappointed to any following term but may continue to serve beyond the expiration of the term until a successor is appointed and has qualified, except that such member may not continue to serve for more than one year after the date on which the term of the member would otherwise expire under this section.

"(d) Any member may be removed by the President only for inefficiency, neglect of duty, or malfeasance in office.

"§ 1203. Chairman; Vice Chairman

"(a) The President shall from time to time, appoint, by and with the advice and consent of the Senate, one of the members of the Merit Systems Protection Board as the Chairman of the Board. The Chairman is the chief executive and administrative officer of the Board.

"(b) The President shall from time to time designate one of the members of the Board as Vice Chairman of the Board. During the absence or disability of the Chairman, or when the office of Chairman is vacant, the Vice Chairman shall perform the functions vested in the Chairman.

"(c) During the absence or disability of both the Chairman and Vice Chairman, or when the offices of Chairman and Vice Chairman are vacant, the remaining Board member shall perform the functions vested in the Chairman.

"§ 1204. Special Counsel; appointment and removal

"The Special Counsel of the Merit Systems Protection Board shall be appointed by the President from attorneys, by and with the advice and consent of the Senate, for a term of 5 years. A Special Counsel appointed to fill a vacancy occurring before the end of a term of office of his predecessor serves for the remainder of the term. The Special Counsel may be removed by the President only for inefficiency, neglect of duty, or malfeasance in office.

"§ 1205. Powers and functions of the Merit Systems Protection Board and Special Counsel

"(a) The Merit Systems Protection Board shall—

"(1) hear, adjudicate, or provide for the hearing or adjudication, of all matters within the jurisdiction of the Board under this title, section 2023 of title 38, or any other law, rule, or regulation, and, subject to otherwise applicable provisions of law, take final action on any such matter;

"(2) order any Federal agency or employee to comply with any order or decision issued by the Board under the authority granted under paragraph (1) of this subsection and enforce compliance with any such order;

"(3) conduct, from time to time, special studies relating to the civil service and to other merit systems in the executive branch, and report to the President and to the Congress as to whether the public interest in a civil service free of prohibited personnel practices is being adequately protected; and

"(4) review, as provided in subsection (c) of this section, rules and regulations of the Office of Personnel Management.

"(b)(1) Any member of the Merit Systems Protection Board, the Special Counsel, any administrative law judge appointed by the Board under section 3105 of this title, and any employee of the Board designated by the Board may administer oaths, examine witnesses, take depositions, and receive evidence.

"(2) Any member of the Board, the Special Counsel, and any administrative law judge appointed by the Board under section 3105 of this title may—

"(A) issue subpenas requiring the attendance and testimony of witnesses and the production of documentary or other evidence from any place in the United States or any territory or possession thereof, the Commonwealth of Puerto Rico, or the District of Columbia; and

"(B) order the taking of depositions and order responses to written interrogatories.

"(3) Witnesses (whether appearing voluntarily or under subpena) shall be paid the same fee and mileage allowances which are paid subpenaed witnesses in the courts of the United States.

"(c) In the case of contumacy or failure to obey a subpena issued under subsection (b)(2) of this section, the United States district court for the judicial district in which the person to whom the subpena is addressed resides or is served may issue an order requiring such person to appear at any designated place to testify or to produce documentary or other evidence. Any failure to obey the order of the court may be punished by the court as a contempt thereof.

"(d)(1) In any proceeding under subsection (a)(1) of this section, any member of the Board may request from the Director of the Office of Personnel Management any advisory opinion concerning the interpretation of any rule, regulation, or other policy directive promulgated by the Office of Personnel Management.

"(2) In enforcing compliance with any order under subsection (a)(2) of this section, the Board may order that any employee charged with complying with such order, other than an employee appointed by the President by and with the advice and consent of the Senate, shall not be entitled to receive payment for service as an employee during any period that the order has not been complied with. The Board shall certify to the Comptroller General of the United States that such an order has been issued and no payment shall be made out of the Treasury of the United States for any service specified in such order.

"(3) In carrying out any study under subsection (a)(3) of this section, the Board shall make such inquiries as may be necessary and, unless otherwise prohibited by law, shall have access to personnel records or information collected by the Office and may require additional reports from other agencies as needed.

"(e)(1) At any time after the effective date of any rule or regulation issued by the Director in carrying out functions under section 1103 of this title, the Board shall review any provision of such rule or regulation—

"(A) on its own motion:

"(B) on the granting by the Board, in its sole discretion, of any petition for such review filed with the Board by any interested person, after consideration of the petition by the Board; or

"(C) on the filing of a written complaint by the Special Counsel requesting such review.

"(2) In reviewing any provision of any rule or regulation pursuant to this subsection the Board shall declare such provision—

"(A) invalid on its face, if the Board determines that such provision would, if implemented by any agency, on its face, require any employee to violate section 2303(b) of this title; or

"(B) invalidly implemented by any agency, if the Board determines that such provision, as it has been implemented by the agency through any personnel action taken by the agency or through any policy adopted by the agency in conformity with such provision, has required any employee to violate section 2302 (b) of this title.

"(3)(A) The Director of the Office of Personnel Management, and the head of any agency implementing any provision of any rule or regulation under review pursuant to this subsection, shall have the right to participate in such review.

"(B) Any review conducted by the Board pursuant to this subsection shall be limited to determining—

"(i) the validity on its face of the provision under review; and

"(ii) whether the provision under review has been validly implemented.

"(C) The Board shall require any agency—

"(i) to cease compliance with any provisions of any rule or regulation which the Board declares under this subsection to be invalid on its face; and "(ii)   to correct any invalid implementation by the agency of any provision of any rule or regulation which the Board declares under this subsection to have been invalidly implemented by the agency.

"(f) The Board may delegate the performance of any of its administrative functions under this title to any employee of the Board.

"(g) The Board shall have the authority to prescribe such regulations as may be necessary for the performance of its functions. The Board shall not issue advisory opinions. All regulations of the Board shall be published in the Federal Register.

"(h) Except as provided in section 518 of title 28, relating to litigation before the Supreme Court, attorneys designated by the Chairman of the Board may appear for the Board, and represent the Board, in any civil action brought in connection with any function carried out by the Board pursuant to this title or as otherwise authorized by law.

"(i) The Chairman of the Board may appoint such personnel as may be necessary to perform the functions of the Board. Any appointment made under this subsection shall comply with the provisions of this title, except that such appointment shall not be subject to the approval or supervision of the Office of Personnel Management or the Executive Office of the President (other than approval required under section 3324 or subchapter VIII of chapter 33 of this title).

"(j) The Board shall prepare and submit to the President, and, at the same time, to the appropriate committees of Congress, an annual budget of the expenses and other items relating to the Board which shall, as revised, be included as a separate item in the budget required to be transmitted to the Congress under section 201 of the Budget and Accounting Act, 1921 (31 U.S.C. 11).

"(k) The Board shall submit to the President, and, at the same time, to each House of Congress, any legislative recommendations of the Board relating to any of its functions under this title.

. . . .

"CHAPTER 43—PERFORMANCE APPRAISAL

"*SUBCHAPTER I—GENERAL PROVISIONS*

"§ 4301. *Definitions*

"For the purpose of this subchapter—

    "(1) 'agency' means—

        "(A) an Executive agency:

        "(B) the Administrative Office of the United States Courts; and

"(C) the Government Printing Office; but does not include—

"(i) a Government corporation;

"(ii) the Central Intelligence Agency, the Defense Intelligence Agency, the National Security Agency, or any Executive agency or unit thereof which is designated by the President and the principal function of which is the conduct of foreign intelligence or counterintelligence activities; or

"(iii) the General Accounting Office;

"(2) 'employee' means an individual employed in or under an agency, but does not include—

"(A) an employee outside the United States who is paid in accordance with local native prevailing wage rates for the area in which employed;

"(B) an individual in the Foreign Service of the United States;

"(C) a physician, dentist, nurse, or other employee in the Department of Medicine and Surgery, Veterans' Administration whose pay is fixed under chapter 73 of title 38;

"(D) an administrative law judge appointed under section 3105 of this title;

"(E) an individual in the Senior Executive Service;

"(F) an individual appointed by the President; or

"(G) an individual occupying a position not in the competitive service excluded from coverage of this subchapter by regulations of the Office of Personnel Management; and

"(3) 'unacceptable performance' means performance of an employee which fails to meet established performance standards in one or more critical elements of such employee's position.

"§ 4302. *Establishment of performance appraisal systems*

"(a) Each agency shall develop one or more performance appraisal systems which—

"(1) provide for periodic appraisals of job performance of employees;

"(2) encourage employee participation in establishing performance standards; and

"(3) use the results of performance appraisals as a basis for training, rewarding, reassigning, promoting, reducing in grade, retaining, and removing employees:

"(b) Under regulations which the Office of Personnel Management shall prescribe, each performance appraisal system shall provide for—

"(1) establishing performance standards which will, to the maximum extent feasible, permit the accurate evaluation of job performance on the basis of objective criteria (which may include the extent of courtesy demonstrated to the public) related to the job in question for each employee or position under the system;

"(2) as soon as practicable, but not later than October 1, 1981, with respect to initial appraisal periods, and thereafter at the beginning of each following appraisal period, communicating to each employee the performance standards and the critical elements of the employee's position;

"(3) evaluating each employee during the appraisal period on such standards;

"(4) recognizing and rewarding employees whose performance so warrants;

"(5) assisting employees in improving unacceptable performance; and

"(6) reassigning, reducing in grade, or removing employees who continue to have unacceptable performance but only after an opportunity to demonstrate acceptable performance.

. . . .

"SUBCHAPTER II—THE SENIOR EXECUTIVE SERVICE

"§ 3131. *The Senior Executive Service*

"It is the purpose of this subchapter to establish a Senior Executve Service to ensure that the executive management of the Government of the United States is responsive to the needs, policies, and goals of the Nation and otherwise is of the highest quality. The Senior Executive Service shall be administered so as to—

"(1) provide for a compensation system, including salaries, benefits, and incentives, and for other conditions of employment, designed to attract and retain highly competent senior executives;

"(2) ensure that compensation, retention, and tenure are contingent on executive success which is measured on the basis of individual and organizational performance (including such factors as improvements in efficiency, and timeliness of performance and success in meeting equal employment opportunity goals);

"(3) assure that senior executives are accountable and responsible for the effectiveness and productivity of employees under them;

"(4) recognize exceptional accomplishment

"(5) enable the head of an agency to reassign senior executives to best accomplish the agency's mission;

"(6) provide for severance pay, early retirement, and placement assistance for senior executives who are removed from the Senior Executive Service for nondisciplinary reasons;

"(7) protect senior executives from arbitrary or capricious actions;

"(8) provide for program continuity and policy advocacy in the management of public programs;

"(9) maintain a merit personnel system free of prohibited personnel practices:

"(10) ensure accountability for honest, economical, and efficient Government;

"(11) ensure compliance with all applicable civil service laws, rules, and regulations, including those related to equal employment opportunity, political activity, and conflicts of interest;

"(12) provide for the initial and continuing systematic development of highly competent senior executives;

"(13) provide for an executive system which is guided by the public interest and free from improper political interference; and

"(14) appoint career executives to fill Senior Executive Service positions to the extent practicable, consistent with the effective and efficient implementation of agency policies and responsibilities.

"§ 3132. *Definitions and exclusions*

"(a) For the purpose of this subchapter—

"(1) 'agency' means an Executive agency, except a Government corporation and the General Accounting Office, but does not include—

"(A) any agency or unit thereof excluded from coverage by the President under subsection (c) of this section: or

"(B) the Federal Bureau of Investigation, the Central Intelligence Agency, the Defense Intelligence Agency, the National Security Agency, as determined by the President, an Executive agency, or unit thereof, whose principal function is the conduct of foreign intelligence or counterintelligence activities;

"(2) 'Senior Executive Service position' means any position in an agency which is in GS–16, 17, or 18 of the General Schedule or in level IV or V of the Executive Schedule, or an equivalent position, which is not required to be filled by an appointment by the President and with the advice and consent of the Senate, and in which an employee—

"(A) directs the work of an organizational unit;

"(B) is held accountable for the success of one or more specific programs or projects;

"(C) monitors progress toward organizational goals and periodically evaluates and makes appropriate adjustments to such goals;

"(D) supervises the work of employees other than personal assistants; or

"(E) otherwise exercises important policy-making, policy-determining, or other executive functions; but does not include—

"(i) any position in the Foreign Service of the United States;

"(ii) an administrative law judge position under section 3105 of this title; or

"(iii) any position in the Drug Enforcement Administration which is excluded from the competitive service under section 201 of the Crime Control Act of 1976 (5 U.S.C. 5108 note; 90 Stat. 2425);

"(3) 'senior executive' means a member of the Senior Executive Service;

"(4) 'career appointee' means an individual in a Senior Executive Service position whose appointment to the position or previous appointment to another Senior Executive Service position was based on approval by the Office of Personnel Management of the executive qualifications of such individual;

"(5) 'limited term appointee' means an individual appointed under a nonrenewable appointment for a term of 3 years or less to a Senior Executive Service position the duties of which will expire at the end of such term;

"(6) 'limited emergency appointee' means an individual appointed under a nonrenewable appointment, not to exceed 18 months, to a Senior Executive Service position established to meet a bona fide, unanticipated, urgent need;

"(7) 'noncareer appointee' means an individual in a Senior Executive Service position who is not a career appointee, a limited term appointee, or a limited emergency appointee;

"(8) 'career reserved position' means a position which is required to be filled by a career appointee and which is designated under subsection (b) of this section; and

"(9) 'general position' means any position, other than a career reserved position, which may be filled by either a career appointee, noncareer appointee, limited emergency appointee, or limited term appointee.

"(b) (1) For the purpose of paragraph (8) of subsection (a) of this section, the Office shall prescribe the criteria and regulations governing the designation of career reserved positions. The criteria and regulations shall provide that a position shall be designated as a career reserved position only if the filling of the position by a career appointee is necessary to ensure impartiality, or the public's confidence in the impartiality, of the Government. The head of each agency shall be responsible for designating career reserved positions in such agency in accordance with such criteria and regulations.

"(2) The Office shall periodically review general positions to determine whether the positions should be designated as career reserved. If the Office determines that any such position should be so designated, it shall order the agency to make the designation.

"(3) Notwithstanding the provisions of any other law, any position to be designated as a Senior Executive Service position (except a position in the Executive Office of the President) which—

  "(A) is under the Executive Schedule, or for which the rate of basic pay is determined by reference to the Executive Schedule, and

  "(B) on the day before the date of the enactment of the Civil Service Reform Act of 1978 was specifically required under section 2102 of this title or otherwise required by law to be in the competitive service,
  shall be designated as a career reserved position if the position entails direct responsibility to the public for the management or operation of particular government programs or functions.

"(4) Not later than March 1 of each year, the head of each agency shall publish in the Federal Register a list of positions in the agency which were career reserved positions during the preceding calendar year.

"(c) An agency may file an application with the Office setting forth reasons why it, or a unit thereof, should be excluded from the coverage of this subchapter. The Office shall—

  "(1) review the application and stated reasons,

  "(2) undertake a review to determine whether the agency or unit should be excluded from the coverage of this subchapter and

  "(3) upon completion of its review, recommend to the President whether the agency or unit should be excluded from the coverage of this subchapter.

"(d) Any agency or unit which is excluded from coverage under subsection (c) of this section shall make a sustained effort to bring its personnel system into conformity with the Senior Executive Service to the extent practicable.

"(e) The Office may at any time recommend to the President that any exclusion previously granted to an agency or unit thereof under subsection(c) of this section be revoked. Upon recommendation of the Office, the President may revoke, by written determination, any exclusion made under subsection (c) of this section.

"(f) If—

"(1) any agency is excluded under subsection (c) of this section, or

"(2) any exclusion is revoked under subsection (e) of this section, the Office shall, within 30 days after the action, transmit to the Congress written notice of the exclusion or revocation.

"§ 3133. *Authorization of positions; authority for appointment*

"(a) During each even-numbered calendar year, each agency shall

"(1) examine its needs for Senior Executive Service positions for each of the 2 fiscal years beginning after such calendar year; and

"(2) submit to the Office of Personnel Management a written request for a specific number of Senior Executive Service positions for each of such fiscal years.

"(b) Each agency request submitted under subsection (a) of this section shall—

"(1) be based on the anticipated type and extent of program activities and budget requests of the agency for each of the 2 fiscal years involved, and such other factors as may be prescribed from time to time by the Office; and

"(2) identify, by position title, positions which are proposed to be designated as or removed from designation as career reserved positions, and set forth justifications for such proposed actions.

"(c) The Office of Personnel Management, in consultation with the Office of Management and Budget, shall review the request of each agency and shall authorize, for each of the 2 fiscal years covered by requests required under subsection (a) of this section, a specific number of Senior Executive Service positions for each agency.

"(d)(1) The Office of Personnel Management may, on a written request of an agency or on its own initiative, make an adjustment in the number of positions authorized for an agency. Each agency request under this paragraph shall be submitted in such form, and shall be based on such factors, as the Office shall prescribe.

"(2) The total number of positions in the Senior Executive Service may not at any time during any fiscal year exceed 105 percent of the total number of positions authorized under subsection (c) of this section for such fiscal year.

"(c)(1) Not later than July 1, 1979, and from time to time thereafter as the Director of the Office of Personnel Management finds appropriate, the Director shall establish, by rule issued in accordance with section 1103(b) of this title, the number of positions out of the total number of positions in the Senior Executive Service, as authorized by this section or section 413 of the Civil Service Reform Act of 1978, which are to be career reserved positions. Except as provided in paragraph (2) of this subsection, the number of positions required by this subsection to be career reserved positions shall not be less than the number of positions then in the Senior Executive Service which before the date of such Act, were authorized to be filled only through competitive civil service examination.

"(2) The Director may, by rule, designate a number of career reserved positions which is less than the number required by paragraph (1) of this subsection only if the Director determines such lesser number necessary in order to designate as general positions (other than positions described in section 3132(b)(3) of this title) which—

"(A) involve policymaking responsibilities which require the advocacy or management of programs of the President and support of controversial aspects of such programs;

"(B) involve significant participation in the major political policies of the President; or

"(C) require the senior executives in the positions to serve as personal assistants of, or advisers to, Presidential appointees.

The Director shall provide a full explanation for his determination in each case.

"§ 3134. *Limitations on noncareer and limited appointments*

"(a) During each calendar year, each agency shall—

"(1) examine its needs for employment of noncareer appointees for the fiscal year beginning in the following year; and

"(2) submit to the Office of Personnel Management, in accordance with regulations prescribed by the Office, a written request for authority to employ a specific number of noncareer appointees for such fiscal year.

"(b) The number of noncareer appointees in each agency shall be determined annually by the Office on the basis of demonstrated need of the agency. The total number of noncareer appointees in all agencies may not exceed 10 percent of the total number of Senior Executive Service positions in all agencies.

"(c) Subject to the 10 percent limitation of subsection (b) of this section, the Office may adjust the number of noncareer positions authorized for any agency under subsection (b) of this section if emergency needs arise that were not anticipated when the original authorizations were made.

"(d) The number of Senior Executive Service positions in any agency which are filled by noncareer appointees may not at any time exceed the greater of—

"(1) 25 percent of the total number of Senior Executive Service positions in the agency; or

"(2) the number of positios in the agency which were filled on the date of the enactment of the Civil Service Reform Act of 1978 by—

"(A) noncareer executive assignments under subpart F of part 305 of title 5, Code of Federal Regulations, as in effect on such date, or

"(B) appointments to level IV or V of the Executive Schedule which were not required on such date to be made by and with the advice and consent of the Senate.

This subsection shall not apply in the case of any agency having fewer than 4 Senior Executive Service positions.

"(e) The total number of limited emergency appointees and limited term appointees in all agencies may not exceed 5 percent of the total number of Senior Executive Service positions in all agencies.

"§ 3135. *Biennial report*

"(a) The Office of Personnel Management shall submit to each House of the Congress, at the time the budget is submitted by the President to the Congress during each odd-numbered calendar year, a report on the Senior Executive Service.

"Subchapter II—Performance Appraisal in the Senior Executive Service

"§4311. *Definitions*

"For the purpose of this subchapter, 'agency', 'senior executive', and 'career appointee' have the meanings set forth in section 3132(a) of this title.

"§4312. Senior Executive Service performance appraisal systems

"(a) Each agency shall, in accordance with standards established by the Office of Personnel Management, develop one or more performance appraisal systems designed to—

"(1) permit the accurate evaluation of performance in any position on the basis of criteria which are related to the position and which specify the critical elements of the position;

"(2) provide for systematic appraisals of performance of senior executives;

"(3) encourage excellence in performance by senior executives and

"(4) provide a basis for making eligibility determinations for retention in the Senior Executive Service and for Senior Executive Service performance awards.

"(b) Each performance appraisal system established by an agency under subsection (a) of this section shall provide—

"(1) that, on or before the beginning of each rating period performance requirements for each senior executive in the agency are established in consultation with the senior executive and communicated to the senior executive;

"(2) that written appraisals of performance are based on the individual and organizational performance requirements established for the rating period involved; and

"(3) that each senior executive in the agency is provided a copy of the appraisal and rating under section 4314 of this title and is given an opportunity to respond in writing and have the rating reviewed by an employee in a higher executive level in the agency before the rating becomes final.

"(c)(1) The Office shall review each agency's performance appraisal system under this section, and determine whether the agency performance appraisal system meets the rquirements of this subchapter.

"(2) The Comptroller General shall from time to time review performance appraisal systems under this section to determine the extent to which any such system meets the requirements under this subchapter and shall periodically report its findings to the Office and to each House of the Congress.

"(3) If the Office determines that an agency performance appraisal system does not meet the requirements under this subchapter (including regulations prescribed under section 4315), the agency shall take such corrective action as may be required by the Office.

"(d) A senior executive may not appeal any appraisal and rating under any performance appraisal system under this section.

"§4313. *Criteria for performance appraisals*

"Appraisals of performance in the Senior Executive Service shall be based on both individual and organizational performance, taking into account such factors as—

"(1) improvements in efficiency, productivity, and quality of work or service, including any significant reduction in paperwork;

"(2) cost efficiency;

"(3) timeliness of performance;

"(4) other indications of the effectiveness, productivity, and performance quality of the employees for whom the senior executive is responsible; and

"(5) meeting affirmative action goals and achievement of equal employment opportunity requirements.

"§4314. *Ratings for performance appraisals*

"(a) Each performance appraisal system shall provide for annual summary ratings of levels of performance as follows:

"(1) one or more fully successful levels,

"(2) a minimally satisfactory level, and

"(3) an unsatisfactory level.

"(b) Each performance appraisal system shall provide that—

"(1) any appraisal and any rating under such system—

"(A) are made only after review and evaluation by a performance review board established under subsection (c) of this section;

"(B) are conducted at least annually, subject to the limitation of subsection (c)(3) of this section;

"(C) in the case of a career appointee, may not be made within 120 days after the beginning of a new presidential administration; and

"(D) are based on performance during a performance appraisal period the duration of which shall be determined under guidelines established by the Office of Personnel Management, but which may be terminated in any case in which the agency making an appraisal determines that an adequate basis exists on which to appraise and rate the senior executive's performance;

"(2) any career appointee receiving a rating at any of the fully successful levels under subsection (a)(1) of this section may be given a performance award under section 5384 of this title;

"(3) any senior executive receiving an unsatisfactory rating under subsection (a)(3) of this section shall be reassigned or transferred within the Senior Executive Service, or removed from the Senior Executive Service, but any senior executive who receives 2 unsatisfactory ratings in any period of 5 consecutive years shall be removed from the Senior Executive Service; and

"(4) any senior executive who twice in any period of 3 consecutive years receives less than fully successful ratings shall be removed from the Senior Executive Service.

"(c)(1) Each agency shall establish, in accordance with regulations prescribed by the Office, one or more performance review boards, as appropriate. It is the function of the boards to make recommendations to the appropriate appointing authority of the agency relating to the performance of senior executives in the agency.

"(2) The supervising official of the senior executive shall provide to the performance review board, an initial appraisal of the senior executive's performance. Before making any recommendation with respect to the senior executive, the board shall review any response by the senior executive to the initial appraisal and conduct such further review as the board finds necessary.

"(3) Performance appraisals under this subchapter with respect to any senior executive shall be made by the appointing authority only after considering the recommendations by the performance review board with respect to such senior executive under paragraph (1) of this subsection.

"(4) Members of performance review boards shall be appointed in such a manner as to assure consistency, stability, and objectivity in performance appraisal. Notice of the appointment of an individual to serve as a member shall be published in the Federal Register.

"(5) In the case of an appraisal of a career appointee, more than one-half of the members of the performance review board shall consist of career appointees. The requirement of the preceding sentence shall not apply in any case in which the Office determines that there exist an insufficient number of career appointees available to comply with the requirement.

"(d) The Office shall include in each report submitted to each House of the Congress under section 3135 of this title a report of—

"(1) the performance of any performance review board established under this section.

"(2) the number of individuals removed from the Senior Executive Service under subchapter V of chapter 35 of this title for less than fully successful executive performance and

"(3) the number of performance awards under section 5384 of this title.

"§4315. Regulations

"The Office of Personnel Management shall prescribe regulation to carry out the purpose of this subchapter.".

(b) The analysis for chapter 43 of title 5, United States Code, amended by inserting at the end thereof the following:

"SUBCHAPTER II—PERFORMANCE APPRAISAL IN THE SENIOR EXECUTIVE SERVICE

"Sec.
"4311. Definitions.
"4312. Senior Executive Service performance appraisal systems.
"4313. Criteria for performance appraisals.
"4314. Ratings for performance appraisals.
"4315. Regulations."

Awarding of Ranks. Sec. 406.(a) Chapter 45 of title 5. United States Code, is amended by adding at the end thereof the following new section:

"§4507. Awarding of ranks in the Senior Executive Service

"(a) For the purpose of this section, 'agency', 'senior executive', and 'career appointee' have the meanings set forth in section 3132(a) of this title.

"(b) Each agency shall submit annually to the Office recommendations of career appointees in the agency to be awarded the rank of Meritorions Executive or Distinguished Executive. The recommendations may take into account the individual's performance over a period of years. The Office shall review such recommendations and provide to the President recommendations as to which of the agency recommended appointees should receive such rank.

"(c) During any fiscal year, the President may, subject to subsection (d) of this section, award to any career appointee recommended by the Office the rank of—

"(1) Meritorious Executive, for sustained accomplishment or

"(2) Distinguished Executive, for sustained extraordinary accomplishment.

A career appointee awarded a rank under paragraph (1) or (2) of this subsection shall not be entitled to be awarded that rank during the following 4 fiscal years.

"(d) During any fiscal year—

"(1) the number of career appointees awarded the rank of Meritorious Executive may not exceed 5 percent of the Senior Executive Service; and

"(2) the number of career appointees awarded the rank of Distinguished Executive may not exceed 1 percent of the Senior Executive Service.

"(e)(1) Receipt by a career appointee of the rank of Meritorious Executive entitles such individual to a lump-sum payment of $10,000, which shall be in addition to the basic pay paid under section 5382 of this title or any award paid under section 5384 of this title.

"(2) Receipt by a career appointee of the rank of Distinguished Executive entitles the individual to a lump-sum payment of $20,000, which shall be in addition to the basic pay paid under section 5382 of this title or any award paid under section 5384 of this title.".

"CHAPTER 54—MERIT PAY AND CASH AWARDS

"Sec.
"5401. Purpose.
"5402. Merit pay system.
"5403. Cash award program.
"5404. Report.
"5405. Regulations.

§ 5401. Purpose

"(a) It is the purpose of this chapter to provide for—

"(1) a merit pay system which shall—

"(A) within available funds, recognize and reward quality performance by varying merit pay adjustments;

"(B) use performance appraisals as the basis for determining merit pay adjustments;

"(C) within available funds, provide for training to improve objectivity and fairness in the evaluation of performance; and

"(D) regulate the costs of merit pay by establishing appropriate control techniques; and

"(2) a cash award program which shall provide cash awards for superior accomplishment and special service.

"(b) (1) Except as provided in paragraph (2) of this subsection, this chapter shall apply to any supervisor or management official (as defined in paragraphs (10) and (11) of section 7103 of this title, respectively) who is in a position which is in GS-13, 14, or 15 of the General Schedule described in section 5104 of this title.

"(2) (A) Upon application under subparagraph (C) of this paragraph, the President may, in writing, exclude an agency or any unit of an agency from the application of this chapter if the President considers such exclusion to be required as a result of conditions arising from—

"(i) the recent establishment of the agency or unit, or the implementation of a new program,

"(ii) an emergency situation, or

"(iii) any other situation or circumstance.

"(B) Any exclusion under this paragraph shall not take effect earlier than 30 calendar days after the President transmits to each House of the Congress a report describing the agency or unit to be excluded and the reasons therefor.

"(C) An application for exclusion under this paragraph of an agency or any unit of an agency shall be filed by the head of the agency with the Office of Personnel Management, and shall set forth reasons why the agency or unit should be excluded from this chapter. The Office shall review the application and reasons, undertake such other review as it considers appropriate to determine whether the agency or unit should be excluded from the coverage of this chapter, and upon completion of its review, recommend to the President whether the agency or unit should be excluded from the coverage of this chapter, and upon completion of its review, recommend to the President whether the agency or unit should be so excluded.

"(D) Any agency or unit which is excluded pursuant to this paragraph shall, insofar as practicable, make a sustained effort to eliminate the conditions on which the exclusion is based.

"(E) The Office shall periodically review any exclusion from coverage and may at any time recommend to the President that an exclusion under this paragraph be revoked. The President may at any time revoke, in writing, any exclusion under this paragraph.

"§ 5042. Merit pay system

"(a) In accordance with the purpose set forth in section 5401 (a) (1) of this title, the Office of Personnel Management shall establish a merit pay system which shall provide for a range of basic pay for each grade to which the system applies, which range shall be limited by the minimum and maximum rates of basic pay payable for each grade under chapter 53 of this title.

"(b)(1) Under regulations prescribed by the Office, the head of each agency may provide for increases within the range of basic pay for any employee covered by the merit pay system.

"(2) Determinations to provide pay increases under this subsection—

"(A) may take into account individual performance and organizational accomplishment, and

"(B) shall be based on factors such as—

"(i) any improvement in efficiency, productivity, and quality of work or service, including any significant reduction in paperwork;

"(ii) cost efficiency;

"(iii) timeliness of performance; and

"(iv) other indications of the effectiveness, productivity, and quality of performance of the employees for whom the employee is responsible;

"(C) shall be subject to review only in accordance with and to the extent provided by procedures established by the head of the agency; and

"(D) shall be made in accordance with regulations issued by the Office which relate to the distribution of increases authorized under this subsection.

"(3) For any fiscal, the head of any agency may exercise authority under paragraph (1) of this subsection only to the extent of the funds available for the purpose of this subsection.

"(4) The funds available for the purpose of this subsection to the head of any agency for any fiscal year shall be determined before the beginning of the fiscal year by the Office on the basis of the amount estimated by the Office to be necessary to reflect—

"(A) within-grade step increases and quality step increases which would have been paid under subchapter III of chapter 53 of this title during the fiscal year to the employees of the agency covered by the merit pay system if the employees were not so covered; and

"(B) adjustments under section 5305 of this title which would have been paid under such subchapter during the fiscal year to such employees if the employees were not so covered, less an amount reflecting the adjustment under subsection (c) (1) of this section in rates of basic pay payable to the employees for the fiscal year.

"(c) (1) Effective at the beginning of the first applicable pay period commencing on or after the first day of the month in which an adjustment takes effect under section 5305 of this title, the rate of basic pay for any position under this chapter shall be adjusted by an amount equal to the greater of—

"(A)   one-half of the percentage of the adjustment in the annual rate of pay which corresponds to the percentage generally applicable to positions not covered by the merit pay system in the same grade as the position; or

"(B)   such greater amount of such percentage of such adjustment in the annual rate of pay as may be determined by the Office.

"(2) Any employee whose position is brought under the merit pay system shall, so long as the employee continues to occupy the position, be entitled to receive basic pay at a rate of basic pay not less than the rate the employee was receiving when the position was brought under the merit pay system, plus any subsequent adjustment under paragraph (1) of this subsection.

"(3) No employee to whom this chapter applies may be paid less than the minimum rate of basic pay of the grade of the employee's position.

"(d) Under regulations prescribed by the Office, the benefit of advancement through the range of basic pay for a grade shall be preserved for any employee covered by the merit pay system whose continuous service is interrupted in the public interest by service with the armed forces, or by service in essential non-Government civilian employment during a period of war or national emergency.

"(e) For the purpose of section 5941 of this title, rates of basic pay of employees covered by the merit pay system shall be considered rates of basic pay fixed by statute.

"§ 5403. Cash award program

"(a) The head of any agency may pay a cash award to, and incur necessary expenses for the honorary recognition of, any employee covered by the merit pay system who—

"(1) by the employee's suggestion, invention, superior accomplishment, or other personal effort, contributes to the efficiency, economy, or other improvement of Government operations or achieves a significant reduction in paperwork: or

"(2) performs a special act or service in the public interest in connection with or related to the employee's Federal employment.

"(b) The President may pay a cash award to, and incur necessary expenses for the honorary recognition of, any employee covered by the merit pay system who—

"(1) by the employee's suggestion, invention, superior accomplishment, or other personal effort, contributes to the efficiency, economy, or other improvement of Government operations or achieves a significant reduction in paperwork; or

"(2) performs an exceptionally meritorious special act or service in the public interest in connection with or related to the employee's Federal employment.

A Presidential cash award may be in addition to an agency cash award under subsection (a) of this section.

"(c) A cash award to any employee under this section is in addition to the basic pay of the employee under section 5402 of this title. Acceptance of a cash award under this section constitutes an agreement that the use by the Government of any idea, method, or device for which the award is made does not form the basis of any claim of any nature against the Government by the employee accepting the award, or the employee's heirs or assigns.

"(d) A cash award to, and expenses for the honorary recognition of, any employee covered by the merit pay system may be paid from the fund or appropriation available to the activity primarily benefiting, or the various activities benefiting, from the suggestion, invention, superior accomplishment, or other meritorious effort of the employee. The head of the agency concerned shall determine the amount to be contributed by each activity to a Presidential award under subsection (b) of this section.

"(e) (1) Except as provided in paragraph (2) of this subsection, a cash award under this section may not exceed $10,000.

"(2) If the head of an agency certifies to the Office of Personnel Management that the suggestion, invention, superior accomplishment, or other meritorious effort of an employee for which a cash award is proposed is highly exceptional and unusually outstanding, a cash award in excess of $10,000 but not in excess of $25,000 may be awarded to the employee on the approval of the Office.

"(f) The President or the head of an agency may pay a cash award under this section notwithstanding the death or separation from the service of an employee, if the suggestion, invention, superior accomplishment, or other meritorious effort of the employee for which the award is proposed was made or performed while the employee was covered by the merit pay system.

"§ 5404. Report

"The Office of Personnel Management shall include in each annual report required by section 1308(a) of this title a report on the operation of the merit pay system and the cash award program established under this chapter. The report shall include—

"(1) an analysis of the cost and effectiveness of the merit pay system and the cash award program; and

"(2) a statement of the agencies and units excluded from the coverage of this chapter under section 5401 (b) (2) of this title, the reasons for which each exclusion was made, and whether the exclusion continues to be warranted.

"§ 5405. Regulations

"The Office of Personnel Management shall prescribe regulations to carry out the purpose of this chapter.".

PART III

The Quest for Improved Budgeting and Financial Management: New Layers of Reform

The Quest for Improved Budgeting and Financial Management: New Layers of Reform

The most striking characteristic of postwar public documents in the budgeting and financial management field has been the repeated attempts to revise fundamentally the way in which public funds should be allocated within the executive branch. Over the years since World War II—from Performance Budgets to Zero Based Budgets—there have been several major reform initiatives (and many, many more minor reform initiatives). Each new reform has had both its defenders and critics and provokes lively, indeed heated, debate within both the academic and administrative circles.

Like an archeologist who investigates the life of ancient peoples through layers of excavation, a student of modern budgeting and financial management can learn much from digging into the public documents contained in Part III, particularly in terms of understanding how each new "layer" of budgetary reform has added another dimension to our contemporary approaches to public sector budgeting and financial management. Selections from the six major reform initiatives from 1949 to 1980 are contained in Part III.

Many of these federal-level reforms in budgeting were suggested, were tried, and took root, sometimes in modified formats, at the state and local levels as well. Clearly, proposals for budgetary revision sell well—very well to the general public, chief executives, and legislatures throughout the country—and no doubt will continue to do so in the future despite the frequent scholarly criticism regarding the sometimes dubious results achieved from adopting a number of the more prominent past revisions of governmental fiscal practices.[1]

For better or worse, or better *and* worse, today's modern public budgets contain bits and pieces of a number of these postwar reforms in fiscal management that have been advocated over the years by administrative specialists, accountants, university-trained economists, businessmen, and political scientists. The perspec-

---

1. Some of the most trenchant criticism of budgetary reform is contained in Aaron Wildavsky's *Politics of the Budgetary Process* (Boston: Little, Brown, 1964); particularly see the 3rd edition (1979), Chapters 4–6.

tives of these professionals have profoundly shaped in piecemeal fashion contemporary budgetary practices.

Each reform reflects, however, a decidedly different set of values. As Allen Schick pointed out some time ago in a perceptive article, "The Road to PPB,"[2] a reform like "Performance Budgeting," shaped largely by businessmen and management specialists serving on the First Hoover Commission, was oriented toward strengthening "management effectiveness"—particularly at the departmental and agency level. "Planning, Programming, Budgeting" (PPB), which was a product principally of the work of planners and economists, was aimed, largely, at improving overall planning capabilities within government. By comparison, the Congressional Budget and Impoundment Act of 1974 was directed at trying to achieve expenditure control limitations. This reform was initiated by Congress in order to extend its control over the executive budgeting processes. Zero Based Budgets, which were adopted in the Carter Administration in 1977, by contrast, emphasized "management values," or a return to values promulgated in the Hoover Report. Present budgets are therefore a complex blend of these primary values of management planning and control.

1.a. U.S. Commission on Organization of the Executive Branch of the Government, "Budget and Accounting Recommendation No. 1" (First Hoover Commission Report, 1949)

b. Budget and Accounting Procedures Act of 1950

One of the most important reforms to come out of the First Hoover Commission Report was contained in its Task Force on Budget and Accounting's Recommendation No. 1, which argued that "the Federal budget is an inadequate document, poorly organized and improperly designed. . . ." The task force's recommendation was to refashion the national budget into a document that emphasized what government "achieves" with the money it spends. The focus, the report argued, should be placed upon "its functions, activities and projects" (outputs) as opposed to the traditional line-item budgetary concerns with personnel, materials, and expenses (inputs). Or, in the words of the First Hoover Report, ". . . upon the work to be done or upon the services to be rendered rather than the things to be acquired." For some time budgetary specialists, like A. E. Buck,[3] had argued for the Performance Budget approach in order to make the budget document more

2. Allen Schick, "The Road to PPB," *Public Administration Review* 26 (December 1966), pp. 243–58.

3. A. E. Buck, *The Budget in Governments of Today* (New York: Macmillan, 1934).

understandable to members of the legislature as well as a more effective management tool for line administrators. The Hoover Report gave the Performance Budgeting concept prominent national attention. The Performance concept, among other financial management reforms, was written into law by the Budget and Accounting Procedures Act of 1950, an act which President Truman at the time called, "the most important legislation enacted by the Congress in the budget and accounting field since the Budget and Accounting Act of 1921."[4]

2.a. *President Lyndon Johnson's Press Statement on PPB* (August 25, 1965)

b. *Bureau of the Budget Bulletin No. 66–3, Planning-Programming-Budgeting* (October 12, 1965)

The defense studies by economists, mathematicians, and social scientists at the RAND Corporation during the 1950s developed important techniques for the Air Force in terms of cost-benefit analysis, systems theory and long-range strategic planning applied to the choice of large complex weapons systems. Many of their ideas were enthusiastically adopted by Robert McNamara's Pentagon "Whiz Kids" for setting the new Kennedy administration's defense priorities in the early 1960s. Out of this bundle of innovative techniques applied for "rationalizing" the choices for large-scale weapon systems emerged a new form of comprehensive, long-term budgetary analysis—the Planning-Programming-Budgeting System (PPB).

President Lyndon Johnson, impressed by Secretary McNamara's application of PPB at the Pentagon, ordered its use throughout government on August 25, 1965. As his press statement indicates, Johnson at the time saw the utilization of PPB as an important tool for implementing his "Great Society" programs. The BOB Bulletin No. 66–3, which was issued more than a month later, outlined the details of the basic concepts and approach of PPB for all federal departments. PPB proved to be a highly complex, difficult, and controversial budgetary system, especially when applied to social programs outside the Defense Department. for a number of reasons—complexity of its methodology, inherent institutional fragmentation of most public social programs, short time horizons of most administrators and politicians as well as the transition to a new Republican administration in 1969—all these factors and others led to PPB's demise at the federal level by 1971.[5]

---

4. As cited in Frederick C. Mosher, *The GAO: The Quest for Accountability in American Government* (Boulder, CO.: Westview Press, 1979), p. 119.

5. For an excellent account of the problems of applying PPB to the "soft area of foreign affairs," read Frederick C. Mosher and John E. Harr, *Programming Systems and Foreign Affairs* (New York: Oxford University Press, 1970).

3.a. President Richard Nixon's Address to the Nation on Domestic Programs ("New Federalism Address," August 8, 1969)

b. Title I of the State and Local Fiscal Assistance Act of 1972

Much of Richard Nixon's campaign for the presidency in 1968 concentrated on the dangers of overcentralized government and the Washington bureaucracy. Early in his first term, August 8, 1969, he called for a "New Federalism" in order to reverse "a third of a century of centralizing power and responsibility in Washington." At the heart of his New Federalism was the idea of Revenue Sharing, which in his words would "turn back to the States a greater measure of responsibility" through "a set portion of the revenues from Federal income taxes . . . remitted directly to the States, with a minimum of Federal restrictions on how those dollars are to be used, and with a requirement that a percentage of them be channelled through for the use of local units."

The Revenue Sharing Proposal was not a new idea in 1969. Representative Melvin Laird (Michigan, Republican) had regularly introduced the proposal in the House of Representatives during the 1950s and 1960s. However, it was not until the early 1970s that the idea became a legislative reality supported by a unique "triangle" of interest groups: (1) conservatives in the Nixon administration favoring its "decentralizating" elements; (2) liberal urban groups supporting its new sources of fiscal relief for cities; and (3) university-based economists who favored redirecting the post-Vietnam "fiscal dividend" for social purposes. The measure was enacted on October 20, 1972, and remains on the books today in substantially the same form, except for several amendments relative to "equalizing" its complex funding formulas. Whether in fact Revenue Sharing "decentralized" government or resulted in the increased fiscal dependency of states and municipalities upon federal largess is very much a moot point. Certainly the measure has been a major source of support for many local capital works projects and social programs in localities throughout America.[6]

4. Congressional Budget and Impoundment Control Act of 1974

In the words of political scientist James P. Pfiffner, "The year 1974 marked a turning point in American Government. President Richard Nixon resigned his office under threat of impeachment by the House of Representatives. The Congress

6. Richard P. Nathan, Allen D. Manvel, and Susannah E. Calkins, *Monitoring Revenue Sharing* (Washington, D.C.: Brookings Institution, 1975).

passed the Congressional Budget and Impoundment Control Act of 1974. . . ."[7] Indeed these two events were inexorably linked together, as Pfiffner points out, for the Congressional Budget Act of 1974 was fundamentally an effort by Congress to gain greater control in fiscal affairs vis-à-vis the president's authority. Stung by Nixon's impoundment of funds for favored Congressional programs in the early 1970s as well as faced with increased difficulty in gaining access to vital budgetary information and independent assessments of the president's budget proposals, Congress passed the 1974 act, which decisively reversed a half century of growth of executive authority over budgetary matters (first marked by passage of the Accounting and Budget Act of 1921). The 1974 act contained a number of critical changes in the way national budgets would be formulated in the future by establishing: (1) a new timetable for budgetary preparation formulation; (2) House and Senate Budget Committees to set overall spending and revenue targets for the budget as a whole; (3) a new Congressional Budget Office that would serve as a source of independent advice, information, and analysis on budget matters for Congress; and (4) an elaborate procedure by which Congress had to be advised of and grant approval (or withhold approval) for future presidential impoundments. Unquestionably the 1974 act is one of the most profound and significant budgetary reforms ever to be enacted by Congress.

5.a. *President Jimmy Carter's Memorandum on Zero Based Budgeting for the Heads of Executive Departments and Agencies* (February 14, 1977)

b. *Office of Management and Budget's Bulletin No. 77–9 on Zero Based Budgeting* (April 19, 1977)

Among Jimmy Carter's campaign promises made during 1976 was the pledge to institute a new form of budgeting at the federal level, Zero Based Budgeting (ZBB). ZBB had been a product of a progressive business enterprise, Texas Instruments, and was later implemented by Carter himself during his term as governor of Georgia. The basic justification for ZBB is outlined in President Carter's February 14, 1977 memo, reflecting many of the same concerns that were similar to PPB's in terms of improving "comprehensiveness," "planning" and "cost-effectiveness" of federal budgets. ZBB differed fundamentally in approach, however, from PPB in that the essence of the ZBB concept promoted good management practices since it

7. James P. Pfiffner, *The President, the Budget and Congress: Impoundment and the 1974 Budget Act* (Boulder, CO.: Westview Press, 1979), p. 1. For the most profound and insightful discussion of the 1974 Congressional Budget Act, read Allen Schick, *Congress and Money* (Washington, D.C.: Urban Institute, 1980).

required program managers to present alternative levels of program expenditures, to analyze alternative benefits of "decision packages," and to justify the "optimum level" of expenditure. ZBB, unlike PBB, essentially maintained organizational integrity and required considerably less comprehensive economic analysis. ZBB, however, generated enormous amounts of paperwork which some critics argued was costly, time-consuming, and served as only more elaborate justification for program increases. Like PPB, ZBB was adopted by many states and localities, and the verdict is "still out" relative to the lasting contributions of ZBB to public budgeting.

1.a. U.S. Commission on Organization of the Executive Branch of Government "Budget and Accounting Recommendations" (First Hoover Commission Report, 1949)

The Budget

REFORM OF THE BUDGET

The budget and appropriation process is the heart of the management and control of the executive branch.

There is a great need for reform in the method of budgeting and in the appropriation structure.

The Federal budget is an inadequate document, poorly organized and improperly designed to serve its major purpose, which is to present an understandable and workable financial plan for the expenditures of the Government. The document has grown larger and larger each year as the Government's requirements have increased, but its general framework and method of presentation have not changed. The latest budget document, that for 1949–50, contains 1,625 closely printed pages, with about 1,500,000 words, and sums covering thousands of specific appropriations.

There is no uniformity in the schedules of appropriations. Some appropriations represent huge sums, others small amounts. Appropriations for the same service appear in many different places. Much of this results from historical accident.

The Bureau of Indian Affairs, for example, had approximately 100 appropriation titles and subtitles for the expenditure during the fiscal year 1947–48 of about $50,000,000. The largest appropriation item for this bureau amounted to more than $11,000,000 while the smallest item was $114.53.

At the other extreme perhaps, is the Veterans Administration, which has an appropriation item of more than a billion dollars for "salaries and expenses," a title which indicates nothing whatever of the work program of that organization.

Report of the Commission on the Organization of the Executive Branch of Government, the Budget (Washington, D.C. U.S. Government Printing Office, 1949) pp. 35–63. Material includes only Recommendation 1 of the report pertaining to Performance Budgets.

A PERFORMANCE BUDGET

Recommendation No. 1

We recommend that the whole budgetary concept of the Federal Government should be refashioned by the adoption of a budget based upon functions, activities, and projects; this we designate as a "performance budget."

Such an approach would focus attention upon the general character and relative importance of the work to be done, or upon the service to be rendered, rather than upon the things to be acquired, such as personal service, supplies, equipment, and so on. These latter objects are, after all, only the means to an end. The all-important thing in budgeting is the work or the service to be accomplished, and what that work or service will cost.

Under performance budgeting, attention is centered on the function or activity—on the accomplishment of the purpose—instead of on lists of employees or authorizations of purchases. In reality, this method of budgeting concentrates Congressional action and executive direction on the scope and magnitude of the different Federal activities. It places both accomplishment and cost in a clear light before the Congress and the public.

We give two examples of the different methods of presenting the budget estimates in Annex I. (pp. 56–63.) To indicate the deficiencies of existing practices, we may cite here the National Naval Medical Center at Bethesda. This hospital now receives allotments from 12 different Navy appropriation titles such as:

> Secretary's Office—Miscellaneous Expenses, Navy
> Bureau of Ships—Maintenance
> Bureau of Ordnance—Ordnance and Ordnance Stores
> Bureau of Supplies and Accounts—Pay, Subsistence, and Transportation
> Bureau of Supplies and Accounts—Maintenance
> Bureau of Supplies and Accounts—Transportation of Things
> Bureau of Medicine and Surgery—Medical Department, Navy
> Five Other Similar Appropriation Titles

There is no one title in the present budget where the total cost of operating a Navy hospital is shown.

We propose, for instance, that by using performance budgeting, the costs of operating the Bethesda Center, along with those of other comparable Naval hospitals, would be shown as an identifiable program under one appropriation title for "Medical Care."

The idea of a performance budget is not new. It has been adopted in the modernization of budgets by some States and several municipalities.

The performance budget does not change or shift legislative responsibility;

control by the Congress still lies in the power to limit expenditures by appropriations. Performance budgeting gives more comprehensive and reliable information to the President, the Congress, and the general public, and helps the individual congressman to understand what the Government is doing, how much it is doing, and what the costs are. Supporting schedules can be fully provided, and in more understandable and effective form.

One of the primary purposes of the performance budget would be to improve Congressional examination of budgetary requirements. Such examination should be largely on the level of accomplishment, and for this reason the Congress needs to know clearly just what the whole of the expenditures is and what the executive and administrative agencies propose to do with the money they request. In the Bethesda case mentioned above, the Congress under the new system would have presented the cost of operating the hospital in detail, so that the Congress might readily compare such cost with that of the preceding year or with the costs of other comparable hospitals.

The Bureau of Ships in the Navy Department, for example, is financed by 27 appropriations, many of which, as shown in the budget, have no apparent connection with the Bureau. Efforts have been made to resolve this confusion through the working out of an adequate budget structure. The ideas thus developed have been applied in part to the new Air Force estimates as set forth in the budget in 1949–50.

In a detailed example, given at the end of this part of the report, of the effect of performance budgeting on the Forest Service, our task force points out that the real operating cost of the Forest Service for the management and protection of the national forests does not appear in full under that heading in the budget, but actually is included in several other places. The total operating cost for the national forests, as displayed by the performance budget, would be shown as about $43,000,000 instead of only $26,000,000 as indicated under the present appropriation headings in the budget.

Example 2—The Forest Service

To illustrate further the application of the performance budget, we take the Forest Service in the Department of Agriculture and show (1) how it is budgeted at present in the 1949–50 budget document and (2) how it can be budgeted on a performance basis.

THE PRESENT METHOD OF BUDGETING THE FOREST SERVICE

As budgeted at the present time, the estimates of the Forest Service cover 18½ closely printed quarto pages of the budget document. The estimates are built around 16 separate items, each of which constitutes an appropriation. Each item has an average of about a page of supporting schedules, setting forth detailed information, principally according to an object classification.

These 16 items or groups now making up the estimates are more or less chance creations; they do not follow either organizational or functional lines. They do not specify accomplishments or indicate performances. Only as one can read meaning into three vertical columns of figures set up on the objective basis can one have any idea of the essential programs, the extent to which these programs succeed or fail, and the effect of changing conditions upon the future character of the programs.

The 16 groups do not make any distinction between current operating costs and captal outlays. Some headings indicate that the amounts requested are to be spent mainly for capital acquisitions; other clearly signify operating costs but, when analyzed, show capital outlays to be included.

The Forest Service has about $24,000,000 of receipts annually which should be indicated in connection with its budget, since percentages of these receipts enter into certain appropriation items, as noted below.

Finally, the 16 items of appropriations made to the Forest Service do not carry all the funds which are required for its operation. Several other appropriations, some of them made directly to the Secretary of Agriculture, contribute to the funds of the Forest Service. By reason of these additional funds the operating requirements of the Service are much larger than actually indicated in the budget. This administrative transfer of funds which takes place on a wide scale within all large governmental departments and agencies makes the present method of budgeting more or less meaningless and defeats the present scheme of appropriations which Congress follows. Only functional budgeting will expose this situation, and allow it to be corrected.

FOREST SERVICE

As Set Up in the Present 1949–50 Budget

(Material in italics below is the Commission's comment and does not appear in the budget quoted.)

	1949–50 Requests
1. General administrative expenses	$ 655,000

           (This item does not by any means include all administrative expenses of the Service. It has not increased appreciably for several years.)

| 2. National forests protection and management . . . . | 26,489,500 |

           (This item contains the bulk of the Service's operating expenses, and it includes considerable capital outlays.)

3. Fighting forest fires.................................   100,000
   (This is a nominal figure. Receipts from payments
   for the suppression of forest fires on State and private
   lands are also made available.)

4. Forest research into forest and range management..........   2,812,500
   (This item covers research into fire control, silvi-
   culture, watershed control, and forest and range
   management. Receipts from the rental and sale of
   equipment and supplies to non-Federal agencies
   which cooperate with the Forest Service in fire con-
   trol are included.)

5. Forest products.....................................   1,172,000
   (This item includes the operation of the great Forest
   Products Laboratory located in Wisconsin, but there
   are no indications as to the volume and general
   character of its work, the nature of the experiments
   and tests being conducted, or the discoveries which
   have resulted.)

6. Forest resources investigations........................   866,000
   (This item provides for a comprehensive forest survey
   and investigation of forest economics. Receipts are
   also available, as under Item 4 above.)

   Subtotal annual specific appropriations......... $32,095,000

7. Forest development roads and trails....................   9,752,000
   (This item is for the construction, reconstruction,
   and maintenance of roads and trails (not main thor-
   oughfares) in national forests. Receipts are also
   available, as under Item 4 above.)

8. Forest fire cooperation   9,000,000
   (This item is the contribution of the Federal Govern-
   ment to the States for fire control in timbered and
   cut-over lands.)

9. Farm and other private forestry cooperation..............   814,500
   (This item is for advice to farmers and other private
   forest owners on sustained-yield management and
   proper utilization of timber resources.)

10. Acquisition of lands for national forests   401,000
    (This item is for the acquisition of forest lands under
    the Weeks Act (1911). It includes the costs of sur-
    veys.)

11. Acquisition of forest land, Superior National Forest, Minnesota 100,000

> *(This item is for the acquisition of forest lands, including surveys, under an Act of 1948.)*

12. Acquisition of lands (in connection with seven National forests in three western states, Utah, Nevada, and California) 142,000

> *(This item includes land appraisal and other work in acquiring lands.)*
>
> > *(Transfers of funds to and from the Forest Service require four pages of schedules at this point.)*

   Total annual specific appropriations $52,304,500

13. Payment to school funds of Arizona and New Mexico. 55,000

> *(This is a permanent appropriation from the general fund.)*

14. Payment to States and Territories 5,995,000

> *(This is a permanent appropriation, consisting of 24% of the net revenue from National forests, paid to states in which the forests are located.)*

15. Roads and trails for States 2,398,000

> *(This is a permanent appropriation, consisting of 10% of the net revenue from National forests, paid to states in which the forests are located.)*

   Total permanent appropriations . . . . $ 8,448,000

   Total Forest Service, general and specific accounts $60,752,500

16. Cooperative work 5,300,000

> *(This item is from privately contributed (trust) funds by users of the forests. It is used for various purposes that benefit both the National and privately owned forests.)*

   Grand Total, Forest Service $66,052,500

The above numbered headings are supported by schedules, mostly on an object basis, amounting to about 18½ closely printed quarto pages of text.

SUGGESTED PERFORMANCE BUDGET FOR THE FOREST SERVICE

It is proposed in the outline below that the two major functions of the Forest Service should be (1) the protection and management of the National forests and (2) forest research.

As far as possible from the facts and figures in hand, all expenditure estimates for each of these functions have been assembled. The first major function has been roughly divided between current operating costs and capital outlays, to illustrate how such a division may be made. The current operating costs, under "protection and management," have then been divided into 10 operating functions or programs. Many of these may be subdivided for purposes of showing important subprograms. In each case, the nature of the work should be explained briefly, the elements involved in carrying it on, some appraisal of results, and the scope or trend of future work. This explanation or justification of the operating programs should be satisfactorily set forth on 4 or 5 pages of the budget document.

The headings under capital investments and improvements indicate the general classes of outlays for which the Forest Service spends funds. It has not been possible to segregate maintenance and other expenses which are frequently included in the capital items; hence the figures are only approximate.

In the total for the national forests, we do, however, show a figure that includes approximately all of the operating costs and outlays in connection with these forests. Some of the programs, like white pine blister rust, pest control, and flood control, are now financed from appropriations made elsewhere in the Department of Agriculture.

Under the second major function of the Forest Service, that of forest research, we show the major subfunctions or subprograms. These are to be treated in the same way as the operating programs under National forests.

Two other major items make up the grand total under the Forest Service. These are (1) cooperative work with the private users of the national forests, and (2) payments under acts relating to State and private cooperation in the forestry field. These items are set up separately because the first involves the use of private or trust funds, and the second is in the nature of a subsidy for promoting certain work with the States and private owners of forests.

FOREST SERVICE

Suggested Set-up under a Performance Budget
(Figures used are approximate)

I. The national forests

	1949–50 Figures Redistributed
A. Protection and management	
1. Over-all managerial and custodial activities	$ 7,300,000
2. Forest fire control.	*7,400,000
3. Insect pest and disease control	2,276,650
4. Timber management (growing and cutting)	4,300,000

    5. Range management (grazing)   1,097,000
    6. Recreation use (health and safety measures)   599,000
    7. Land-use management   620,000
    8. Water resources management   44,000
    9. Maintenance of improvements   13,297,000
    10. Payments to states in lieu of taxes   6,050,000
        Total protection and management $42,983,650

B. Capital investments and improvements
    1. Acquisition of lands for national forests.......... $ 1,225,750
    2. Flood control works   1,941,600
    3. Construction of roads and trails   1,752,000
    4. Construction of other improvements.............   213,000
    5. Reforestation of forest lands..................   1,268,000
    6. Revegetation of forest lands..................   758,000
        Total capital investments and improvements .... $ 7,158,350

        Grand Total national forests............. $50,142,000
Revenues, national forests, from use of
    lands and sale of products $23,980,000
*Estimated supplement of $4,000,000 additional needed for fire control.

II. *Forest research*
A. Forest and range management research.............. $ 2,862,000
B. Forest products utilization....................... $1,200,950
        1. Forest Products Laboratory ($858,000)
C. Forest resources surveys   885,300
        Total forest research....................... $ 4,948,250

III. *Cooperative work—Forest Service and private users of national forests*
A. Protection and management
    1. Forest and range management .... $ 275,000
    2. Custodial services   109,000
    3. Forest fire control..........................   985,000
    4. Maintenance of improvements   550,000
    5. Timber management.........................   2,736,000
    6. Refunds to cooperators......................   100,000
        Total protection and management .... $ 4,755,000
B. Capital improvements
    1. Construction of improvements .... $ 520,000

    2. Reforestation 25,000

        Total capital improvements .... $ 545,000

        Total cooperative work (trust account) .... $ 5,300,000

IV. *State and private cooperation*

  A. Forest fire prevention and protection............... $ 9,000,000
      (Clarke-McNary Act)

  B. Farm and other private forestry.................... 814,500
      (Clarke-McNary and Norris-Doxey Acts)

        Total State and private cooperation .... $ 9,814,500

1.b. Budget and Accounting Procedures Act of 1950

An Act

To authorize the President to determine the form of the national budget and of departmental estimates, to modernize and simplify governmental accounting and auditing methods and procedures, and for other purposes.

Be it enacted by the Senate and House of Representatives of the United States of America in Congress assembled, That this Act may be cited as the "Budget and Accounting Procedures Act of 1950".

TITLE I—BUDGETING AND ACCOUNTING

Part I—Budgeting

Sec. 101. Section 2 of the Budget and Accounting Act, 1921 (42 Stat. 20), is amended by adding at the end thereof the following:

"The term 'appropriations' includes, in appropriate context, funds and authorizations to create obligations by contract in advance of appropriations, or any other authority making funds available for obligation or expenditure."

Sec. 102. (a) Section 201 of such Act is amended to read as follows:

"Sec. 201. The President shall transmit to Congress during the first fifteen days of each regular session, the Budget, which shall set forth his Budget message, summary data and text, and supporting detail. The budget shall set forth in such form and detail as the President may determine—

"(a) functions and activities of the Government;

"(b) any other desirable classifications of data;

"(c) a reconciliation of the summary data on expenditures with proposed appropriations;

"(d) estimated expenditures and proposed appropriations necessary in

Title I, Part I, Public Law 81–784 (September 12, 1950). Part II, relating to Accounting and Auditing, is omitted here.

his judgment for the support of the Government for the ensuing fiscal year, except that estimated expenditures and proposed appropriations for such year for the legislative branch of the Government and the Supreme Court of the United States shall be transmitted to the President on or before October 15 of each year, and shall be included by him in the budget without revision;

"(e) estimated receipts of the Government during the ensuing fiscal year, under (1) laws existing at the time the Budget is transmitted and also (2) under the revenue proposals, if any, contained in the Budget;

"(f) actual appropriations, expenditures, and receipts of the Government during the last completed fiscal year;

"(g) estimated expenditures and receipts, and actual or proposed appropriations of the Government during the fiscal year in progress;

"(h) balanced statements of (1) the condition of the Treasury at the end of the last completed fiscal year, (2) the estimated condition of the Treasury at the end of the fiscal year in progress and (3) the estimated condition of the Treasury at the end of the ensuing fiscal year if the financial proposals contained in the Budget are adopted;

"(i) all essential facts regarding the bonded and other indebtedness of the Government; and

"(j) such other financial statements and data as in his opinion are necessary or desirable in order to make known in all practicable detail the financial condition of the Government."

(b) Section 203 of such Act is amended to read as follows:

"Sec. 203. (a) The President from time to time may transmit to Congress such proposed supplemental or deficiency appropriations as in his judgment (1) are necessary on account of laws enacted after the transmission of the Budget, or (2) are otherwise in the public interest. He shall accompany such proposals with a statement of the reasons therefor, including the reasons for their omission from the Budget.

"(b) Whenever such proposed supplemental or deficiency appropriations reach an aggregate which, if they had been contained in the Budget, would have required the President to make a recommendation under subsection (a) of section 202, he shall thereupon make such recommendation."

(c) Section 204 of such Act is amended to read as follows:

"Sec. 204. (a) Except as otherwise provided in this Act, the contents, order, and arrangement of the proposed appropriations and the statements of expenditures and estimated expenditures contained in the

Budget or transmitted under section 203, and the notes and other data submitted therewith, shall conform to requirements prescribed by the President.

"(b) The Budget, and statements furnished with any proposed supplemental or deficiency appropriations, shall be accompanied by information as to personal services and other objects of expenditure in the same manner and form as in the Budget for the fiscal year 1950: *Provided*, That this requirement may be waived or modified, either generally or in specific cases, by joint action of the committees of Congress having jurisdiction over appropriation: *And provided further*, That nothing in this Act shall be construed to limit the authority of committees of Congress to request and receive such information in such form as they may desire in consideration of and action upon budget estimates."

(d) Section 205 of such Act is amended to read as follows:
"Sec. 205. Whenever any basic change is made in the form of the Budget, the President, in addition to the Budget, shall transmit to Congress such explanatory notes and tables as may be necessary to show where the various items embraced in the Budget of the prior year are contained in the new Budget."

(e) The last sentence of section 207 of such Act is amended to read as follows: "The Bureau, under such rules and regulations as the President may prescribe, shall prepare the Budget, and any proposed supplemental or deficiency appropriations, and to this end shall have authority to assemble, correlate, revise, reduce, or increase the requests for appropriations of the several departments or establishments."

(f) Section 214 of such Act is amended to read as follows:
"Sec. 214. The head of each department and establishment shall prepare or cause to be prepared in each year his requests for regular, supplemental or deficiency appropriations."

(g) Section 215 of such Act is amended to read as follows:
"Sec. 215. The head of each department and establishment shall submit his requests for appropriations to the Bureau on or before a date which the President shall determine. In case of his failure to do so, the President shall cause such requests to be prepared as are necessary to enable him to include such requests with the Budget in respect to the work of such department or establishment."

(h) Section 216 of such Act is amended to read as follows:
"Sec. 216. Requests for regular, supplemental, or deficiency appropriations which are submitted to the Bureau by the head of any department or

establishment shall be prepared and submitted as the President may determine in accordance with the provisions of section 201.

GOVERNMENT STATISTICAL ACTIVITIES

Sec. 103. The President, through the Director of the Bureau of the Budget, is authorized and directed to develop programs and to issue regulations and orders for the improved gathering, compiling, analyzing, publishing, and disseminating of statistical information for any purpose by the various agencies in the executive branch of the Government. Such regulations and orders shall be adhered to by such agencies.

IMPROVED ADMINISTRATION OF EXECUTIVE AGENCIES

Sec. 104. The President, through the Director of the Bureau of the Budget, is authorized and directed to evaluate and develop improved plans for the organization, coordination, and management of the executive branch of the Government with a view to efficient and economical service.

BUSINESS-TYPE BUDGETS

Sec. 105. The first two sentences of section 102 of the Government Corporation Control Act of 1945 (59 Stat. 597), are amended to reads as follows: "Each wholly owned Government corporation shall cause to be prepared annually a business-type budget which shall be submitted to the Bureau of the Budget, under such rules and regulations as the President may establish as to the date of submission, the form and content, the classifications of data, and the manner in which such budget program shall be prepared and presented."

2.a. President Lyndon Johnson's Press Statement on PPB to Members of the Cabinet and Heads of Agencies (1965)

I have asked you to meet with me this morning to discuss the introduction of a new planning and budgeting system throughout the Government.

The objective of this program is simple:

To use the most modern management tools so that the full promise of a finer life can be brought to every American at the least possible cost.

This program is aimed at finding new ways to do new jobs faster, better, less expensively; to insure sounder judgment through more accurate information; to pinpoint those things we ought to do more, and to spotlight those things we ought to do less; to make our decision-making process as up to date as our space-exploring equipment; in short, we want to trade in our surreys for automobiles, our old cannon for new missiles.

Everything I have done in both legislation and the construction of a budget has been guided by my deep concern for the American people—consistent with wise management of the taxpayer's dollar.

In translating this principle in action, and with the help of an outstanding Congress, we have passed more progressive legislation than in any comparable period in history.

We have been compassionate. We have also been prudent.

But we can and must do better if we are to bring the Great Society closer to all the people.

Good Government demands excellence.

It demands the fullest value for each dollar spent. It demands that we take advantage of the most modern management techniques.

This is what I want to introduce today—a new planning-programming-budgeting system developed by our top management experts led by Budget Director Charles Schultze. Once in operation, it will enable us to:

(1) identify our national goals with precision and on a continuing basis

(2) choose among those goals the ones that are most urgent

Press Release from Office of the White House Press Secretary, August 25, 1965.

(3) search for alternative means of reaching those goals most effectively at the least cost

(4) inform ourselves not merely on next year's costs—but on the second, and third, and subsequent year's costs—of our programs

(5) measure the performance of our programs to insure a dollars worth of service for each dollar spent.

This system will improve our ability to control our programs and our budgets rather than having them control us. It will operate year round. Studies, goals, program proposals and reviews will be scheduled throughout the year instead of being crowded into "budget time."

To establish this system and carry out the necessary studies, each of you will need a Central Staff for Program and Policy Planning accountable directly to you. To make this work will take good people, the best you now have and the best you can find.

I intend to have the 1968 budget and later-year programs presented in this new form by next Spring.

With these programs will go the first studies produced by your planning and policy staffs.

It is important to remember one thing: no system, no matter how refined, can make decisions for you. You and I have that responsibility in the Executive Branch. But our judgment is not better than our information. This system will present us with the alternatives and the information on the basis of which we can, together, make better decisions. The people will be the beneficiary.

The Budget Director has already talked to most of you about the need for this new approach. He is now preparing plans for setting it up. He is ready to help you in any way he can.

Within the next several weeks he will send out detailed instructions for incorporating fiscal year 1968 and later-year programs into this system. But to make this new plan a success, he will need your full support. I know that you will give him that support.

2.b.   Bureau of the Budget Bulletin No. 66–3 Planning-Programming-Budgeting (1965)

1. PURPOSE.   The President has directed the introduction of an integrated Planning-Programming-Budgeting system in the executive branch. This Bulletin contains instructions for the establishment of such a system. It will be followed by additional instructions, including more explicit policy and procedural guidelines for use of the system in the annual Budget Preview.

2. APPLICATION OF INSTRUCTIONS.   This Bulletin applies in all respects to the agencies listed in Section A of Exhibit 1. The agencies listed in Section B of that Exhibit are encouraged to apply the principles and procedures for the development and review of programs to the extent practical. (In this Bulletin, the word "agency" is used to designate departments and establishments; the word "bureau" is used to designate principal subordinate units.)

3. BACKGROUND AND NEED.   A budget is a financial expression of a program plan. Both formal instructions (such as those contained in Bureau of the Budget Circular No. A–11) and training materials on budgeting have stressed that setting goals, defining objectives, and developing planned programs for achieving those objectives are important integral parts of preparing and justifying a budget submission.

Under present practices, however, program review for decision making has frequently been concentrated within too short a period; objectives of agency programs and activities have too often not been specified with enough clarity and concreteness; accomplishments have not always been specified concretely; alternatives have been insufficiently presented for consideration by top management; in a number of cases the future year costs of present decisions have not been laid out systematically enough; and formalized planning and systems analysis have had too little effect on budget decisions.

To help remedy these shortcomings the planning and budget system in each agency should be made to provide more effective information and analyses to assist line managers, the agency head, and the President in judging needs and in deciding on the use of resources and their allocation among competing claims. The

Issued from Executive Office of the President, Bureau of the Budget, Washington, D.C., Bureau of the Budget, Bulletin No. 66–3, October 12, 1965. The more technical details and examples of the implementation of PPB have been omitted from the text.

establishment of a Planning, Programming, and Budgeting System in accordance with this Bulletin will make needed improvement possible.

While the improved system is intended for year-round use within each agency, its results will be especially brought into focus in connection with the spring Preview. It should lead to more informed and coordinated budget recommendations.

4. BASIC CONCEPTS AND DESIGN. a. The new Planning-Programming-Budgeting system is based on three concepts:

(1) The existence in each agency of an *Analytic* capability which carries out continuing in-depth analyses by permanent specialized staffs of the agency's objectives and its various programs to meet these objectives.

(2) The existence of a multi-year *Planning and Programming* process which incorporates and uses an information system to present data in meaningful categories essential to the making of major decisions by agency heads and by the President.

(3) The existence of a *Budgeting* process which can take broad program decisions, translate them into more refined decisions in a budget context, and present the appropriate program and financial data for Presidential and Congressional action.

b. Essential to the system are:

(1) An output-oriented (this term is used interchangeably with mission-oriented or objectives-oriented) program structure (sometimes also called a program format) which presents data on all of the operations and activities of the agency in categories which reflect the agency's end purposes or objectives. This is discussed in more detail in paragraph 5, below.

(2) Analyses of possible alternative objectives of the agency and of alternative programs for meeting these objectives. Many different techniques of analysis will be appropriate, but central should be the carrying out of broad systems analyses in which alternative programs will be compared with respect to both their costs and their benefits.

(3) Adherence to a time cycle within which well-considered information and recommendations will be produced at the times needed for decision-making and for the development of the President's budget and legislative program. An illustrative cycle which does this is described in paragraph 9.

(4) Acceptance by line officials (from operating levels up to the agency head), with appropriate staff support, of responsibility for the establishment and effective use of the system.

c. The products of the system will include:

(1) A comprehensive multi-year *Program and Financial Plan* systematically updated.

(2) *Analyses,* including Program Memoranda, prepared annually and used in the

budget Preview, Special Studies in depth from time to time, and other information which will contribute to the annual budget process.

d. The overall system is designed to enable each agency to:

(1) Make available to top management more concrete and specific data relevant to broad decisions;

(2) Spell out more concretely the objectives of Government programs;

(3) Analyze systematically and present for agency head and Presidential review and decision possible alternative objectives and alternative programs to meet those objectives;

(4) Evaluate thoroughly and compare the benefits and costs of programs;

(5) Produce total rather than partial cost estimates of programs;

(6) Present on a multi-year basis the prospective costs and accomplishments of programs;

(7) Review objectives and conduct program analyses on a continuing, year-round basis, instead of on a crowded schedule to meet budget deadlines.

e. The entire system must operate within the framework of overall policy guidance—from the President to the agency head, and from the agency head to his central planning, programming, and budgeting staffs and to his line managers. Fiscal policy considerations and other aspects of Presidential policy will be provided by the Bureau of the Budget in accordance with the President's program. Modifications will also have to be made from time to time to reflect changing external conditions, Congressional action, and other factors.

5. THE PROGRAM STRUCTURE. a. An early and essential step for each agency is the determination of a series of output-oriented categories which, together, cover the total work of the agency. These will serve as a basic framework for the planning, programming, and budgeting processes (including work on systems analysis, reporting, evaluation of accomplishments, and other aspects of management) and for relating these processes to each other. The following principles should guide the development of such output categories.

(1) *Program categories* are groupings of agency programs (or activities or operations) which serve the same broad objective (or mission) or which have generally similar objectives. Succinct captions or headings describing the objective should be applied to each such grouping. Obviously, each program category will contain programs which are complementary or are close substitutes in relation to the objectives to be attained. For example, a broad program objective is improvement of higher education. This could be a *program category*, and as such would contain Federal programs aiding undergraduate, graduate and vocational education, including construction of facilities, as well as such auxiliary Federal activities as library support and relevant research programs. For purposes of illustration and to aid understanding, Exhibit 2 shows some program structures as they might be

applied to two organizational units within different agencies; the same approach, of course, applies to the agency as a whole.

(2) *Program subcategories* are subdivisions which should be established within each program category, combining agency programs (or activities or operations) on the basis of narrower objectives contributing directly to the broad objectives for the program category as a whole. Thus, in the example given above, improvement of engineering and science and of language training could be two program subcategories within the program category of improvement of higher education.

(3) *Program elements* are usually subdivisions of program subcategories and comprise the specific products (i.e., the goods and services) that contribute to the agency's objectives. Each program element is an integrated activity which combines personnel, other services, equipment and facilities. An example of a program element expressed in terms of the objectives served would be the number of teachers to be trained in using new mathematics.

b. The program structure will not necessarily reflect organization structure. It will be appropriate and desirable in many cases to have the basic program categories cut across bureau lines to facilitate comparisons and suggest possible trade-offs among elements which are close substitutes. It is also desirable to develop program formats which facilitate comparisons across agency lines (e.g., in urban transportation and in recreation).

c. Basic research activities may not be and frequently are not mission or output oriented. Whenever this is the case, such activities should be identified as a separate program category or subcategory as appropriate. However, applied research and development is usually associated with a specific program objective and should be included in the same program category as the other activities related to that objective.

d. To facilitate top level review, the number of program categories should be limited. For example, a Cabinet Department should have as many as 15 program categories in only a rare and exceptional case.

e. Program categories and subcategories should not be restricted by the present appropriation pattern or budget activity structure. (Eventually, however, it may be necessary and desirable for the "Program by Activity" portion of the schedules in the Budget Appendix to be brought into line with the program structure developed according to this Bulletin.)

6. THE MULTI-YEAR PROGRAM AND FINANCIAL PLAN.

a. The entire process is designed to provide information essential to the making of major decisions in a compact and logical form. A principal product of the process will be a document, the Multi-Year Program and Financial Plan of the agency.

b. Thus, the process is concerned with developing for agency head review, and, after his official approval or modification, for Bureau of the Budget and Presidential review (as summarized in Program Memoranda, per paragraph 7c) a translation of concretely specified agency objectives into combinations of agency activities and operations designed to reach such objectives in each of the stated time periods.

c. The Program and Financial Plan will:

(1) Be set forth on the basis of the program structure described in paragraph 5, above.

(2) Cover a period of years, usually five, although the number will vary with the considerations pertinent to particular agencies; for example, a longer time span would be appropriate for timber production and for large multiple-purpose water resource projects. The multi-year feature is not to be compromised by the expiration of legislation at an earlier date, since extension or renewal, with possible modification, of the legislation should be reflected in the Plan.

(3) Include activities under contemplated or possible new legislation as well as those presently authorized.

(4) Show the program levels which the agency head thinks will be appropriate over the entire period covered by the multi-year plan.

(5) Express objectives and planned accomplishments, wherever possible, in *quantitive* non-financial terms. For example, physical description of program elements might include the additional capacity (in terms of numbers to be accommodated) of recreational facilities to be built in national forests, the number of youths to be trained in Job Corps camps along with measures of the kinds and intensity of training, the number of hours of Spanish language broadcasts of the Voice of America, the number of children to receive pre-school training, and the number of patients in Federally-supported mental hospitals. In some programs, it may not be possible to obtain or develop adequate measures in quantitative physical terms such as these but it is important to do so wherever feasible. In any case, objectives and performance should be described in as specific and concrete terms as possible.

(6) Where relevant, relate the physical description of Federal programs to the entire universe to be served. For example, a poverty program plan directed at aged poor should describe not only the numbers receiving specific Federal benefits but might well show what proportion of the entire aged poor population is being benefited.

(7) Associate financial data with the physical data to show the cost of carrying out the activity described. Cost data should be expressed in systems terms. That is, *all* costs—such as capital outlay, research and development, grants and subsidies, and current costs of operations (including maintenance)—which are associated with a program element should be assigned to that element. These component costs generally can be derived from existing appropriation and accounting categories. Where there are receipts, such as the collection of user charges or proceeds from sales of commodities or other assets, an estimate of receipts should also be included.

(8) Translate the costs and receipts used for analytic purposes, as described in

the preceding subparagraph, into the financial terms used in Federal budget preparation, presentation, and reporting.

d. The Program and Financial Plan as approved by the agency head will be submitted to the Bureau of the Budget. The Bureau of the Budget will also be kept abreast of significant revisions and updatings (see subparagraphs *e* and *f*, immediately below).

e. The Program and Financial Plan, as approved or modified by the agency head in conformity with guidance received from the Bureau of the Budget and the President (usually following the annual spring Preview), will form the basis for the agency's budget requests. Therefore, it should not be changed except in accordance with a procedure approved by the agency head. Appropriate arrangements should be made for participation of the Budget Bureau in significant changes.

f. Provision will be made for a thorough reappraisal and updating of the Program and Financial Plan annually. In this process, one year is added on to the Plan. Other changes to the Plan are to be expected from time to time and a procedure may be useful for making minor changes to the Plan without requiring agency head approval.

7. *ANALYSIS*. An analytic effort will be undertaken to examine deeply program objectives and criteria of accomplishments. Whenever applicable this effort will utilize systems analysis, operations research, and other pertinent techniques. The analysis should raise important questions, compare the benefits and costs of alternative programs and explore future needs in relationship to planned programs. The sources of data used will be many, including most importantly, the Program and Financial Plan, special studies done throughout the agency, and budget, accounting and operating data. It is important to have continuity in the work of staffs doing this work and to build expertise in them over a period of years. As expertise is developed, more and more of the agency's activities can be subjected to these analytical techniques.

a. *Special Studies* on specific topics should be carried out in response to requests by the agency top management, the Budget Bureau, or at the initiative of the analysic staff itself. Suggestions should also be made by line operating managers. The special studies may involve intensive examination of a narrow subject or broad review of a wide field. The broad program studies envisioned here will often be hampered by a dearth of information and gaps in our knowledge which can be filled only by project studies and other micro-economic studies. Nevertheless, these broad studies should be assigned top priority in the agency's analytic effort.

b. *Questions* should be posed by the analytic staffs to other elements of the agency on program objectives, measures of performance, costs and the like.

c. A broad *Program Memorandum* should be prepared annually on each of the program categories of the agency. The Program Memorandum will summarize the Program and Financial Plan approved by the agency head for that category and present a succinct evaluation and justification. It should appraise the national needs to be met for several years in the future (covering at least as many years as the Program and Financial Plan), assess the adequacy, effectiveness, and efficiency of the previously approved Plan to meet those needs, and propose any necessary modifications in the previously approved Plan, including new legislative proposals. Thus, the Program Memorandum should:

(1) Spell out the specific programs recommended by the agency head for the multi-year time period being considered, show how these programs meet the needs of the American people in this area, show the total costs of recommended programs, and show the specific ways in which they differ from current programs and those of the past several years.

(2) Describe program objectives and expected concrete accomplishments and costs for several years into the future.

(3) Describe program objectives insofar as possible in quantitative physical terms.

(4) Compare the effectiveness and the cost of alternative objectives, of alternative *types* of programs designed to meet the same or comparable objectives, and of different *levels* within any given program category. This comparison should identify past experience, the alternatives which are believed worthy of consideration, earlier differing recommendations, earlier cost and performance estimates, and the reasons for change in these estimates.

(5) Make explicit the assumptions and criteria which support recommended programs.

(6) Identify and analyze the main uncertainties in the assumptions and in estimated program effectiveness or costs, and show the sensitivity of recommendations to these uncertainties.

d. In sum, the analytic effort will:

(1) Help define major agency objectives and subobjectives.

(2) Analyze and review criteria by which program performance is measured and judged, and help to develop new, improved criteria.

(3) Compare alternative programs, both in terms of their effectiveness and their costs, old as well as new.

(4) Develop reliable estimates of total systems costs of alternatives over the relevant span of years.

(5) Analyze the validity of cost data.

(6) Identify and analyze program uncertainties; test the sensitivity of conclusions and recommendations against uncertain variables.

(7) Carry out systems analyses to aid in making program choices.

8. RELATION OF THE SYSTEM TO THE BUDGET PROCESS. a. Two products of the system will be utilized in the spring Budget Preview: the Program Memoranda (which incorporate in summarized form the relevant portions of the Program and Financial Plan) and Special Studies.

b. All annual budget requests in the fall will be based on and related to the first year of the current multi-year Program and Financial Plan, subject to such modifications as may be required by changing circumstances since the Plan was last reviewed and approved by the agency head. Within this framework the detailed formulation and review of the budget will take place.

c. The introduction of the Planning, Programming, and Budgeting system will not, by itself, require any changes in the form in which budget appropriation requests are sent to Congress. Further, this Bulletin is not to be interpreted to set forth changes in the format of annual budget submissions to the Budget Bureau. Circular No. A–11 will be revised as needed to provide guidance on such budget submissions.

d. Over the next few years agency operating budgets used to allocate resources and control the day to day operations are to be brought into consistency with the Program and Financial Plan. Performance reports that show physical and financial accomplishments in relation to operating budgets should also be related to the basic plan.

e. The Planning, Programming and Budgeting functions are closely related and there must be close coordination in the work of the various staffs.

9. AN ILLUSTRATIVE ANNUAL CYCLE. Program review is a year-round process of reevaluating and updating objectives, performance, and costs. The annual cycle described below is presented for purposes of illustration and will be refined and changed over time. It is intended to identify check-points to assure that essential steps are taken and that current reviews, revisions and recommendations are given consideration at appropriate times in the budget cycle. Insofar as this schedule affects internal agency operations and does not affect Bureau of the Budget scheduling, it may be modified by each agency head to suit his needs. The illustrative annual cycle shows in outline form how the system would work after it is established and operating for an agency participating in the Preview.

January. Changes are made by the agency to the prior multi-year program plan to conform to Presidential decisions as reflected in the budget sent to the Congress.

March. By March bureaus or similar major organizational units within the agency will submit to the agency head their current appraisals of approved program objectives and multi-year plans and their proposals for (a) needed modifications, including measures to meet new needs and to take account of changing and expiring needs, and (b) extension of plans to cover an added year (e.g., 1972). The Director of the Bureau of the Budget will advise the agency head of any change in the overall policies and objectives upon which the currently approved plan is based.

April. On the basis of instructions from the agency head following his review of bureau submissions, bureaus develop *specific* program plans.

May. Analytic staffs complete Program Memoranda. Agency had reviews program plans and approves Program Memoranda for submission to the Bureau of the Budget. He may want to assign additional studies on the basis of this review.

May–June. The budget preview is conducted by the Bureau of the Budget. The basic documents for this preview are the Program memoranda prepared by agencies which are to be submitted to the Bureau of the budget by May 1, and Special Studies to be submitted over a period of several months preceding this date. Presidential guidance will be obtained, where necessary, on major policy issues and on the fiscal outlook.

July–August. Appropriate changes to program plans are made on the basis of the guidance received and of congressional legislation and appropriations. Budget estimates, including those for new legislative proposals, are developed on the basis of the first year of the currently approved program plans (e.g., 1968).

September. Budget estimates and agency legislative programs are submitted to the Bureau of the Budget.

October–December. Budget Bureau reviews budget estimates, consults with agencies, and makes its recommendations to the President. Presidential decisions are transmitted to agencies, the budget is prepared for submission to Congress, and the legislative program is prepared.

January. Changes are again made by the agency to the multi-year program plan to conform to Presidential decisions as reflected in the budget sent to the Congress.

10. RESPONSIBILITY AND STAFFING. a. Personal responsibility for the Planning, Programming, and Budgeting system rests with the head of each agency. Since planning, programming, and budgeting are all essential elements of management, line managers at appropriate levels in the agency must also take responsibility for, and participate in, the system. Responsibility should be so fixed that the agency head receives the recommendations of his principal managers (e.g., bureau chiefs) on program plans as well as on the findings and recommendations of centrally prepared analytical studies. Similarly, arrangements should be made for obtaining original suggestions, recommendations, and views from other echelons in a manner consistent with the assignment of responsibility and authority.

b. Specialized staff assistance is also essential in all but the smallest agencies. Such assistance will be especially useful in the preparation and review of Program and Financial Plans and in the preparation of the appropriate analytical studies. Each agency will, therefore, establish an adequate central staff or staffs for analysis, planning and programming. Some bureaus and other subordinate organizations should also have their own analytical planning and programming staffs.

c. No single form of organization is prescribed since agency circumstances differ. Planning-Programming-Budgeting activities are functionally linked but it is not essential that they be located in the same office so long as they are well coordinated. However, it is important that the head of the central analytic staff be directly responsible to the head of the agency or his deputy.

11. INITIAL ACTION UNDER THIS BULLETIN. The head of each agency listed in Exhibit 1 should see that the following steps are taken by the dates indicated. It is recognized that this is a tight schedule. Nonetheless, the President's interest in the prompt establishment of the new Programming, Planning, and Budgeting system requires that each agency exert every possible effort to adhere to this schedule.

3.a.   President Richard Nixon's Address to the Nation on Domestic Programs: "New Federalism" Address (1969)

Good evening my fellow Americans:

As you know, I returned last Sunday night from a trip around the world—a trip that took me to eight countries in 9 days.

The purpose of this trip was to help lay the basis for a lasting peace, once the war in Vietnam is ended. In the course of it, I also saw once again the vigorous efforts so many new nations are making to leap the centuries into the modern world.

Every time I return to the United States after such a trip, I realize how fortunate we are to live in this rich land. We have the world's most advanced industrial economy, the greatest wealth ever known to man, the fullest measure of freedom ever enjoyed by any people, anywhere.

Yet we, too, have an urgent need to modernize our institutions—and our need is no less than theirs.

We face an urban crisis, a social crisis—and at the same time, a crisis of confidence in the capacity of government to do its job.

A third of a century of centralizing power and responsibility in Washington has produced a bureaucractic monstrosity, cumbersome, unresponsive, ineffective.

A third of a century of social experiment has left us a legacy of entrenched programs that have outlived their time or outgrown their purposes.

A third of a century of unprecedented growth and change has strained our institutions, and raised serious questions about whether they are still adequate to the times.

It is no accident, therefore, that we find increasing skepticism—and not only among our young people, but among citizens everywhere—about the continuing capacity of government to master the challenges we face.

Nowhere has the failure of the government been more tragically apparent than in its efforts to help the poor and especially in its system of public welfare.

TARGET: REFORMS

Since taking office, one of my first priorities has been to repair the machinery of government, to put it in shape for the 1970's. I have made many changes designed

From the *Public Papers of the President of the United States Richard Nixon*, 1969, Book I, USGPO, 1971, pp. 637–645. Nixon's statements not pertaining to New Federalism have been deleted. This presidential address was televised on August 8, 1969.

to improve the functioning of the executive branch. And I have asked Congress for a number of important structural reforms; among others, a wide-ranging postal reform, a comprehensive reform of the draft, a reform of unemployment insurance, a reform of our hunger programs, a reform of the present confusing hodge-podge of Federal grants-in-aid.

Last April 21, I sent Congress a message asking for a package of major tax reforms, including both the closing of loopholes and the removal of more than 2 million low-income families from the tax rolls altogether. I am glad that Congress is now acting on tax reform, and I hope the Congress will begin to act on the other reforms that I have requested.

The purpose of all these reforms is to eliminate unfairness; to make government more effective as well as more efficient; and to bring an end to its chronic failure to deliver the service that it promises.

My purpose tonight, however, is not to review the past record, but to present a new set of reforms—a new set of proposals—a new and drastically different approach to the way in which government cares for those in need, and to the way the responsibilities are shared between the State and the Federal Government.

I have chosen to do so in a direct report to the people because these proposals call for public decisions of the first importance; because they represent a fundamental change in the Nation's approach to one of its most pressing social problems; and because, quite deliberately, they also represent the first major reversal of the trend toward ever more centralization of government in Washington, D.C. After a third of a century of power flowing from the people and the States to Washington it is time for a New Federalism in which power, funds, and responsibility will flow from Washington to the States and to the people.

During last year's election campaign, I often made a point that touched a responsive chord wherever I traveled.

I said that this Nation became great not because of what government did for people, but because of what people did for themselves.

This new approach aims at helping the American people do more for themselves. It aims at getting everyone able to work off welfare rolls and onto payrolls.

It aims at ending the unfairness in a system that has become unfair to the welfare recipient, unfair to the working poor, and unfair to the taxpayer.

This new approach aims to make it possible for people—wherever in America they live—to receive their fair share of opportunity. It aims to ensure that people receiving aid, and who are able to work, contribute their fair share of productivity.

This new approach is embodied in a package of four measures: First, a complete replacement of the present welfare system; second, a comprehensive new job training and placement program; third, a revamping of the Office of Economic Opportunity; and fourth, a start on the sharing of Federal tax revenues with the States.

. . . .

REVENUE SHARING

We come now to a proposal which I consider profoundly important to the future of our Federal system of shared responsibilities. When we speak of poverty or jobs or opportunity or making government more effective or getting it closer to the people, it brings us directly to the financial plight of our States and cities.

We can no longer have effective government at any level unless we have it at all levels. There is too much to be done for the cities to do it alone, for Washington to do it alone, or for the States to do it alone.

For a third of a century, power and responsibility have flowed toward Washington, and Washington has taken for its own the best sources of revenue.

We intend to reverse this tide, and to turn back to the States a greater measure of responsibility—not as a way of avoiding problems, but as a better way of solving problems.

Along with this would go a share of Federal revenues. I shall propose to the Congress next week that a set portion of the revenues from Federal income taxes be remitted directly to the States, with a minimum of Federal restrictions on how those dollars are to be used, and with a requirement that a percentage of them be channeled through for the use of local governments.

The funds provided under this program will not be great in the first year. But the principle will have been established, and the amounts will increase as our budgetary situation improves.

This start on revenue sharing is a step toward what I call the New Federalism. It is a gesture of faith in America's State and local governments and in the principle of democratic self-government.

With this revenue sharing proposal we follow through on a commitment I made in the last campaign. We follow through on a mandate which the electorate gave us last November.

In recent years, we all have concentrated a great deal of attention on what we commonly call the "crisis of the cities." These proposals I have made are addressed in part to that, but they also are focused much more broadly.

They are addressed to the crisis of government—to adapting its structures and making it manageable.

They are addressed to the crisis of poverty and need, which is rural as well as urban. This administration is committed to full opportunity on the farm as well as in the city; to a better life for rural America; to ensuring that government is responsive to the needs of rural America as well as urban America. These proposals will advance these goals.

I have discussed these four matters together because together they make both a package and a pattern. They should be studied together, debated together, and seen in perspective.

Now these proposals will be controversial, just as any new program is controversial. They also are expensive. Let us face that fact frankly and directly.

The first-year costs of the new family assistance program, including the child care centers and job training, would be $4 billion. I deliberated long and hard over whether we could afford such an outlay. I decided in favor of it for two reasons: First, because the costs will not begin until fiscal year 1971, when I expect the funds to be available within the budget; and second, because I concluded that this is a reform we cannot afford not to undertake. The cost of continuing the present system, in financial as well as human terms, is staggering if projected into the 1970's.

Revenue sharing would begin in the middle of fiscal 1971, at a half-year cost of a half billion dollars. This cuts into the Federal budget, but it represents relief for the equally hard-pressed States. It would help curb the rise in State and local taxes which are such a burden to millions of American families.

Overall, we would be spending more—in the short run—to help people who now are poor and who now are unready for work or unable to find work.

But I see it this way: Every businessman, every workingman knows what "start-up costs" are. They are a heavy investment made in early years in the expectation that they will more than pay for themselves in future years.

The investment in these proposals is a human investment; it also is a "start-up cost" in turning around our dangerous decline into welfarism in America. We cannot produce productive people with the antiquated, wheezing, overloaded machine we now call the welfare system.

If we fail to make this investment in work incentives now, if we merely try to patch up the system here and there, we will only be pouring good money after bad in ever-increasing amounts.

If we do invest in this modernization, the heavily burdened taxpayer at least will have the chance to see the end of the tunnel. And the man who now only looks ahead only to a lifetime of dependency will see hope—hope for a life of work and pride and dignity.

In the final analysis, we cannot talk our way out of poverty; we cannot legislate our way out of poverty; but this Nation can work its way out of poverty. What America needs now is not more welfare, but more "workfare."

The task of this Government, the great task of our people, is to provide the training for work, the incentive to work, the opportunity to work, and the reward for work. Together these measures are a first long step in that direction.

For those in the welfare system today who are struggling to fight their way out of poverty, these measures offer a way to independence through the dignity of work.

For those able to work, these measures provide new opportunities to learn work, to find work.

For the working poor—the forgotten poor—these measures offer a fair share in the assistance given to the poor.

This new system establishes a direct link between the Government's willingness to help the needy and the willingness of the needy to help themselves.

It removes the present incentive not to work and substitutes an incentive to work;

it removes the present incentive for families to break apart and substitutes an incentive for families to stay together.

It removes the blatant inequities and injustices and indignities of the welfare system.

It establishes a basic Federal floor so that children in any State can have at least the minimum essentials of life.

Together, these measures cushion the impact of welfare costs on States and localities, many of which have found themselves in fiscal crisis as costs have escalated.

They bring reason, order, and purpose into a tangle of overlapping programs, and show that Government can be made to work.

Poverty will not be defeated by a stroke of a pen signing a check, and it will not be reduced to nothing overnight with slogans or ringing exhortations.

Poverty is not only a state of income. It is also a state of mind, a state of health. Poverty must be conquered without sacrificing the will to work, for if we take the route of the permanent handout, the American character will itself be impoverished.

In my recent trip around the world, I visited countries in all stages of economic development; countries with different social systems, different economic systems, different political systems.

In all of them, however, I found that one event had caught the imagination of the people and lifted their spirits almost beyond measure: the trip of Apollo II to the moon and back. On that historic day, when the astronauts set foot on the moon, the spirit of Apollo truly swept through this world. It was a spirit of peace and brotherhood and adventure, a spirit that thrilled to the knowledge that man had dreamed the impossible, dared the impossible, and done the impossible.

Abolishing poverty, putting an end to dependency—like reaching the moon a generation ago—may seem to be impossible. But in the spirit of Apollo, we can lift our sights and marshal our best efforts. We can resolve to make this the year not that we reached the goal, but that we turned the corner—turned the corner from a dismal cycle of dependency toward a new birth of independence; from despair toward hope; from an ominously mounting impotence of government toward a new effectiveness of government, and toward a full opportunity for every American to share the bounty of this rich land.

Thank you and goodnight.

NOTE: President Richard Nixon delivered the address on nationwide radio and television at 10 p.m.

The advance text of the President's address is printed in the Weekly Compilation of Presidential Documents (vol. 5, p. 1103).

3.b.   Title I of the State and Local Fiscal Assistance Act of 1972

An Act

To provide fiscal assistance to State and local governments, to authorize Federal collection of State Individual Income taxes, and for other purposes.

Be it enacted by the Senate and House of Representatives of the United States of America in Congress assembled,

TITLE I—FISCAL ASSISTANCE TO STATE AND LOCAL GOVERNMENTS

SUBTITLE A— ALLOCATION AND PAYMENT OF FUNDS

Sec. 101. Short Title.
This title may be cited as the "State and Local Fiscal Assistance Act of 1972".
Sec. 102. Payments to State and Local Governments.
Except as otherwise provided in this title, the Secretary shall, for each entitlement period, pay out of the Trust Fund to—

(1) each State government a total amount equal to the entitlement of such State government determined under section 107 for such period, and

(2) each unit of local government a total amount equal to the entitlement of such unit determined under section 108 for such period.

In the case of entitlement periods ending after the date of the enactment of this Act, such payments shall be made in installments, but not less often than once for each quarter, and, in the case of quarters ending after September 30, 1972, shall be paid not later than 5 days after the close of each quarter. Such payments for any entitlement period may be initially made on the basis of estimates. Proper adjustment shall be made in the amount of any payment to a State government or a unit of local government to the extent that the payments previously made to such government under this subtitle were in excess of or less than the amounts required to be paid.

Public Law 92–512, (October 20, 1972). Subtitle B and C pertaining to Administrative and General Provisions were omitted.

Sec. 103. Use of Funds by Local Governments for Priority Expenditures.

(a) In General.—Funds received by units of local government under this subtitle may be used only for priority expenditures. For purposes of this title, the term "priority expenditures" means only—

    (1) ordinary and necessary maintenance and operating expenses for—

        (A) public safety (including law enforcement, fire protection, and building code enforcement),

        (B) environmental protection (including sewage disposal, sanitation, and pollution abatement),

        (C) public transportation (including transit systems and streets and roads),

        (D) health,

        (E) recreation,

        (F) libraries,

        (G) social services for the poor or aged, and

        (H) financial administration; and

    (2) ordinary and necessary capital expenditures authorized by law.

(b) Certificates by Local Governments.—The Secretary is authorized to accept a certification by the chief executive officer of a unit of local government that the unit of local government has used the funds received by it under this subtitle for an entitlement period only for priority expenditures, unless he determines that such certification is not sufficiently reliable to enable him to carry out his duties under this title.

Sec. 104. Prohibition on Use as Matching Funds by State or Local Governments.

(a) In General.—No State government or unit of local government may use, directly or indirectly, any part of the funds it receives under this subtitle as a contribution for the purpose of obtaining Federal funds under any law of the United States which requires such government to make a contribution in order to receive Federal funds.

(b) Determinations by Secretary of the Treasury.—If the Secretary has reason to believe that a State government or unit of local government has used funds received under this subtitle in violation of subsection (a), he shall give reasonable notice and opportunity for hearing to such government. If, thereafter, the Secretary of the Treasury determines that such government has used funds in violation of subsection (a), he shall notify such government of his determination and shall request repayment to the United States of an amount equal to the funds so used. To the extent that such government fails to repay such amount, the Secretary shall withhold from subsequent payments to such government under this subtitle an amount equal to the funds so used.

(c) Increased State or Local Government Revenues.—No State government or unit of local government shall be determined to have used funds in violation of subsection (a) with respect to any funds received for any entitlement period to the extent that the net revenues received by it from its own sources during such period exceed the net revenues received by it from its own sources during the one-year period beginning July 1, 1971 (or one-half of such net revenues, in the case of an entitlement period of 6 months).

(d) Deposits and Transfers to General fund.—Any amount repaid by a State government or unit of local government under subsection (b) shall be deposited in the general fund of the Treasury. An amount equal to the reduction in payments to any State government or unit of local government which results from the application of this section (after any judicial review under section 143) shall be transferred from the Trust Fund to the general fund of the Treasury on the day on which such reduction becomes final.

(e) Certificates by State and Local Governments.—The Secretary is authorized to accept a certification by the Governor of a State or the chief executive officer of a unit of local government that the State government or unit of local government has not used any funds received by it under this subtitle for an entitlement period in violation of subsection (a); unless he determines that such certification is not sufficiently reliable to enable him to carry out his duties under this title.

Sec. 105. Creation of Trust Fund; Appropriations.

    (a) Trust Fund.—

        (1) In general.—There is hereby established on the books of the Treasury of the United States a trust fund to be known as the "State and Local Government Fiscal Assistance Trust Fund" (referred to in this subtitle as the "Trust Fund"). The Trust Fund shall remain available without fiscal year limitation and shall consist of such amounts as may be appropriated to it and deposited in it as provided in subsection (b). Except as provided in this title, amounts in the Trust Fund may be used only for the payments to State and local governments provided by this subtitle.

        (2) Trustee.—The Secretary of the Treasury shall be the trustee of the Trust Fund and shall report to the Congress not later than March 1 of each year on the operation and status of the Trust Fund during the preceding fiscal year.

    (b) Appropriations.—

        (1) In general.—There is appropriated to the Trust Fund, out of amounts in the general fund of the Treasury attributable to the collections of the Federal individual income taxes not otherwise appropriated—

            (A) for the period beginning January 1, 1972, and ending June 30, 1972, $2,650,000,000;

(B) for the period beginning July 1, 1972, and ending December 31, 1972, $2,650,000,000;

(C) for the period beginning January 1, 1973, and ending June 30, 1973, $2,987,500,000;

(D) for the fiscal year beginning July 1, 1973, $6,050,000,000;

(E) for the fiscal year beginning July 1, 1974, $6,200,000,000;

(F) for the fiscal year beginning July 1, 1975, $6,350,000,000; and

(G) for the period beginning July 1, 1976, and ending December 31, 1976, $3,325,000,00.

(2) Noncontiguous States adjustment amounts.—There is appropriated to the Trust Fund, out of amounts in the general fund of the Treasury attributable to the collections of the Federal individual income taxes not otherwise appropriated—

(A) for the period beginning January 1, 1972, and ending June 30, 1972, $2,390,000;

(B) for the period beginning July 1, 1972, and ending December 31, 1972, $2,390,000;

(C) for the period beginning January 1, 1973, and ending June 30, 1973, $2,390,000;

(D) for each of the fiscal years beginning July 1, 1973, July 1, 1974, and July 1, 1975, $4,780,000; and

(E) for the period beginning July 1, 1976, and ending December 31, 1976, $2,390,000.

(3) Deposits.—Amounts appropriated by paragraph (1) or (2) for any fiscal year or other period shall be deposited in the Trust Fund on the later of (A) the first day of such year or period, or (B) the day after the date of enactment of this Act.

(c) Transfers From Trust Fund to General Fund.—The Secretary shall from time to time transfer from the Trust Fund to the general fund of the Treasury any moneys in the Trust Fund which he determines will not be needed to make payments to State governments and units of local government under this subtitle.

Sec. 106. Allocation Among States.

In General.—There shall be allocated to each State for each entitlement period, out of amounts appropriated under section 105(b) (1) for that entitlement period, an amount which bears the same ratio to the amount appropriated under that section for that period as the amount allocable to that State under subsection (b) bears to the sum of the amounts allocable to all States under subsection (b).

(b) Determination of Allocable Amount.—

(1) In general.—For purposes of subsection (a), the amount allocable to a State under this subsection for any entitlement period shall be determined under paragraph (2), except that such amount shall be determined under paragraph (3) if the amount allocable to it under paragraph (3) is greater than the sum of the amounts allocable to it under paragraph (2) and subsection (c).

(2) Three factor formula.—For purposes of paragraph (1), the amount allocable to a State under this paragraph for any entitlement period is the amount which bears the same ratio to $5,300,000,000 as—

    (A) the population of that State, multiplied by the general tax effort factor of that State, multiplied by the relative income factor of that State, bears to

    (B) the sum of the products determined under subparagraph (A) for all States.

(3) Five factor formula.—For purposes of paragraph (1), the amount allocable to a State under this paragraph for any entitlement period is the amount to which that State would be entitled if—

    (A) ⅓ of $3,500,000,000 were allocated among the States on the basis of population.

    (B) ⅓ of $3,500,000,000 were allocated among the States on the basis of urbanized population.

    (C) ⅓ of $3,500,000,000 were allocated among the States on the basis of population inversely weighted for per capita income,

    (D) ½ of $1,800,000,000 were allocated among the States on the basis of income tax collections, and

    (E) ½ of $1,800,000,000 were allocated among the States on the basis of general tax effort.

(c) Noncontiguous States Adjustment.—

(1) In general.—In addition to amounts allocated among the States under subsection (a), there shall be allocated for each entitlement period, out of amounts appropriated under section 105(b) (2), an additional amount to any State (A) whose allocation under subsection (b) is determined by the formula set forth in paragraph (2) of that subsection and (B) in which civilian employees of the United States Government receive an allowance under section 5941 of title 5, United States Code.

(2) Determination Of Amount.—The additional amount allocable to any State under this subsection for any entitlement period is an amount equal to a percentage of the amount allocable to that State under subsection (b) (2) for that period which is the same as the percentage of basic pay received

by such employees stationed in that State as an allowance under such section 5941. If the total amount appropriated under section 105 (b) (2) for any entitlement period is not sufficient to pay in full the additional amounts allocable under this subsection for that period, the Secretary shall reduce proportionately the amounts so allocable.

Sec. 107. Entitlements of State Governments.

(a) Division Between State and Local Governments.—The State government shall be entitled to receive one-third of the amount allocated to that State for each entitlement period. The remaining portion of each State's allocation shall be allocated among the units of local government of that State as provided in section 108.

(b) State Must Maintain Transfers to Local Governments.—

   (1) General Rule.—The entitlement of any State government for any entitlement period beginning or after July 1, 1973, shall be reduced by the amount (if any) by which—

   (A) the average of the aggregate amounts transferred by the State government (out of its own sources) during such period and the preceding entitlement period to all units of local government in such State, is less than,

   (B) the similar aggregate amount for the one-year period beginning July 1, 1971.

   For purposes of subparagraph (A), the amount of any reduction in the entitlement of a State government under this subsection for any entitlement period shall, for subsequent entitlement periods, be treated as an amount transferred by the State government (out of its own sources) during such period to units of local government in such State.

   (2) Adjustment Where State Assumes Reponsibility for Category of Expenditures.—If the State government establishes to the satisfaction of the Secretary that since June 30, 1972, it has assumed responsibility for a category of expenditures which (before July 1, 1972) was the responsibility of local governments located in such State, then, under regulations prescribed by the Secretary, the aggregate amount taken into account under paragraph (1)(B) shall be reduced to the extent that increased State government spending (out of its own sources) for such category has replaced corresponding amounts which for the one-year period beginning July 1, 1971, it trannsferred to units of local government.

   (3) Adjustment Where New Taxing Powers Are Conferred Upon Local Governments.—If a State establishes to the satisfaction of the Secretary that since June 30, 1972, one or more units of local government within such

State have had conferred upon them new taxing authority, then, under regulations prescribed by the Secretary, the aggregate amount taken into account under paragraph (1)(B) shall be reduced to the extent of the larger of—

(A) an amount equal to the amount of the taxes collected by reason of the exercise of such new taxing authority by such local governments, or

(B) an amount equal to the amount of the loss of revenue to the State by reason of such new taxing authority being conferred on such local governments.

No amount shall be taken into consideration under subparagraph (A) if such new taxing authority is an increase in the authorized rate of tax under a previously authorized kind of tax, unless the State is determined by the Secretary to have decreased a related State tax.

(4) Special Rule for Period Beginning July 1, 1973.—In the case of the entitlement period beginning July 1, 1973, the preceding entitlement period for purposes of paragraph (1)(A) shall be treated as being the one-year period beginning July 1, 1972.

(5) Special Rule for Period Beginning July 1, 1976.—In the case of the entitlement period beginning July 1, 1976, and ending December 31, 1976, the aggregate amount taken into account under paragraph (1)(A) for the preceding entitlement period and the aggregate amount taken into account under paragraph (1)(B) shall be one-half of the amounts which (but for this paragraph) would be taken into account.

(6) Reduction in Entitlement.—If the Secretary has reason to believe that paragraph (1) requires a reduction in the entitlement of any State government for any entitlement period, he shall give reasonable notice and oportunity for hearing to the State. If, thereafter, he determines that paragraph (1) requires the reduction of such entitlement, he shall also determine the amount of such reduction and shall notify the Governor of such State of such determinations and shall withhold from subsequent payments to such State government under this subtitle an amount equal to such reduction.

(7) Transfer to General Fund.—An amount equal to the reduction in the entitlement of any State government which results from the application of this subsection (after any judicial review under section 143) shall be transferred from the Trust Fund to the general fund of the Treasury on the day on which such reduction becomes final.

Sec. 108. Entitlements of Local Governments.

(a) Allocation Among County Areas.—The amount to be allocated to the units of local government within a State for any entitlement period shall be allocated among the county areas located in the State so that each county area will receive an amount which bears the same ratio to the total amount to be allocated to the units of local government within that State as—

(1) the population of that county area, multiplied by the general tax effort factor of that county area, multiplied by the relative income factor of that county area, bears to

(2) the sum of the products determined under paragraph (1) for all county areas within that State.

(b) Allocation to County Governments, Municipalities, Townships, Etc.—

(1) County Governments.—The county government shall be allocated that portion of the amount allocated to the county area for the entitlement period under subsection (a) which bears the same ratio to such amount as the adjusted taxes of the county government bear to the adjusted taxes of the county government and all other units of local government located in the county area.

(2) Other Units of Local Government.—The amount remaining for allocation within a county area after the application of paragraph (1) shall be allocated among the units of local government (other than the county government and other than township governments) located in that county area so that each unit of local government will receive an amount which bears the same ratio to the total amount to be allocated to all such units as—

(A) the population of that local government, multiplied by the general tax effort factor of that local government, multiplied by the relative income factor of that local government, bears to

(B) the sum of the products determined under subparagraph (A) for all such units.

(3) Township Governments.—If the county area includes one or more township governments, then before applying paragraph (2)—

(A) there shall be set aside for allocation under subparagraph (B) to such township governments that portion of the amount allocated to the county area for the entitlement period which bears the same ratio to such amount as the sum of the adjusted taxes of all such township governments bears to the aggregate adjusted taxes of the county government, such township governments, and all other units of local government located in the county area, and

(B) that portion of each amount set aside under subparagraph (A) shall be allocated to each township government on the same basis as amounts are allocated to units of local government under paragraph (2).

If this paragraph applies with respect to any county area for any entitlement period, the remaining portion allocated under paragraph (2) to the units of local government located in the county area (other than the county government and the township governments) shall be appropriately reduced to reflect the amounts set aside under subparagraph (A).

(4) Indian Tribes and Alaskan Native Villages.—If within a county area there is an Indian tribe or Alaskan native village which has a recognized governing body which performs substantial governmental functions, then before applying paragraph (1) there shall be allocated to such tribe or village a portion of the amount allocated to the county area for the entitlement period which bears the same ratio to such amount as the population of that tribe or village within that county area bears to the populations of that county area. If this paragraph applies with respect to any county area for any entitlement period, the amount to be allocated under paragraph (1) shall be appropriately reduced to reflect the amount allocated under the preceding sentence. If the entitlement of any such tribe or village is waived for any entitlement period by the governing body of that tribe or village, then the provisions of this paragraph shall not apply with respect to the amount of such entitlement for such period.

(5) Rule for Small Units of Government.—If the Secretary determines that in any county area the data available for any entitlement period are not adequate for the application of the formulas set forth in paragraphs (2) and (3)(B) with respect to units of local government (other than a county government) with a population below a number (not more than 500) prescribed for that county area by the Secretary, he may apply paragraph (2) or (3)(B) by allocating for such entitlement period to each such unit located in that county area an amount which bears the same ratio to the total amount to be allocated under paragraph (2) or (3)(B) for such entitlement period as the population of such unit bears to the population of all units of local government in that county area to which allocations are made under such paragraph. If the preceding sentence applies with respect to any county area, the total amount to be allocated under paragraph (2) or (3)(B) to other units of local government in that county area for the entitlement period shall be appropriately reduced to reflect the amounts allocated under the preceding sentence.

(6) Entitlement.—

(A) In General.—Except as otherwise provided in this paragraph, the entitlement of any unit of local government for any entitlement period shall be the amount allocated to such unit under this subsection (after taking into account any applicable modification under subsection (c).

(B) Maximum and Minimum Per Capita Entitlement.—Subject to the provisions of subparagraphs (C) and (D), the per capita amount allocated to any county area or any unit of local government (other than a county government) within a State under this section for any entitlement period shall not be less than 20 percent, nor more than 145 percent, of two-thirds of the amount allocated to the State under section 106, divided by the population of that State.

(C) Limitation.—The amount allocated to any unit of local government under this section for any entitlement period shall not exceed 50 percent of the sum of (i) such government's adjusted taxes, and (ii) the intergovernmental transfers of revenue to such government (other than transfers to such government under this subtitle).

(D) Entitlement Less Than $200, or Governing Body Waives Entitlement.—If (but for this subparagraph) the entitlement of any unit of local government below the level of county government—

(i) would be less then $200 for any entitlement period ($100 for an entitlement period of 6 months), or

(ii) is waived for any entitlement period by the governing body of such unit,

then the amount of such entitlement for such period shall (in lieu of being paid to such unit) be added to, and shall become a part of, the entitlement for such period of the county government of the county area in which such unit is located.

(7) Adjustment of Entitlement.—

(A) In General.—In adjusting the allocation of any county area or unit of local government, the Secretary shall make any adjustment required under paragraph (6)(B) first, any adjustment required under paragraph (6)(C) next, and any adjustment required under paragraph (6)(D) last.

(B) Adjustment for Application of Maximum or Minimum Per Capita Entitlement.—The Secretary shall adjust the allocations made under this section to county areas or to units of local governments in any State in order to bring those allocations into compliance with the provisions of paragraph (6)(B). In making such adjustments he shall make any necessary adjustments with respect to county areas before making any necessary adjustments with respect to units of local government.

(C) Adjustment for Application of Limitation.—In any case in which the amount allocated to a unit of local government is reduced under paragraph (6)(C) by the Secretary, the amount of that reduction—

(i) in the case of a unit of local government (other than a county government), shall be added to and increase the allocation of the county government of the county area in which it is located, unless (on acount of the application of paragraph (6)) that county government may not receive it, in which case the amount of the reduction shall be added to and increase the entitlement of the State government of the State in which that unit of local government is located; and

(ii) in the case of a county government, shall be added to and increase the entitlement of the State government of the State in which it is located.

(c) Special Allocation Rules.—

(1) Optional Formula—A State may by law provide for the allocation of funds among county areas, or among units of local government (other than county governments), on the basis of the population multiplied by the general tax effort factors of such areas or units of local government, on the basis of the population multiplied by the relative income factors of such areas or units of local government, or on the basis of a combination of those two factors. Any State which provides by law for such a variation in the allocation formula provided by subsection (a), or by paragraphs (2) and (3) of subsection (b), shall notify the Secretary of such law not later than 30 days before the beginning of the first entitlement period to which such law is to apply. Any such law shall—

(A) provide for allocating 100 percent of the aggregate amount to be allocated under subsection (a), or under paragraphs (2) and (3) of subsection (b);

(B) apply uniformly throughout the State; and

(C) apply during the period beginning on the first day of the first entitlement period to which it applies and ending on December 31, 1976.

(2) Certification.—Paragraph (1) shall apply within a State only if the Secretary certifies that the State law complies with the requirements of such paragraph. The Secretary shall not certify any such law with respect to which he receives notification later than 30 days prior to the first entitlement period during which it is to apply.

(d) Governmental Definitions and Related Rules.—For purposes of this title—

(1) Units of Local Government.—The term "unit of local government" means the government of a county, municipality, township, or other unit of

government below the State which is a unit of general government (determined on the basis of the same principles as are used by the Bureau of the Census for general statistical purposes). Such term also means, except for purposes of paragraphs (1), (2), (3), (5), (6)(C), and (6)(D) of subsection (b), and, except for purposes of subsection (c), the recognized governing body of an Indian tribe or Alaskan native village which performs substantial governmental functions.

(2) Certain areas treated as counties.—In any State in which any unit of local government (other than a county government) constitutes the next level of government below the State government level, then, except as provided in the next sentence, the geographic area of such unit of government shall be treated as a county area (and such unit of government shall be treated as a county government) with respect to that portion of the State's geographic area. In any State in which any county area is not governed by a county government but contains two or more units of local government, such units shall not be treated as county governments and the geographic areas of such units shall not be treated as county areas.

(3) Townships.—The term "township" includes equivalent subdivisions of government having different designations (such as "towns"), and shall be determined on the basis of the same principles as are used by the Bureau of the Census for general statistical purposes.

(4) Units of local government located in larger entity.—A unit of local government shall be treated as located in a larger entity if part or all of its geographic area is located in the larger entity.

(5) Only part of unit located in larger entity.—If only part of a unit of local government is located in a larger entity, such part shall be treated for allocation purposes as a separate unit of local government, and all computations shall, except as otherwise provided in regulations, be made on the basis of the ratio which the estimated population of such part bears to the population of the entirety of such unit.

(6) Boundary changes, governmental reorganization, etc.—If, by reason of boundary line changes, by reason of State statutory or constitutional changes, by reason of annexations or other governmental reorganizations, or by reason of other circumstances, the application of any provision of this section to units of local government does not carry out the purposes of this subtitle, the application of such provision shall be made, under regulations prescribed by the Secretary, in a manner which is consistent with such purposes.

Sec. 109. Definitions and Special Rules for Application of Allocation Formulas.
(a) In General.—For purposes of this subtitle—

(1) Population.—Population shall be determined on the same basis as resi-

dent population is determined by the Bureau of the Census for general statistical purposes.

(2) Urbanized population.—Urbanized population means the population of any area consisting of a central city or cities of 50,000 or more inhabitants (and of the surrounding closely settled territory for such city or cities) which is treated as an urbanized area by the Bureau of the Census for general statistical purposes.

(3) Income.—Income means total money income received from all sources, as determined by the Bureau of the Census for general statistical purposes.

(4) Personal income.—Personal income means the income of individuals, as determined by the Department of Commerce for national income accounts purposes.

(5) Dates for determining allocations and entitlements.—Except as provided in regulations, the determination of allocations and entitlements for any entitlement period shall be made as of the first day of the third month immediately preceding the beginning of such period.

(6) Intergovernmental transfers.—The intergovernmental transfers of revenue to any government are the amounts of revenue received by that government from other governments as a share in financing (or as reimbursement for) the performance of governmental functions, as determined by the Bureau of the Census for general statistical purposes.

(7) Data used; uniformity of data.—

   (A) General rule.—Except as provided in subparagraph (B), the data used shall be the most recently available data provided by the Bureau of the Census or the Department of Commerce, as the case may be.

   (B) Use of estimates, etc.—Where the Secretary determines that the data referred to in subparagraph (A) are not current enough or are not comprehensive enough to provide for equitable allocations, he may use such additional data (including data based on estimates) as may be provided for in regulations.

(b) Income Tax Amount of States.—For purposes of this subtitle—

   (1) In general.—The income tax amount of any State for any entitlement period is the income tax amount of such State as determined under paragraphs (2) and (3).

   (2) Income tax amount.—The income tax amount of any State for any entitlement period is 15 percent of the net amount collected from the State individual income tax of such State during 1972 or (if later) during the last calendar year ending before the beginning of such entitlement period.

(3) Ceiling and floor.—The income tax amount of any State for any entitlement period—

(A) shall not exceed 6 percent, and

(B) shall not be less than 1 percent, of the Federal individual income tax liabilities attributed to such State for taxable years ending during 1971 or (if later) during the last calendar year ending before the beginning of such entitlement period.

(4) State individual income tax.—The individual income tax of any State is the tax imposed upon the income of individuals by such State and described as a State income tax under section 164(a)(3) of the Internal Revenue Code of 1954.

(5) Federal individual income tax liabilities.—Federal individual income tax liabilities attributed to any State for any period shall be determined on the same basis as such liabilities are determined for such period by the Internal Revenue Service for general statistical purposes.

(c) General Tax Effort of States.—

(1) In general.—For purposes of this subtitle—

(A) General tax effort factor.—The general tax effort factor of any State for any entitlement period is (i) the net amount collected from the State and local taxes of such State during the most recent reporting year, divided by (ii) the aggregate personal income (as defined in paragraph (4) of subsection (a)) attributed to such State for the same period.

(B) General tax effort amount.—The general tax effort amount of any State for any entitlement period is the amount determined by multiplying—

(i) the net amount collected from the State and local taxes of such State during the most recent reporting year by

(ii) the general tax effort factor of that State.

(2) State and local taxes.—

(A) Taxes taken into account.—The State and local taxes taken into account under paragraph (1) are the compulsory contributions exacted by the State (or by any unit of local government or other political subdivision of the State) for public purposes (other than employee and employer assessments and contributions to finance retirement and social insurance systems, and other than special assessments for capital outlay), as such contributions are determined by the Bureau of the Census for general statistical purposes.

(B) Most recent reporting year.—The most recent reporting year with respect to any entitlement period consists of the years taken into account by the Bureau of the Census in its most recent general determination of State and local taxes made before the close of such period.

(d) General Tax Effort Factor of County Area.—For purposes of this subtitle, the general tax effort factor of any county area for any entitlement period is—

(1) the adjusted taxes of the county government plus the adjusted taxes of each other unit of local government within that county area, divided by

(2) the aggregate income (as defined in paragraph (3) of subsection (a)) attributed to that county area.

(e) General Tax Effort Factor of Unit of Local Government.—For purposes of this subtitle—

(1) In general.—The general tax effort factor of any unit of local government for any entitlement period is—

(A) the adjusted taxes of that unit of local government, divided by

(B) the aggregate income (as defined in paragraph (3) of subsection (a)) attributed to that unit of local government.

(2) Adjusted taxes.—

(A) In general.—the adjusted taxes of any unit of local government are—

(i) the compulsory contributions exacted by such government for public purposes (other than employee and employer assessments and contributions to finance retirement and social insurance systems, and other than special assessments for capital outlay), as such contributions are determined by the Bureau of the Census for general statistical purposes,

(ii) adjusted (under regulations prescribed by the Secretary) by excluding an amount equal to that portion of such compulsory contributions which is properly allocable to expenses for education.

(B) Certain sales taxes collected by counties.—In any case where—

(i) a county government exacts sales taxes within the geographic area of a unit of local government and transfers part or all of such taxes to such unit without specifying the purposes for which such unit may spend the revenues, and

(ii) the Governor of the State notifies the Secretary that the requirements of this subparagraph have been met with respect to such taxes, then the taxes so transferred shall be treated as the taxes of the unit of local government (and not the taxes of the county government).

(f) Relative Income Factor.—For purposes of this subtitle, the relative income factor is a fraction—

(1) in the case of a State, the numerator of which is the per capita income of the United States and the denominator of which is the per capita income of that State;

(2) in the case of a county area, the numerator of which is the per capita income of the State in which it is located and the denominator of which is the per capita income of that county area; and

(3) in the case of a unit of local government, the numerator of which is the per capita income of the county area in which it is located and the denominator of which is the per capita income of the geographic area of that unit of local government.

For purposes of this subsection, per capita income shall be determined on the basis of income as defined in paragraph (3) of subsection (a).

(g) Allocation Rules for Five Factor Formula.—For purposes of section 106(b)(3)—

(1) Allocation on basis of population.—Any allocation among the States on the basis of population shall be made by allocating to each State an amount which bears the same ratio to the total amount to be allocated as the population of such State bears to the population of all the States.

(2) Allocation on basis of urbanized population.—Any allocation among the States on the basis of urbanized population shall be made by allocating to each State an amount which bears the same ratio to the total amount to be allocated as the urbanized population of such State bears to the urbanized population of all the States.

(3) Allocation on basis of population inversely weighted for per capita income.—Any allocation among the States on the basis of population inversely weighted for per capita income shall be made by allocating to each State an amount which bears the same ratio to the total amount to be allocated as—

(A) the population of such State, multiplied by a fraction the numerator of which is the per capita income of all the States and the denominator of which is the per capita income of such State, bears to

(B) the sum of the products determined under subparagraph (A) for all the States.

(4) Allocation on basis of income tax collections.—Any allocation among the

States on the basis of income tax collections shall be made by allocating to each State an amount which bears the same ratio to the total amount to be allocated as the income tax amount of such State bears to the sum of the income tax amounts of all the States.

(5) Allocation on basis of general tax effort.—Any allocation among the States on the basis of general tax effort shall be made by allocating to each State an amount which bears the same ratio to the total amount to be allocated as the general tax effort amount of such State bears to the sum of the general tax effort amounts of all the States.

4. Congressional Budget and Impoundment Control Act of 1974

An Act

To establish a new congressional budget process; to establish Committees on the Budget in each House; to establish a Congressional Budget Office; to establish a procedure providing congressional control over the impoundment of funds by the executive branch; and for other purposes.

Be it enacted by the Senate and House of Representatives of the United States of America in Congress assembled,

SHORT TITLES; TABLE OF CONTENTS

Section 1. (a) Short Titles.—This Act may be cited as the "Congressional Budget and Impoundment Control Act of 1974". Titles I through IX may be cited as the "Congressional Budget Act of 1974", and title X may be cited as the "Impoundment Control Act of 1974".

. . . .

DECLARATION OF PURPOSES

Sec. 2. The Congress declares that it is essential—

(1) to assure effective congressional control over the budgetary process;

(2) to provide for the congressional determination each year of the appropriate level of Federal revenues and expenditures;

(3) to provide a system of impoundment control;

(4) to establish national budget priorities; and

(5) to provide for the furnishing of information by the executive branch in a manner that will assist the Congress in discharging its duties.

. . . .

Public Law 93–344 (July 12, 1974). The more technical aspects of this act have been omitted. Specific parts deleted include: (1) Title IV—Additional Provisions; (2) Title V—Change of Fiscal Year; (3) Title VI—Amendments; (4) Title VIII—Fiscal and Budgetary Information and Control; and Title IX—Miscellaneous Provisions.

TITLE I—ESTABLISHMENT OF HOUSE AND SENATE BUDGET COMMITTEES

BUDGET COMMITTEE OF THE HOUSE OF REPRESENTATIVES

Sec. 101. (a) Clause 1 of Rule X of the Rules of the House of Representatives is amended by redesignating paragraphs (e) through (n) as paragraphs (f) through (v), respectively, and by inserting after paragraph (d) the following new paragraph:

"(e) Committee on the Budget, to consist of twenty-three Members as follows:

"(1) five Members who are members of the Committee on Appropriations;

"(2) five Members who are members of the Committee on Ways and Means;

"(3) eleven Members who are members of other standing committees;

"(4) one Member from the leadership of the majority party; and

"(5) one Member from the leadership of the minority party.

No Member shall serve as a member of the Committee on the Budget during more than two Congresses in any period of five successive Congresses beginning after 1974 (disregarding for this purpose any service performed as a member of such committee for less than a full session in any Congress). All selections of Members to serve on the committee shall be made without regard to seniority."

(b) Rule X of the Rules of the House of Representatives is amended by adding at the end thereof the following new clause:

"6. For carrying out the purposes set forth in clause 5 of Rule XI, the Committee on the Budget or any subcommittee thereof is authorized to sit and act at such times and places within the United States, whether the House is in session, has recessed, or has adjourned, to hold such hearings, to require the attendance of such witnesses and the production of such books or papers or documents or vouchers by subpena or otherwise, and to take such testimony and records, as it deems necessary. Subpenas may be issued over the signature of the chairman of the committee or of any member of the committee designated by him; and may be served by any person designated by such chairman or member. The chairman of the committee, or any member thereof, may administer oaths to witnesses."

(c) Rule XI of the Rules of the House of Representatives is amended by redesignating clauses 5 through 33 as clauses 6 through 34, respectively, and by inserting after clause 4 the following new clause:

"5. Committee on the Budget

"(a) All concurrent resolutions on the budget (as defined in section 3(a)(4) of the Congressional Budget Act of 1974) and other matters required to be referred to the committee under titles III and IV of that Act.

"(b) The committee shall have the duty—

"(1) to report the matters required to be reported by it under titles III and IV of the Congressional Budget Act of 1974;

"(2) to make continuing studies of the effect on budget outlays of relevant existing and proposed legislation and to report the results of such studies to the House on a recurring basis;

"(3) to request and evaluate continuing studies of tax expenditures, to devise methods of coordinating tax expenditures, policies, and programs with direct budget outlays, and to report the results of such studies to the House on a recurring basis; and

"(4) to review, on a continuing basis, the conduct by the Congressional Budget Office of its functions and duties."

BUDGET COMMITTEE OF THE SENATE

Sec. 102. (a) Paragraph 1 of rule XXV of the Standing Rules of the Senate is amended by adding at the end thereof the following new subparagraph:

"(r)(1) Committee on the Budget, to which committee shall be referred all concurrent resolutions on the budget (as defined in section 3(a)(4) of the Congressional Budget Act of 1974) and all other matters required to be referred to that committee under titles III and IV of that Act, and messages, petitions, memorials, and other matters relating thereto.

"(2) Such committee shall have the duty—

"(A) to report the matters required to be reported by it under titles III and IV of the Congressional Budget Act of 1974;

"(B) to make continuing studies of the effect on budget outlays of relevant existing and proposed legislation and to report the results of such studies to the Senate on a recurring basis;

"(C) to request and evaluate continuing studies of tax expenditures, to devise methods of coordinating tax expenditures, policies, and programs with direct budget outlays, and to report the results of such studies to the Senate on a recurring basis; and

"(D) to review, on a continuing basis, the conduct by the Congressional Budget Office of its functions and duties."

(b) The table contained in paragraph 2 of rule XXV of the Standing Rules of the Senate is amended by inserting after—

"Banking, Housing and Urban Affairs. . . . .   15" the following:

"Budget . . . . 15".

(c) Paragraph 6 of rule XXV of the Standing Rules of the Senate is amended by adding at the end thereof the following new subparagraph:

"(h) For purposes of the first sentence of subparagraph (a), membership on the Committee on the Budget shall not be taken into account until that date occurring during the first session of the Ninety-fifth Congress, upon which the appointment of the majority and minority party members of the standing committees of the Senate is initially completed."

(d) Each meeting of the Committee on the Budget of the Senate, or any subcommittee thereof, including meetings to conduct hearings, shall be open to the public, except that a portion or portions of any such meeting may be closed to the public if the committee or subcommittee, as the case may be, determines by record vote of a majority of the members of the committee or subcommittee present that the matters to be discussed or the testimony to be taken at such portion or portions—

(1) will disclose matters necessary to be kept secret in the interests of national defense or the confidential conduct of the foreign relations of the United States;

(2) will relate solely to matters of committee staff personnel or internal staff management or procedure;

(3) will tend to charge an individual with crime or misconduct, to disgrace or injure the professional standing of an individual, or otherwise to expose an individual to public contempt or obloquy, or will represent a clearly unwarranted invasion of the privacy of an individual;

(4) will disclose the identity of any informer or law enforcement agent or will disclose any information relating to the investigation or prosecution of a criminal offense that is required to be kept secret in the interests of effective law enforcement; or

(5) will disclose information relating to the trade secrets or financial or commercial information pertaining specifically to a given person if—

(A) an Act of Congress requires the information to be kept confidential by Government officers and employees; or

(B) the information has been obtained by the Government on a confidential basis, other than through an application by such person for a specific Government financial or other benefit, and is required to be kept secret in order to prevent undue injury to the competitive position of such person.

(e) Paragraph 7(b) of rule XXV of the Standing Rules of the Senate and section 133A(b) of the Legislative Reorganization Act of 1946 shall not apply to the Committee on the Budget of the Senate.

TITLE II—CONGRESSIONAL BUDGET OFFICE

ESTABLISHMENT OF OFFICE

Sec. 201. (a) In General—

(1) There is established an office of the Congress to be known as the Congressional Budget Office (hereinafter in this title referred to as the "Office"). The Office shall be headed by a Director; and there shall be a Deputy Director who shall perform such duties as may be assigned to him by the Director and, during the absence or incapacity of the Director or during a vacancy in that office, shall act as Director.

(2) The Director shall be appointed by the Speaker of the House of Representatives and the President pro tempore of the Senate after considering recommendations received from the Committees on the Budget of the House and the Senate, without regard to political affiliation and solely on the basis of his fitness to perform his duties. The Deputy Director shall be appointed by the Director.

(3) The term of office of the Director first appointed shall expire at noon on January 3, 1979, and the terms of office of Directors subsequently appointed shall expire at noon on January 3 of each fourth year thereafter. Any individual appointed as Director to fill a vacancy prior to the expiration of a term shall serve only for the unexpired portion of that term. An individual serving as Director at the expiration of a term may continue to serve until his successor is appointed. Any Deputy Director shall serve until the expiration of the term of office of the Director who appointed him (and until his successor is appointed), unless sooner removed by the Director.

(4) The Director may be removed by either House by resolution.

(5) The Director shall receive compensation at a per annum gross rate equal to the rate of basic pay, as in effect from time to time, for level III of the Executive Schedule in section 5314 of title 5, United States Code. The Deputy Director shall receive compensation at a per annum gross rate equal to the rate of basic pay, as so in effect, for level IV of the Executive Schedule in section 5315 of such title.

(b) Personnel.—The Director shall appoint and fix the compensation of such personnel as may be necessary to carry out the duties and functions of the Office. All personnel of the Office shall be appointed without regard to political affiliation and solely on the basis of their fitness to perform their duties. The Director may prescribe the duties and responsibilities of the personnel of the Office, and delegate to them authority to perform any of the duties, powers, and functions imposed on the Office or on the Director. For purposes of pay (other than pay of the Director and Deputy Director) and employment benefits, rights, and privileges, all personnel of the Office shall be treated as if they were employees of the House of Representatives.

(c) Experts and Consultants.—In carrying out the duties and functions of the Office, the Director may procure the temporary (not to exceed one year) or intermittent services of experts or consultants or organizations thereof by contract as independent contractors, or, in the case of individual experts or consultants, by employment at rates of pay not in excess of the daily equivalent of the highest rate of basic pay payable under the General Schedule of section 5332 of title 5, United States Code.

(d) Relationship to Executive Branch.—The Director is authorized to secure information, data, estimates, and statistics directly from the various departments, agencies, and establishments of the executive branch of Government and the regulatory agencies and commissions of the Government. All such departments, agencies, establishments, and regulatory agencies and commissions shall furnish the Director any available material which he determines to be necessary in the performance of his duties and functions (other than material the disclosure of which would be a violation of law). The Director is also authorized, upon agreement with the head of any such department, agency, establishment, or regulatory agency or commission, to utilize its services, facilities, and personnel with or without reimbursement; and the head of each such department, agency, establishment, or regulatory agency or commission is authorized to provide the Office such services, facilities, and personnel.

(e) Relationship to Other Agencies in Congress—In carrying out the duties and functions of the Office, and for the purpose of coordinating the operations of the Office with those of other congressional agencies with a view to utilizing most effectively the information, services, and capabilities of all such agencies in carrying out the various responsibilities assigned to each, the Director is authorized to obtain information, data, estimates, and statistics developed by the General Accounting Office, the Library of Congress, and the Office of Technology Assessment, and (upon agreement with them) to utilize their services, facilities, and personnel with or without reimbursement. The Comptroller General, the Librarian of Congress, and the Technology Assessment Board are authorized to provide the Office with the information, data, estimates, and statistics, and the services, facilities, and personnel, referred to in the preceding sentence.

(f) Appropriations.—There are authorized to be appropriated to the Office for each fiscal year such sums as may be necessary to enable it to carry out its duties and functions. Until sums are first appropriated pursuant to the preceding sentence, but for a period not exceeding 12 months following the effective date of this subsection, the expenses of the Office shall be paid from the contingent fund of the Senate, in accordance with the paragraph relating to the contingent fund of the Senate under the heading "UNDERLYING LEGISLATIVE" in the Act of October 1, 1888 (28 Stat. 546; 2 U.S.C. 68), and upon vouches approved by the Director.

Sec. 202.(a) Assistance to Budget Committees.—It shall be the duty and function of the Office to provide to the Committees on the Budget of both Houses information which will assist such committees in the discharge of all matters within their jurisdictions, including (1) information with respect to the budget, appropriation bills, and other bills authorizing or providing budget authority or tax expenditures, (2) information with respect to revenues, receipts, estimated future revenues and receipts, and changing revenue conditions, and (3) such related information as such Committees may request.

(b) Assistance to Committees on Appropriations, Ways and Means, and Finance.—At the request of the Committee on Appropriations of either House, the Committee on Ways and Means of the House of Representatives, or the Committee on Finance of the Senate, the Office shall provide to such Committee any information which will assist it in the discharge of matters within its jurisdiction, including information described in clauses (1) and (2) of subsection (a) and such related information as the Committee may request.

(c) Assistance to Other Committees and Members.—

(1) At the request of any other committee of the House of Representatives, or the Senate or any joint committee of the Congress, the Office shall provide to such committee or joint committee any information compiled in carrying out clauses (1) and (2) of subsection (a), and, to the extent practicable, such additional information related to the foregoing as may be requested.

(2) At the request of any Member of the House or Senate, the Office shall provide to such Member any information compiled in carrying out clauses (1) and (2) of subsection (a), and, to the extent available such additional information related to the foregoing as may be requested.

(d) Assignment of Office Personnel to Committees and Joint Committees.—At the request of the Committee on the Budget of either House, personnel of the Office shall be assigned, on a temporary basis, to assist such committee. At the request of any other committee of either House or any joint committee of the Congress, personnel of the Office may be assigned, on a temporary basis, to assist such committee or joint committee with respect to matters directly related to the applicable provisions of subsection (b) or (c).

(e) Transfer of Functions of Joint Committee on Reduction of Federal Expenditures.—

   (1) The duties, functions, and personnel of the Joint Committee on Reduction of Federal Expenditures are transferred to the Office, and the Joint Committee is abolished.

   (2) Section 601 of the Revenue Act of 1941 (55 Stat. 726) is repealed.

(f) Reports to Budget Committees.—

   (1) On or before April 1 of each year, the Director shall submit to the Committees on the Budget of the House of Representatives and the Senate a report, for the fiscal year commencing on October 1 of that year, with respect to fiscal policy, including (A) alternative levels of total revenues, total new budget authority, and total outlays (including related surpluses and deficits), and (B) the levels of tax expenditures under existing law, taking into account projected economic factors and any changes in such levels based on proposals in the budget submitted by the President for such fiscal year. Such report shall also include a discussion of national budget priorities, including alternative ways of allocating budget authority and budget outlays for such fiscal year among major programs or functional categories, taking into account how such alternative allocations will meet, major national needs and affect balanced growth and development of the United States.

   (2) The Director shall from time to time submit to the Committees on the Budget of the House of Representatives and the Senate such further reports (including reports revising the report required by paragraph (1)) as may be necessary or appropriate to provide such Committees with information, data, and analyses for the performance of their duties and functions.

(g) Use of Computers and Other Techniques.—The Director may equip the Office with up-to-date computer capability (upon approval of the Committee on House Administration of the House of Representatives and the Committee on Rules and Administration of the Senate), obtain the services of experts and consultants in computer technology, and develop techniques for the evaluation of budgetary requirements.

PUBLIC ACCESS TO BUDGET DATA

Sec. 203.(a) Right to Copy.—Except as provided in subsections (c) and (d), the Director shall make all information, data, estimates, and statistics obtained under sections 201(d) and 201(e) available for public copying during normal business hours, subject to reasonable rules and regulations, and shall to the extent practicable, at the request of any person, furnish a copy of any such information, data, estimates, or statistics upon payment by such person of the cost of making and furnishing such copy.

(b) Index.—The Director shall develop and maintain filing, coding, and indexing systems that identify the information, data, estimates, and statistics to which subsection (a) applies and shall make such systems available for public use during normal business hours.

(c) Exceptions.—Subsection (a) shall not apply to information, data, estimates, and statistics—

(1) which are specifically exempted from disclosure by law; or

(2) which the Director determines will disclose—

    (A) matters necessary to be kept secret in the interests of national defense or the confidential conduct of the foreign relations of the United States;

    (B) information relating to trade secrets or financial or commercial information pertaining specifically to a given person if the information has been obtained by the Government on a confidential basis, other than through an application by such person for a specific financial or other benefit, and is required to be kept secret in order to prevent undue injury to the competitive position of such person; or

    (C) personnel or medical data or similar data the disclosure of which would constitute a clearly unwarranted invasion of personal privacy; unless the portions containing such matters, information, or data have been excised.

(d) Information Obtained for Committees and Members.—Subsection (a) shall apply to any information, data, estimates, and statistics obtained at the request of any committee, joint committee, or Member unless such committee, joint committee, or Member has instructed the Director not to make such information, data, estimates, or statistics available for public copying.

TITLE III—CONGRESSIONAL BUDGET PROCESS

TIMETABLE

Sec. 300. The timetable with respect to the congressional budget process for any fiscal year is as follows:

On or before:	Action to be completed:
November 10.................	President submits current services budget.
15th day after Congress meets	President submits his budget.
March 15....................	Committees and joint committees submit reports to Budget Committees.
April 1	Congressional Budget Office submits report to Budget Committees.
April 15	Budget Committees report first concurrent resolution on the budget to their Houses.
May 15	Committees report bills and resolutions authorizing new budget authority.
May 15	Congress completes action on first concurrent resolution on the budget.
7th day after Labor Day	Congress completes action on bills and resolutions providing new budget authority and new spending authority.
September 15	Congress completes action on second required concurrent resolution on the budget.
September 25	Congress completes action on reconciliation bill or resolution, or both, implementing second required concurrent resolution.
October 1	Fiscal year begins.

ADOPTION OF FIRST CONCURRENT RESOLUTION

Sec. 301. (a) Action To Be Completed by May 15—On or before May 15 of each year, the Congress shall complete action on the first concurrent resolution on the budget for the fiscal year beginning on October 1 of such year. The concurrent resolution shall set forth—

(1) the appropriate level of total budget outlays and of total new budget authority;

(2) an estimate of budget outlays and an appropriate level of new budget authority for each major functional category, for contingencies, and for undistributed intragovernmental transactions, based on allocations of the appropriate level of total budget outlays and of total new budget authority;

(3) the amount, if any, of the surplus or the deficit in the budget which is appropriate in light of economic conditions and all other relevant factors;

(4) the recommended level of Federal revenues and the amount, if any, by which the aggregate level of Federal revenues should be increased or decreased by bills and resolutions to be reported by the appropriate committees;

(5) the appropriate level of the public debt, and the amount, if any, by which the statutory limit on the public debt should be increased or decreased by bills and resolutions to be reported by the appropriate committees; and

(6) such other matters relating to the budget as may be appropriate to carry out the purposes of this Act.

(b) Additional Matters in Concurrent Resolution.—The first concurrent resolution on the budget may also require—

(1) a procedure under which all or certain bills and resolutions providing new budget authority or providing new spending authority described in section 401(c)(2)(C) for such fiscal year shall not be enrolled until the concurrent resolution required to be reported under section 310(a) has been agreed to, and, if a reconciliation bill or reconciliation resolution, or both, are required to be reported under section 310(c), until Congress has completed action on that bill or resolution, or both; and

(2) any other procedure which is considered appropriate to carry out the purposes of this Act.

Not later than the close of the Ninety-fifth Congress, the Committee on the Budget of each House shall report to its House on the implementation of procedures described in this subsection.

(c) Views and Estimates of Other Committees.—On or before March 15 of each year, each standing committee of the House of Representatives shall submit to the Committee on the Budget of the House, each standing committee of the Senate shall submit to the Committee on the Budget of the Senate, and the Joint Economic Committee and Joint Committee on Internal Revenue Taxation shall submit to the Committees on the Budget of both Houses—

(1) its views and estimates with respect to all matters set forth in subsection (a) which relate to matters within the respective jurisdiction or functions of such committee or joint committee; and

(2) except in the case of such joint committees, the estimate of the total amounts of new budget authority, and budget outlays resulting therefrom, to be provided or authorized in all bills and resolutions within the jurisdiction of such committee which such committee intends to be effective during the fiscal year beginning on October 1 of such year.

The Joint Economic Committee shall also submit to the Committees on the Budget of both Houses, its recommendations as to the fiscal policy appropriate to the goals of the Employment Act of 1946. Any other committee of the House or Senate may submit to the Committee on the Budget of its House, and any other joint committee of the Congress may submit to the Committees on the Budget of both Houses, its views and estimates with respect to all matters set forth in subsection (a) which relate to matters within its jurisdiction or functions.

(d) Hearings and Report.—In developing the first concurrent resolution on the budget referred to in subsection (a) for each fiscal year, the Committee on the Budget of each House shall hold hearings and shall receive testimony from Members of Congress and such appropriate representatives of Federal departments and agencies, the general public, and national organizations as the committee deems desirable. On or before April 15 of each year, the Committee on the Budget of each House shall report to its House the first concurrent resolution on the budget referred to in subsection (a) for the fiscal year beginning on October 1 of such year. The report accompanying such concurrent resolution shall include, but not be limited to—

(1) a comparison of revenues estimated by the committee with those estimated in the budget submitted by the President;

(2) a comparison of the appropriate levels of total budget outlays and total new budget authority, as set forth in such concurrent resolution, with total budget outlays estimated and total new budget authority requested in the budget submitted by the President;

(3) with respect to each major functional category, an estimate of budget outlays and an appropriate level of new budget authority for all proposed programs and for all existing programs (including renewals thereof), with the estimate and level for existing programs being divided between permanent authority and funds provided in appropriation Acts, and each such division being subdivided between controllable amounts and all other amounts;

(4) an allocation of the level of Federal revenues recommended in the concurrent resolution among the major sources of such revenues;

(5) the economic assumptions and objectives which underlie each of the matters set forth in such concurrent resolution and alternative economic assumptions and objectives which the committee considered;

(6) projections, not limited to the following, for the period of five fiscal years beginning with such fiscal year of the estimated levels of total budget outlays, total new budget outlays, total new budget authority, the estimated revenues to be received, and the estimated surplus or deficit, if any, for each fiscal year in such period, and the estimated levels of tax expenditures (the tax expenditures budget) by major functional categories;

(7) a statement of any significant changes in the proposed levels of Federal assistance to State and local governments; and

(8) information, data, and comparisons indicating the manner in which, and the basis on which, the committee determined each of the matters set forth in the concurrent resolution, and the relationship of such matters to other budget categories.

MATTERS TO BE INCLUDED IN JOINT STATEMENT OF MANAGERS; REPORTS BY COMMITTEES

Sec. 302. (a) Allocation of Totals.—The joint explanatory statement accompanying a conference report on a concurrent resolution on the budget shall include an estimated allocation, based upon such concurrent resolution as recommended in such conference report, of the appropriate levels of total budget outlays and total new budget authority among each committee of the House of Representatives and the Senate which has jurisdiction over bills and resolutions providing such new budget authority.

(b) Reports by Committees.—As soon as practicable after a concurrent resolution on the budget is agreed to—

(1) the Committee on Appropriations of each House shall, after consulting with the Committee on Appropriations of the other House, (A) subdivide among its subcommittees the allocation of budget outlays and new budget authority allocated to it in the joint explanatory statement accompanying the conference report on such concurrent resolution, and (B) further subdivide the amount with respect to each such subcommittee between controllable amounts and all other amounts; and

(2) every other committee of the House and Senate to which an allocation was made in such joint explanatory statement shall, after consulting with the committee or committees of the other House to which all or part of its allocation was made, (A) subdivide such allocation among its subcommittees or among programs over which it has jurisdiction, and (B) further subdivide the amount with respect to each subcommittee or program between controllable amounts and all other amounts.

Each such committee shall promptly report to its House the subdivisions made by it pursuant to this subsection.

(c) Subsequent Concurrent Resolutions.—In the case of a concurrent resolution on the budget referred to in section 304 or 310, the allocation under subsection (a) and the subdivisions under subsection (b) shall be required only to the extent necessary to take into account revisions made in the most recently agreed to concurrent resolution on the budget.

FIRST CONCURRENT RESOLUTION ON THE BUDGET MUST BE ADOPTED BEFORE LEGISLATION PROVIDING NEW BUDGET AUTHORITY, NEW SPENDING AUTHORITY, OR CHANGES IN REVENUES OR PUBLIC DEBT LIMIT IS CONSIDERED

Sec. 303. (a) In General.—It shall not be in order in either the House of Representatives or the Senate to consider any bill or resolution (or amendment thereto) which provides—

(1) new budget authority for a fiscal year;

(2) an increase or decrease in revenues to become effective during a fiscal year;

(3) an increase or decrease in the public debt limit to become effective during a fiscal year; or

(4) new spending authority described in section 401(c)(2)(C) to become effective during a fiscal year;

until the first concurrent resolution on the budget for such year has been agreed to pursuant to section 301.

(b) Exceptions.—Subsection (a) does not apply to any bill or resolution—

(1) providing new budget authority which first becomes available in a fiscal year following the fiscal year to which the concurrent resolution applies; or

(2) increasing or decreasing revenues which first become effective in a fiscal year following the fiscal year to which the concurrent resolution applies.

(c) Waiver in the Senate.—

(1) The committee of the Senate which reports any bill or resolution to which subsection (a) applies may at or after the time it reports such bill or resolution, report a resolution to the Senate (A) providing for the waiver of subsection (a) with respect to such bill or resolution, and (B) stating the reasons why the waiver is necessary. The resolution shall then be referred to the Committee on the Budget of the Senate. That committee shall report the resolution to the Senate within 10 days after the resolution is referred to it (not counting any day on which the Senate is not in session) beginning with the day following the day on which it is so referred, accompanied by that committee's recommendations and reasons for such recommendations with respect to the resolution. If the committee does not report the resolution within such 10-day period, it shall automatically be

discharged from further consideration of the resolution and the resolution shall be placed on the calendar.

(2) During the consideration of any such resolution, debate shall be limited to one hour, to be equally divided between, and controlled by, the majority leader and minority leader or their designees, and the time on any debatable motion or appeal shall be limited to twenty minutes, to be equally divided between, and controlled by, the mover and the manager of the resolution. In the event the manager of the resolution is in favor of any such motion or appeal, the time in opposition thereto shall be controlled by the minority leader or his designee. Such leaders, or either of them, may, from the time under their control on the passage of such resolution, allot additional time to any Senator during the consideration of any debatable motion or appeal. No amendment to the resolution is in order.

(3) If, after the Committee on the Budget has reported (or been discharged from further consideration of) the resolution, the Senate agrees to the resolution, then subsection (a) of this section shall not apply with respect to the bill or resolution to which the resolution so agreed to applies.

PERMISSIBLE REVISIONS OF CONCURRENT RESOLUTIONS OF THE BUDGET

Sec. 304. At any time after the first concurrent resolution on the budget for a fiscal year has been agreed to pursuant to section 301, and before the end of such fiscal year, the two Houses may adopt a concurrent resolution on the budget which revises the concurrent resolution on the budget for such fiscal year most recently agreed to.

PROVISIONS RELATING TO THE CONSIDERATION OF CONCURRENT RESOLUTIONS ON THE BUDGET

Sec. 305. (a) Procedure in House of Representatives After Report of Committee; Debate—

(1) When the Committee on the Budget of the House has reported any concurrent resolution on the budget, it is in order at any time after the tenth day (excluding Saturdays, Sundays, and legal holidays) following the day on which the report upon such resolution has been available to Members of the House (even though a previous motion to the same effect has been disagreed to) to move to proceed to the consideration of the concurrent resolution. The motion is highly privileged and is not debatable. An amendment to the motion is not in order, and it is not in order to move to reconsider the vote by which the motion is agreed to or disagreed to.

(2) General debate on any concurrent resolution on the budget in the House of Representatives shall be limited to not more than 10 hours, which shall be divided equally between the majority and minority parties. A motion further to limit debate is not debatable. A motion to recommit the concurrent resolution is not in order, and it is not in order to move to reconsider the vote by which the concurrent resolution is agreed to or disagreed to.

(3) Consideration of any concurrent resolution on the budget by the House of Representatives shall be in the Committee of the Whole, and the resolution shall be read for amendment under the five-minute rule in accordance with the applicable provisions of rule XXIII of the Rules of the House of Representatives. After the Committee rises and reports the resolution back to the House, the previous question shall be considered as ordered on the resolution and any amendments thereto to final passage without intervening motion; except that it shall be in order at any time prior to final passage (notwithstanding any other rule or provision of law) to adopt an amendment (or a series of amendments changing any figure or figures in the resolution as so reported to the extent necessary to achieve mathematical consistency.

(4) Debate in the House of Representatives on the conference report on any concurrent resolution on the budget shall be limited to not more than 5 hours, which shall be divided equally between the majority and minority parties. A motion further to limit debate is not debatable. A motion to recommit the conference report is not in order, and it is not in order to move to reconsider the vote by which the conference report is agreed to or disagreed to.

(5) Motions to postpone, made with respect to the consideration of any concurrent resolution on the budget, and motions to proceed to the consideration of other business, shall be decided without debate.

(6) Appeals from the decisions of the Chair relating to the application of the Rules of the House of Representatives to the procedure relating to any concurrent resolution on the budget shall be decided without debate.

(b) Procedure in Senate After Report of Committee; Debate; Amendments—

(1) Debate in the Senate on any concurrent resolution on the budget, and all amendments thereto and debatable motions and appeals in connection therewith, shall be limited to not more than 50 hours, except that, with respect to the second required concurrent resolution referred to in section 310(a), all such debate shall be limited to not more than 15 hours. The time shall be equally divided between, and controlled by, the majority leader and the minority leader of their designees.

(2) Debate in the Senate on any amendment to a concurrent resolution on the

budget shall be limited to 2 hours, to be equally divided between, and controlled by, the mover and the manager of the concurrent resolution, and debate on any amendment to an amendment, debatable motion, or appeal shall be limited to 1 hour, to be equally divided between, and controlled by, the mover and the manager of the concurrent resolution, except that in the event the manager of the concurrent resolution is in favor of any such amendment, motion, or appeal, the time in opposition thereto shall be controlled by the minority leader or his designee. No amendment that is not germane to the provisions of such concurrent resolution shall be received. Such leaders, or either of them, may, from the time under their control on the passage of the concurrent resolution, allot additional time to any Senator during the consideration of any amendment, debatable motion, or appeal.

(3) A motion to further limit debate is not debatable. A motion to recommit (except a motion to recommit with instructions to report back within a specified number of days, not to exceed 3, not counting any day on which the Senate is not in session) is not in order. Debate on any such motion to recommit shall be limited to 1 hour, to be equally divided between, and controlled by, the mover and the manager of the concurrent resolution.

(4) Notwithstanding any other rule, an amendment, or series of amendments, to a concurrent resolution on the budget proposed in the Senate shall always be in order if such amendment or series of amendments proposes to change any figure or figures then contained in such concurrent resolution so as to make such concurrent resolution mathematically consistent or so as to maintain such consistency.

(c) Action on Conference Reports in the Senate—

(1) The conference report on any concurrent resolution on the budget shall be in order in the Senate at any time after the third day (excluding Saturdays, Sundays, and legal holidays) following the day on which such a conference report is reported and is available to Members of the Senate. A motion to proceed to the consideration of the conference report may be made even though a previous motion to the same effect has been disagreed to.

(2) During the consideration in the Senate of the conference report on any concurrent resolution on the budget, debate shall be limited to 10 hours, to be equally divided between, and controlled by, the majority leader and minority leader or their designees. Debate on any debatable motion or appeal related to the conference report shall be limited to 1 hour, to be equally divided between, and controlled by, the mover and the manager of the conference report.

(3) Should the conference report be defeated, debate on any request for a new conference and the appointment of conferees shall be limited to 1 hour, to be equally divided between, and controlled by, the manager of the conference report and the minority leader or his designee, and should any motion be made to instruct the conferees before the conferees are named, debate on such motion shall be limited to one-half hour, to be equally divided between, and controlled by, the mover and the manager of the conference report. Debate on any amendment to any such instructions shall be limited to 20 minutes, to be equally divided between and controlled by the mover and the manager of the conference report. In all cases when the manager of the conference report is in favor of any motion, appeal, or amendment, the time in opposition shall be under the control of the minority leader or his designee.

(4) In any case in which there are amendments in disagreement, time on each amendment shall be limited to 30 minutes, to be equally divided between, and controlled by, the manager of the conference report and the minority leader or his designee. No amendment that is not germane to the provisions of such amendments shall be received.

(d) Required Action by Conference Committee.—If, at the end of 7 days (excluding Saturdays, Sundays, and legal holidays) after the conferees of both Houses have been appointed to a committee of conference on a concurrent resolution on the budget, the conferees are unable to reach agreement with respect to all matters in disagreement between the two Houses, then the conferees shall submit to the respective Houses, on the first day thereafter on which their House is in session—

(1) a conference report recommending those matters on which they have agreed and reporting in disagreement those matters on which they have agreed: or

(2) a conference report in disagreement, if the matter in disagreement is an amendment which strikes out the entire text of the concurrent resolution and inserts a substitute text.

(e) Concurrent Resolution Must Be Consistent in the Senate—It shall not be in order in the Senate to vote on the question of agreeing to—

(1) a concurrent resolution on the budget unless the figures then contained in such resolution are mathematically consistent; or

(2) a conference report on a concurrent resolution on the budget unless the figures contained in such resolution, as recommended in such conference report, are mathematically consistent.

LEGISLATION DEALING WITH CONGRESSIONAL BUDGET MUST BE HANDLED BY BUDGET COMMITTEES

Sec. 306. No bill or resolution, and no amendment to any bill or resolution, dealing with any matter which is within the jurisdiction of the Committee on the Budget of either House shall be considered in that House unless it is a bill or resolution which has been reported by the Committee on the Budget of that House (or from the consideration of which such committee has been discharged) or unless it is an amendment to such a bill or resolution.

HOUSE COMMITTEE ACTION ON ALL APPROPRIATION BILLS TO BE COMPLETED BEFORE FIRST APPROPRIATION BILL IS REPORTED

Sec. 307. Prior to reporting the first regular appropriation bill for each fiscal year, the Committee on Appropriations of the House of Representatives shall, to the extent practicable, complete subcommittee markup and full committee action on all regular appropriation bills for that year and submit to the House a summary report comparing the committee's recommendations with the appropriate levels of budget outlays and new budget authority as set forth in the most recently agreed to concurrent resolution on the budget for that year.

REPORTS, SUMMARIES, AND PROJECTIONS OF CONGRESSIONAL BUDGET ACTIONS

Sec. 308. (a) Reports on Legislation Providing New Budget Authority or Tax Expenditures.—Whenever a committee of either House reports a bill or resolution to its House providing new budget authority (other than continuing appropriations) or new or increased tax expenditures for a fiscal year, the report accompanying that bill or resolution shall contain a statement, prepared after consultation with the Director of the Congressional Budget Office, detailing—

    (1) in the case of a bill of resolution providing new budget authority—

        (A) how the new budget authority provided in that bill or resolution compares with the new budget authority set forth in the most recently agreed to concurrent resolution on the budget for such fiscal year and the reports submitted under section 202;

        (B) a projection for the period of 5 fiscal years beginning with such fiscal year of budget outlays, associated with the budget authority provided in that bill or resolution, in each fiscal year in such period; and

(C) the new budget authority, and budget outlays resulting therefrom, provided by that bill or resolution for financial assistance to State and local government; and

(2) in the case of a bill of resolution providing new or increased tax expenditures

(A) how the new or increased tax expenditures provided in that bill or resolution will affect the levels of tax expenditures under existing law as set forth in the report accompanying the first concurrent resolution on the budget for such fiscal year, or, if a report accompanying a subsequently agreed to concurrent resolution for such year sets forth such levels, then as set forth in that report; and

(B) a projection for the period of 5 fiscal years beginning with such fiscal year of the tax expenditures which will result from that bill or resolution in each fiscal year in such period. No projection shall be required for a fiscal year under paragraph (1)(B) or (2)(B) if the committee determines that a projection for that fiscal year is impracticable and states in its report the reason for such impracticability.

(b) Up-to-Date Tabulation of Congressional Budget Actions.—The Director of the Congressional Budget Office shall issue periodic reports detailing and tabulating the progress of congressional action on bills and resolutions providing new budget authority and changing revenues and the public debt limit for a fiscal year. Such reports shall include, but are not limited to—

(1) an up-to-date tabulation comparing the new budget authority for such fiscal year in bills and resolutions on which Congress has completed action and estimated outlays, associated with such new budget authority, during such fiscal year to the new budget authority and estimated outlays set forth in the most recently agreed to concurrent resolution on the budget for such fiscal year and the reports submitted under section 302;

(2) an up-to-date status report on all bills and resolutions providing new budget authority and changing revenues and the public debt limit for such fiscal year in both Houses;

(3) an up-to-date comparison of the appropriate level of revenues contained in the most recently agreed to concurrent resolution on the budget for such fiscal year with the latest estimate of revenues for such year (including new revenues anticipated during such year under bills and resolutions on which the Congress has completed action); and

(4) an up-to-date comparison of the appropriate level of the public debt

contained in the most recently agreed to concurrent resolution on the budget for such fiscal year with the latest estimate of the public debt during such fiscal year.

(c) Five-Year Projection of Congressional Budget Action.—As soon as practicable after the beginning of each fiscal year, the Director of the Congressional Budget Office shall issue a report projecting for the period of 5 fiscal years beginning with such fiscal year—

> (1) total new budget authority and total budget outlays for each fiscal year in such period;
>
> (2) revenues to be received and the major sources thereof, and the surplus or deficit, if any, for each fiscal year in such period; and
>
> (3) tax expenditures for each fiscal year in such period.

COMPLETION OF ACTION ON BILLS PROVIDING NEW BUDGET AUTHORITY AND CERTAIN NEW SPENDING AUTHORITY

Sec. 309. Except as otherwise provided pursuant to this title, not later than the seventh day after Labor Day of each year, the Congress shall complete action on all bills and resolutions—

> (1) providing new budget authority for the fiscal year beginning on October 1 of such year, other than supplemental, deficiency, and continuing appropriation bills and resolutions, and other than the reconciliation bill for such year, if required to be reported under section 310(c); and
>
> (2) providing new spending authority described in section 401(c)(2)(C) which is to become effective during such fiscal year.

Paragraph (1) shall not apply to any bill or resolution if legislation authorizing the enactment of new budget authority to be provided in such bill or resolution has not been timely enacted.

SECOND REQUIRED CONCURRENT RESOLUTION AND RECONCILIATION PROCESS

Sec. 310.(a) Reporting of Concurrent Resolution.—The Committee on the Budget of each House shall report to its House a concurrent resolution on the budget which reaffirms or revises the concurrent resolution on the budget most recently agreed to with respect to the fiscal year beginning on October 1 of such year. Any such concurrent resolution on the budget shall also, to the extent necessary—

(1) specify the total amount by which—

    (A) new budget authority for such fiscal year;

    (B) budget authority initially provided for prior fiscal years; and

    (C) new spending authority described in section 401(c)(2)(C) which is to become effective during such fiscal year, contained in laws, bills, and resolutions within the jurisdiction of a committee, is to be changed and direct that committee to determine and recommend changes to accomplish a change of such total amount;

(2) specify the total amount by which revenues are to be changed and direct that the committees having jurisdiction to determine and recommend changes in the revenue laws, bills, and resolutions to accomplish a change of such total amount;

(3) specify the amount by which the statutory limit on the public debt is to be changed and direct the committees having jurisdiction to recommend such change; or

(4) specify and direct any combination of the matters described in paragraphs (1), (2), and (3).

    Any such concurrent resolution may be reported, and the report accompanying it may be filed, in either House notwithstanding that that House is not in session on the day on which such concurrent resolution is reported.

  (b) Completion of Action on Concurrent Resolution.—Not later than September 15 of each year, the Congress shall complete action on the concurrent resolution on the budget referred to in subsection (a).

  (c) Reconciliation Process.—If a concurrent resolution is agreed to in accordance with subsection (a) containing directions to one or more committees to determine and recommend changes in laws, bills, or resolutions, and—

(1) only one committee of the House or the Senate is directed to determine and recommend changes, that committee shall promptly make such determination and recommendations and report to its House a reconciliation bill or reconciliation resolution, or both, containing such recommendations; or

(2) more than one committee of the House or the Senate is directed to determine and recommend changes, each such committee so directed shall promptly make such determination and recommendations, whether such changes are to be contained in a reconciliation bill or reconciliation resolution, and submit such recommendations to the Committee on the Budget of its House, which upon receiving all such recommendations,

shall report to its House a reconciliation bill or reconciliation resolution, or both, carrying out all such recommendations without any substantive revision.

For purposes of this subsection, a reconciliation resolution is a concurrent resolution directing the Clerk of the House of Representatives or the Secretary of the Senate, as the case may be, to make specified changes in bills and resolutions which have not been enrolled.

(d) Completion of Reconciliation Process.—Congress shall complete action on any reconciliation bill or reconciliation resolution reported under subsection (c) not later than September 25 of each year.

(e) Procedure in the Senate.—

   (1) Except as provided in paragraph (2), the provisions of section 305 for the consideration in the Senate of concurrent resolutions on the budget and conference reports thereon shall also apply to the consideration in the Senate of reconciliation bills and reconciliation resolutions reported under subsection (c) and conference reports thereon.

   (2) Debate in the Senate on any reconciliation bill or resolution reported under subsection (c), and all amendments thereto and debatable motions and appeals in connection therewith, shall be limited to not more than 20 hours.

(f) Congress May Not Adjourn Until Action Is Completed.—It shall not be in order in either the House of Representatives or the Senate to consider any resolution providing for the adjournment sine die of either House unless action has been completed on the concurrent resolution on the budget required to be reported under subsection (a) for the fiscal year beginning on October 1 of such year, and, if a reconciliation bill or resolution, or both, is required to be reported under subsection (c) for such fiscal year, unless the Congress has completed action on that bill or resolution, or both.

NEW BUDGET AUTHORITY, NEW SPENDING AUTHORITY AND REVENUE LEGISLATION MUST BE WITHIN APPROPRIATE LEVELS

Sec. 311.(a) Legislation Subject to Point of Order.—After the Congress has completed action on the concurrent resolution on the budget required to be reported under section 310(a) for a fiscal year and, if a reconciliation bill or resolution, or both, for such fiscal year are required to be reported under section 310(c), after that bill has been enacted into law or that resolution has been agreed to, it shall not be in order in either the House of Representatives or the Senate to consider any bill, resolution, or amendment providing additional new budget authority for such fiscal year, providing new spending authority described in section 401(c)(2)(C) to become effective during the fiscal year, or reducing revenues for such fiscal year, or any conference report on any such bill or resolution, if—

(1) the enactment of such bill or resolution as reported;

(2) the adoption and enactment of such amenement; or

(3) the enactment of such bill or resolution in the form recommended in such conference report;

would cause the appropriate level of total new budget authority or total budget outlays set forth in the most recently agreed to concurrent resolution on the budget for such fiscal year to be exceeded, or would cause revenues to be less than the appropriate level of revenues set forth in such concurrent resolution.

(b) Determination of Outlays and Revenues.—For purposes of subsection (a), the budget outlays to be made during a fiscal year and revenues to be received during a fiscal year shall be determined on the basis of estimates made by the Committee on the Budget of the House of Representatives or the Senate, as the case may be.

. . . .

TITLE V—CHANGE OF FISCAL YEAR

FISCAL YEAR TO BEGIN OCTOBER 1

Sec. 501. Section 237 of the Revised Statutes (32 U.S.C. 1020) is amended to read as follows:

"Sec. 237.(a) The fiscal year of the Treasury of the United States, in all matters of accounts, receipts, expenditures, estimates, and appropriations—

"(1) shall, through June 30, 1976, commence on July 1 of each year and end on June 30 of the following year; and

"(2) shall, beginning on October 1, 1976, commence on October 1 of each year and end on September 30 of the following year.

"(b) All accounts of receipts and expenditures required by law to be published annually shall be prepared and published for each fiscal year as established by subsection (a)."

. . . .

TITLE VII—PROGRAM REVIEW AND EVALUATION

REVIEW AND EVALUATION BY STANDING COMMITTEES

Sec. 701. Section 136(a) of the Legislative Reorganization Act of 1946 (2 U.S.C. 190d) is amended by adding at the end thereof the following new sentences: "Such committees may carry out the required analysis, appraisal, and evaluation themselves, or by contract, or may require a Government agency to do so and furnish a report thereon to the Congress. Such committees may rely on such techniques as pilot testing, analysis of costs in comparison with benefits, or provision for evaluation after a defined period of time."

REVIEW AND EVALUATION BY THE COMPTROLLER GENERAL

Sec. 702.(a) Section 204 of the Legislative Reorganization Act of 1970 (31 U.S.C. 1154) is amended to read as follows:

"REVIEW AND EVALUATION

"Sec. 204.(a) The Comptroller General shall review and evaluate the results of Government programs and activities carried on under existing law when ordered by either House of Congress, or upon his own initiative, or when requested by any committee of the House of Representatives or the Senate, or any joint committee of the two Houses, having jurisdiction over such programs and activities.

"(b) The Comptroller General, upon request of any committee of either House or any joint committee of the two Houses, shall—

"(1) assist such committee or joint committee in developing a statement of legislative objectives and goals and methods for assessing and reporting actual program performance in relation to such legislative objectives and goals. Such statements shall include, but are not limited to, recommendations as to methods of assessment, information to be reported, responsibility for reporting, frequency of reports, and feasibility of pilot testing; and

"(2) assist such committee or joint committee in analyzing and assessing program reviews or evaluation studies prepared by and for any Federal agency.

Upon request of any Member of either House, the Comptroller General shall furnish to such Member a copy of any statement or other material compiled in carrying out paragraphs (1) and (2) which has been released by the committee or joint committee for which it was compiled.

"(c) The Comptroller General shall develop and recommend to the Congress methods for review and evaluation of Government programs and activities carried on under existing law.

"(d) In carrying out his responsibilities under this section, the Comptroller General is authorized to establish an Office of Program Review and Evaluation within the General Accounting Office. The Comptroller General is authorized to employ not to exceed ten experts on a permanent, temporary, or intermittent basis and to obtain services as authorized by section 3109 of title 5, United States Code, but in either case at a rate (or the daily equivalent) for individuals not to exceed that prescribed, from time to time, for level V of the Executive Schedule under section 5316 of title 5. United States Code.

"(e) The Comptroller General shall include in his annual report to the Congress a review of his activities under this section, including his recommendations of methods for review and evaluation of Government programs and activities under subsection (c)."

(b) Item 204 in the table of contents of such Act is amended to read as follows: "Sec. 204. Review and evaluation."

CONTINUING STUDY OF ADDITIONAL BUDGET REFORM PROPOSALS

Sec. 703. (a) The Committees on the Budget of the House of Representatives and the Senate shall study on a continuing basis proposals designed to improve and facilitate methods of congressional budget-making. The proposals to be studied shall include, but are not limited to, proposals for—

(1) improving the information base required for determining the effectiveness of new programs by such means as pilot testing, survey research, and other experimental and analytical techniques;

(2) improving analytical and systematic evaluation of the effectiveness of existing programs;

(3) establishing maximum and minimum time limitations for program authorization; and

(4) developing techniques of human resource accounting and other means of providing noneconomic as well as economic evaluation measures.

(b) The Committee on the Budget of each House shall, from time to time, report to its House the results of the study carried on by it under subsection (a), together with its recommendations.

(c) Nothing in this section shall preclude studies to improve the budgetary process by any other committee of the House of Representatives or the Senate or any joint committee of the Congress.

. . . .

TITLE X—IMPOUNDMENT CONTROL

Part A—General Provisions

DISCLAIMER

Sec. 1001. Nothing contained in this Act, or in any amendments made by this Act, shall be construed as—

(1) asserting or conceding the constitutional powers or limitations of either the Congress or the President;

(2) ratifying or approving any impoundment heretofore or hereafter executed or approved by the President or any other Federal officer or employee, except insofar as pursuant to statutory authorization then in effect;

(3) affecting in any way the claims or defenses of any party to litigation concerning any impoundment; or

(4) superseding any provision of law which requires the obligation of budget authority or the making of outlays thereunder.

AMENDMENT TO ANTIDEFICIENCY ACT

Sec. 1002. Section 3679(c)(2) of the Revised Statutes, as amended (31 U.S.C. 665), is amended to read as follows:

"(2) In apportioning any appropriation, reserves may be established solely to provide for contingencies, or to effect savings whenever savings are made possible by or through changes in requirements or greater efficiency of operations. Whenever it is determined by an officer designated in subsection (d) of this section to make apportionments and reapportionments that any amount so reserved will not be required to carry out the full objectives and scope of the appropriation concerned, he shall recommend the rescission of such amount in the manner provided in the Budget and Accounting Act, 1921, for estimates of appropriations. Except as specifically provided by particular appropriations Acts or other laws, no reserves shall be established other than as authorized by this subsection. Reserves established pursuant to this subsection shall be reported to the Congress in accordance with the Impoundment Control Act of 1974."

REPEAL OF EXISTING IMPOUNDMENT REPORTING PROVISION

Sec. 1003. Section 203 of the Budget and Accounting Procedures Act of 1950 is repealed.

Part B—Congressional Consideration of Proposed Rescissions, Reservations, and Deferrals of Budget Authority

DEFINITIONS

Sec. 1011. For purposes of this part—

(1) "deferral of budget authority" includes—

   (A) withholding or delaying the obligation or expenditure of budget authority (whether by establishing reserves or otherwise) provided for projects or activities; or

   (B) any other type of Executive action or inaction which effectively precludes the obligation or expenditure of budget authority, including authority to obligate by contract in advance of appropriations as specifically authorized by law;

(2) "Comptroller General" means the Comptroller General of the United States;

(3) "rescission bill" means a bill or joint resolution which only rescinds, in whole or in part, budget authority proposed to be rescinded in a special message transmitted by the President under section 1012, and upon which the Congress completes action before the end of the first period of 45 calendar days of continuous session of the Congress after the date on which the President's message is received by the Congress;

(4) "impoundment resolution" means a resolution of the House of Representatives or the Senate which only expresses its disapproval of a proposed deferral of budget authority set forth in a special message transmitted by the President under section 1013; and

(5) continuity of a session of the Congress shall be considered as broken only by an adjournment of the Congress sine die, and the days on which either House is not in session because of an adjournment of more than 3 days to a day certain shall be excluded in the computation of the 45-day period referred to in paragraph (3) of this section and in section 1012, and the

25-day periods referred to in sections 1016 and 1017(b)(1). If a special message is transmitted under section 1012 during any Congress and the last session of such Congress adjourns sine die before the expiration of 45 calendar days of continuous session (or a special message is so transmitted after the last session of the Congress adjourns sine die), the message shall be deemed to have been retransmitted on the first day of the succeeding Congress and the 45-day period referred to in paragraph (3) of this section and in section 1012 (with respect to such message) shall commence on the day after such first day.

RESCISSION OF BUDGET AUTHORITY

Sec. 1012. (a) Transmittal of Special Message.—Whenever the President determines that all or part of any budget authority will not be required to carry out the full objectives or scope of programs for which it is provided or that such budget authority should be rescinded for fiscal policy or other reasons (including the termination of authorized projects or activities for which budget authority has been provided), or whenever all or part of budget authority provided for only one fiscal year is to be reserved from obligation for such fiscal year, the President shall transmit to both Houses of Congress a special message specifying—

(1) the amount of budget authority which he proposes to be rescinded or which is to be so reserved;

(2) any account, department, or establishment of the Government to which such budget authority is available for obligation, and the specific project or governmental functions involved;

(3) the reasons why the budget authority should be rescinded or is to be so reserved;

(4) to the maximum extent practicable, the estimated fiscal, economic, and budgetary effect of the proposed rescission or of the reservation; and

(5) all facts, circumstances, and considerations relating to or bearing upon the proposed rescission or the reservation and the decision to effect the proposed rescission or the reservation, and to the maximum extent practicable, the estimated effect of the proposed rescission or the reservation upon the objects, purposes, and programs for which the budget authority is provided.

(b) Requirement to Make Available for Obligation.—Any amount of budget authority proposed to be rescinded or that is to be reserved as set forth in such special message shall be made available for obligation unless, within the prescribed 45-day period, the Congress has completed action on a rescission bill rescinding all or part of the amount proposed to be rescinded or that is to be reserved.

DISAPPROVAL OF PROPOSED DEFERRALS OF BUDGET AUTHORITY

Sec. 1013. (a) Transmittal of Special Message.—Whenever the President, the Director of the Office of Management and Budget, the head of any department or agency of the United States, or any officer or employee of the United States proposes to defer any budget authority provided for a specific purpose or project, the President shall transmit to the House of Representatives and the Senate a special message specifying—

(1) the amount of the budget authority proposed to be deferred;

(2) any account, department, or establishment of the Government to which such budget authority is available for obligation and the specific projects or governmental functions involved;

(3) the period of time during which the budget authority is proposed to be deferred;

(4) the reasons for the proposed deferral, including any legal authority invoked by him to justify the proposed deferral;

(5) to the maximum extent practicable, the estimated fiscal, economic, and budgetary effect of the proposed deferral; and

(6) all facts, circumstances, and considerations relating to or bearing upon the proposed deferral and the decision to effect the proposed deferral, including an analysis of such facts, circumstances, and considerations in terms of their application to any legal authority and specific elements of legal authority invoked by him to justify such proposed deferral, and to the maximum extent practicable, the estimated effect of the proposed deferral upon the objects, purposes, and programs for which the budget authority is provided.

A special message may include one or more proposed deferrals of budget authority. A deferral may not be proposed for any period of time extending beyond the end of the fiscal year in which the special message proposing the deferral is transmitted to the House and the Senate.

(b) Requirement to Make Available for Obligation.—Any amount of budget authority proposed to be deferred, as set forth in a special message transmitted under subsection (a), shall be made available for obligation if either House of Congress passes an impoundment resolution disapproving such proposed deferral.

(c) Exception.—The provisions of this section do not apply to any budget authority proposed to be rescinded or that is to be reserved as set forth in a special message required to be transmitted under section 1012.

TRANSMISSION OF MESSAGES; PUBLICATION

Sec. 1014. (a) Delivery to House and Senate.—Each special message transmitted under section 1012 or 1013 shall be transmitted to the House of Representatives and the Senate on the same day, and shall be delivered to the Clerk of the House of Representatives if the House is not in session, and to the Secretary of the Senate if the Senate is not in session. Each special message so transmitted shall be referred to the appropriate committee of the House of Representatives and the Senate. Each such message shall be printed as a document of each House.

(b) Delivery to Comptroller General.—A copy of each special message transmitted under section 1012 or 1013 shall be transmitted to the Comptroller General on the same day it is transmitted to the House of Representatives and the Senate. In order to assist the Congress in the exercise of its functions under sections 1012 and 1013, the Comptroller General shall review each such message and inform the House of Representatives and the Senate as promptly as practicable with respect to—

(1) in the case of a special message transmitted under section 1012, the facts surrounding the proposed rescission or the reservation of budget authority (including the probable effects thereof); and

(2) in the case of a special message transmitted under section 1013, (A) the facts surrounding each proposed deferral of budget authority (including the probable effects thereof) and (B) whether or not (or to what extent), in his judgment, such proposed deferral is in accordance with existing statutory authority.

(c) Transmission of Supplementary Messages.—If any information contained in a special message transmitted under section 1012 or 1013 is subsequently revised, the President shall transmit to both Houses of Congress and the Comptroller General a supplementary message stating and explaining such revision. Any such supplementary message shall be delivered, referred, and printed as provided in subsection (a). The Comptroller General shall promptly notify the House of Representatives and the Senate of any changes in the information submitted by him under subsection (b) which may be necessitated by such revision.

(d) Printing in Federal Register.—Any special message transmitted under section 1012 or 1013, and any supplementary message transmitted under subsection (c), shall be printed in the first issue of the Federal Register published after such transmittal.

(e) Cumulative Reports of Proposed Rescissions, Reservations, and Deferrals of Budget Authority.—

(1) The President shall submit a report to the House of Representatives and the Senate not later than the 10th day of each month during a fiscal year,

listing all budget authority for that fiscal year with respect to which, as of the first day of such month—

(A) he has transmitted a special message under section 1012 with respect to a proposed rescission or a reservation; and

(B) he has transmitted a special message under section 1013 proposing a deferral.

Such report shall also contain, with respect to each such proposed rescission or deferral, or each such reservation, the information required to be submitted in the special message with respect thereto under section 1012 or 1013.

(2) Each report submitted under paragraph (1) shall be printed in the first issue of the Federal Register published after its submission.

REPORTS BY COMPTROLLER GENERAL

Sec. 1015. (a) Failure To Transmit Special Message.—If the Comptroller General finds that the President, the Director of the Office of Management and Budget, the head of any department or agency of the United States, or any other officer or employee of the United States—

(1) is to establish a reserve or proposes to defer budget authority with respect to which the President is required to transmit a special message under section 1012 or 1013; or

(2) has ordered, permitted, or approved the establishment of such a reserve or a deferral of budget authority;

and that the President has failed to transmit a special message with respect to such reserve or deferral, the Comptroller General shall make a report on such reserve or deferral and any available information concerning it to both Houses of Congress. The provisions of this part shall apply with respect to such reserve or deferral in the same manner and with the same effect as if such report of the Comptroller General were a special message transmitted by the President under section 1012 or 1013, and, for purposes of this part, such report shall be considered a special message transmitted under section 1012 or 1013.

(b) Incorrect Classification of Special Message.—If the President has transmitted a special message to both Houses of Congress in accordance with section 1012 or 1013, and the Comptroller General believes that the President so transmitted the special message in accordance with one of those sections when the special message should have been transmitted in accordance with the other of those sections, the Comptroller General shall make a report to both Houses of the Congress setting forth his reasons.

SUITS BY COMPTROLLER GENERAL

Sec. 1016. If, under section 1012(b) or 1013(b), budget authority is required to be made available for obligation and such budget authority is not made available for obligation, the Comptroller General is hereby expressly empowered, through attorneys of his own selection, to bring a civil action in the United States District Court for the District of Columbia to require such budget authority to be made available for obligation, and such court is hereby expressly empowered to enter in such civil action, against any department, agency, officer, or employee of the United States, any decree, judgment, or order which may be necessary or appropriate to make such budget authority available for obligation. The courts shall give precedence to civil actions brought under this section, and to appeals and writs from decisions in such actions, over all other civil actions, appeals, and writs. No civil action shall be brought by the Comptroller General under this section until the expiration of 25 calendar days of continuous session of the Congress following the date on which an explanatory statement by the Comptroller General of the circumstances giving rise to the action contemplated has been filed with the Speaker of the House of Representatives and the President of the Senate.

PROCEDURE IN HOUSE AND SENATE

Sec. 1017. (a) Referral.—Any rescission bill introduced with respect to a special message or impoundment resolution introduced with respect to a proposed deferral of budget authority shall be referred to the appropriate committee of the House of Representatives or the Senate, as the case may be.

(b) Discharge of Committee.—

(1) If the committee to which a rescission bill or impoundment resolution has been referred has not reported it at the end of 25 calendar days of continuous session of the Congress after its introduction, it is in order to move either to discharge the committee from further consideration of the bill or resolution or to discharge the committee from further consideration of any other rescission bill with respect to the same special message or impoundment resolution with respect to the same proposed deferral, as the case may be, which has been referred to the committee.

(2) A motion to discharge may be made only by an individual favoring the bill or resolution, may be made only if supported by one-fifth of the Members of the House involved (a quorum being present), and is highly privileged in the House and privileged in the Senate (except that it may not be made after the committee has reported a bill or resolution with respect to the same special message or the same proposed deferral, as the case may be); and debate thereon shall be limited to not more than 1 hour, the time to

be divided in the House equally between those favoring and those opposing the bill or resolution, and to be divided in the Senate equally between, and controlled by, the majority leader and the minority leader or
their designees. An amendment to the motion is not in order, and it is not
in order to move to reconsider the vote by which the motion is agreed to or
disagreed to.

(c) Floor Consideration in the House.—

(1) When the committee of the House of Representatives has reported, or has
been discharged from further consideration of, a rescission bill or impoundment resolution, it shall at any time thereafter be in order (even
though a previous motion to the same effect has been disagreed to) to
move to proceed to the consideration of the bill or resolution. The motion
shall be highly privileged and not debatable. An amendment to the
motion shall not be in order, nor shall it be in order to move to reconsider
the vote by which the motion is agreed to or disagreed to.

(2) Debate on a rescission bill or impoundment resolution shall be limited to
not more than 2 hours, which shall be divided equally between those
favoring and those opposing the bill or resolution. A motion further to
limit debate shall not be debatable. In the case of an impoundment
resolution, no amendment to, or motion to recommit, the resolution shall
be in order. It shall not be in order to move to reconsider the vote by
which a recission bill or impoundment resolution is agreed to or disagreed
to.

(3) Motions to postpone, made with respect to the consideration of a rescission bill or impoundment resolution, and motions to proceed to the consideration of other business, shall be decided without debate.

(4) All appeals from the decisions of the Chair relating to the application of
the Rules of the House of Representatives to the procedure relating to any
rescission bill or impoundment resolution shall be decided without debate.

(5) Except to the extent specifically provided in the preceding provisions of
this subsection, consideration of any rescission bill or impoundment
resolution and amendments thereto (or any conference report thereon)
shall be governed by the Rules of the House of Representatives applicable to other bills and resolutions, amendments, and conference reports
in similar circumstances.

(d) Floor Consideration in the Senate.—

(1) Debate in the Senate on any rescission bill or impoundment resolution,
and all amendments thereto (in the case of a rescission bill) and debat-

able motions and appeals in connection therewith, shall be limited to not more than 10 hours. The time shall be equally divided between, and controlled by, the majority leader and the minority leader or their designees.

(2) Debate in the Senate on any amendment to a rescission bill shall be limited to 2 hours, to be equally divided between, and controlled by, the mover and the manager of the bill. Debate on any amendment to an amendment, to such a bill, and debate on any debatable motion or appeal in connection with such a bill or an impoundment resolution shall be limited to 1 hour, to be equally divided between, and controlled by, the mover and the manager of the bill or resolution, except that in the event the manager of the bill or resolution is in favor of any such amendment, motion, or appeal, the time in opposition thereto, shall be controlled by the minority leader or his designee. No amendment that is not germane to the provisions of a rescission bill shall be received. Such leaders, or either of them, may, from time under their control on the passage of a rescission bill or impoundment resolution, allot additional time to any Senator during the consideration of any amendment, debatable motion, or appeal.

(3) A motion to further limit debate is not debatable. In the case of a rescission bill, a motion to recommit (except a motion to recommit with instructions to report back within a specified number of days, not to exceed 3, not counting any day on which the Senate is not in session) is not in order. Debate on any such motion to recommit shall be limited to one hour, to be equally divided between, and controlled by, the mover and the manager of the concurrent resolution. In the case of an impoundment resolution, no amendment or motion to recommit is in order.

(4) The conference report on any rescission bill shall be in order in the Senate at any time after the third day (excluding Saturdays, Sundays, and legal holidays) following the day on which such a conference report is reported and is available to Members of the Senate. A motion to proceed to the consideration of the conference report may be made even though a previous motion to the same effect has been disagreed to.

(5) During the consideration in the Senate of the conference report on any rescission bill, debate shall be limited to 2 hours, to be equally divided between, and controlled by, the majority leader and minority leader or their designees. Debate on any debatable motion or appeal related to the conference report shall be limited to 30 minutes, to be equally divided between, and controlled by, the mover and the manager of the conference report.

(6) Should the conference report be defeated, debate on any request for a new

conference and the appointment of conferees shall be limited to one hour, to be equally divided between, and controlled by, the manager of the conference report and the minority leader or his designee, and should any motion be made to instruct the conferees before the conferees are named, debate on such motion shall be limited to 30 minutes, to be equally divided between, and controlled by, the mover and the manager of the conference report. Debate on any amendment to any such instructions shall be limited to 20 minutes, to be equally divided between, and controlled by, the mover and the manager of the conference report. In all cases when the manager of the conference report is in favor of any motion, appeal, or amendment, the time in opposition shall be under the control of the minority leader or his designee.

(7) In any case in which there are amendments in disagreement, time on each amendment shall be limited to 30 minutes, to be equally divided between, and controlled by, the manager of the conference report and the minority leader or his designee. No amendment that is not germane to the provisions of such amendments shall be received.

Approved July 12, 1974.

5.a. President Jimmy Carter's ZBB Memorandum for the Heads of Executive Departments and Agencies (1977)

During the campaign, I pledged that immediately after the inauguration I would issue an order establishing zero-base budgeting throughout the Federal Government. This pledge was made because of the success of the zero-base budget system adopted by the State of Georgia under my direction as Governor.

A zero-base budgeting system permits a detailed analysis and justification of budget requests by an evaluation of the importance of each operation performed.

An effective zero-base budgeting system will benefit the Federal Government in several ways. It will

- Focus the budget process on a comprehensive analysis of objectives and needs.
- Combine planning and budgeting into a single process.
- Cause managers to evaluate in detail the cost-effectiveness of their operations.
- Expand management participation in planning and budgeting at all levels of the Federal Government.

The Director of the Office of Management and Budget will review the Federal budget process for the preparation, analysis, and justification of budget estimates and will revise those procedures to incorporate the appropriate techniques of the zero-base budgeting system. He will develop a plan for applying the zero-base budgeting concept to preparation, analysis, and justifications of the budget estimates of each department and agency of the Executive Branch.

I ask each of you to develop a zero-base system within your agency in accordance with instructions to be issued by the Office of Management and Budget. The Fiscal Year 1979 budget will be prepared using this system.

By working together under a zero-base budgeting system, we can reduce costs and make the Federal Government more efficient and effective.

Jimmy Carter

Press Release from the White House, Washington, D.C. (February 14, 1977).

5.b.   Office of Management and Budget Bulletin No. 77–9 on Zero Based Budgeting (1977)

To the Heads of Executive Departments and Establishments
Subject: Zero-Base Budgeting

1. PURPOSE.   The President, in a memorandum of February 14, 1977 (Attachment), asked each agency head to develop a zero-base budgeting system to be used in the preparation of the 1979 Budget. In accordance with the President's direction, these instructions provide guidance on the use of zero-base budgeting techniques for the preparation and justification of 1979 budget requests within each agency. *Separate instructions will be issued in OMB Circular No. A–11 to advise agencies of budget materials to be submitted to OMB.* The instructions in this Bulletin lay the foundation for agency budget submissions in September in accordance with Circular No. A–11.

2. COVERAGE.   These instructions apply to all agencies in the executive branch whose budgets are subject to Presidential review (see OMB Circular No. A–11, section 11.1). These concepts and guidelines are a framework within which each agency should develop necessary procedures to meet its individual requirements. Agencies should insure that the fundamental characteristics of zero-base budgeting are retained. Agencies excluded from the coverage of this bulletin are encouraged to develop zero-base budgeting procedures.

3. DEFINITION OF TERMS.   a. *Decision unit.* The program or organizational entity for which budgets are prepared and for which a manager makes significant decisions on the amount of spending and the scope or quality of work to be performed.

   b. *Decision package.* A brief justification document that includes the information necessary for managers to make judgments on program or activity levels and resource requirements. A series of decision packages (a decision package set) is

Executive Office of the President, Office of Management and Budget, Washington, D.C. Charts and technical details omitted. Issued April 19, 1977.

prepared for each decision unit and cumulatively represents the total budget request for that unit.

c. *Consolidated decision packages*. Packages prepared at higher management levels that summarize and supplement information contained in decision packages received from lower level units. Consolidated packages may reflect different priorities, including the addition of new programs or the abolition of existing ones.

d. *Ranking*. The process by which managers array program or activity levels (as shown in decision packages) in decreasing order of priority. This ranking process identifies the relative priority assigned to each decision package increment contained in the manager's budget request based on the benefits to be gained at and the consequences of various spending levels.

e. *Minimum level*. The program, activity, or funding level below which it is not feasible to continue the program, activity, or entity because no constructive contribution can be made toward fulfilling its objective. The minimum level:

—may not be a fully acceptable level from the program manager's perspective; and

—may not completely achieve the desired objectives of the decision unit.

f. *Current level*. The level that would be reflected in the budget if fiscal year 1978 activities were carried on at 1978 service or other output levels without major policy changes. A concept, not unlike current services, that nevertheless permits internal realignments of activities within existing statutory authorization. Estimates of personnel compensation and other objects of expenditure will be made in accordance with OMB Circular No. A–11.

4. THE ZERO-BASE BUDGETING CONCEPT. Zero-base budgeting is a management process that provides for systematic consideration of all programs and activities in conjunction with the formulation of budget requests and program planning.

The principal objectives of zero-base budgeting are to:

—involve managers at all levels in the budget process;

—justify the resource requirements for existing activities as well as for new activities;

—focus the justification on the evaluation of discrete programs or activities of each decision unit;

—establish, for all managerial levels in an agency, objectives against which accomplishments can be identified and measured;

—assess alternative methods of accomplishing objectives;

—analyze the probable effects of different budget amounts or performance levels on the achievement of objectives; and

—provide a credible rationale for reallocating resources, especially from old activities to new activities.

To accomplish these objectives zero-base budgeting requires these decision-makers to:

—use "decision packages" as the major tool for budgetary review, analysis, and decision making, and

—rank program or activity levels in order of priority.

5. BENEFITS ANTICIPATED IN THE FEDERAL GOVERNMENT.

This new system can provide significant benefits at all levels throughout the federal government. These benefits include:

—focusing the budget process on a comprehensive analysis of objectives, and the development of plans to accomplish those objectives;

—providing better coordination of program and activity planning, evaluation, and budgeting;

—causing managers at all levels to evaluate in detail the cost effectiveness of their operations and specific activities—both new and old—all of which are clearly identified;

—requiring that alternative ways to meet objectives are identified;

—identifying trade-offs between and within programs; and

—providing managers at all levels with better information on the relative priority associated with budget requests and decisions.

Many agency management processes are aimed at providing some if not all of these same benefits. In many instances, however, such processes do not operate agency-wide and the information relevant to the processes is not gathered, analyzed and reviewed in a systematic manner for all programs and activities. The value of zero-base budgeting is that it provides a process requiring systematic evaluation of the total budget request and all program objectives.

6. THE ZERO-BASE BUDGETING PROCESS.

Agencies should develop their internal zero-base budgeting procedures within the following framework.

a. *Identification of objectives.* An important early step in zero-base budgeting is the identification of objectives for all managers preparing and reviewing decision packages.

Top level agency management should be involved in setting objectives for lower level agency managers to:

(1) help ensure that appropriate guidance is furnished to managers throughout the agency;

(2) aid managers preparing the decision packages in defining, explaining, and

justifying their work to be performed and the associated resources; and

(3) aid top and intermediate level managers in understanding and evaluating the budget requests.

Program and organization objectives should be explicit statements of intended output, clearly related to the basic need for which the program or organization exists. The task of identifying objectives requires the participation by managers at all levels to determine the ultimate realistic outputs or accomplishments expected from a program or organization (major objectives) and the services or products to be provided for a given level of funding during the budget year (short-term objectives).

However, lack of precise identification and quantification of such objectives does not preclude the development and implementation of zero-based budgeting procedures.

As objectives are identified, managers should simultaneously determine the key indicators by which performance and results are to be measured. Agencies should specify measures of effectiveness, efficiency, and workload for each decision unit. These measures can often be obtained from existing evaluation and workload measurement systems. If such systems do not exist, or if data are not readily available, desirable performance indicators should not be rejected because of apparent difficulties in measurement. Indirect or proxy indicators should be considered initially, while evaluation and workload systems are developed to provide the necessary data for subsequent budget cycles.

b. *Identification of decision units.* Another of the first steps in zero-base budgeting is the identification of the entities in the program or organization structure whose managers will prepare the initial decision packages. In all instances, the identification of the decision units should be determined by the information needs of higher level management. *Agencies should ensure that the basic decision units selected are not so low in the structure as to result in excessive paperwork and review. On the other hand, the units selected should not be so high as to mask important considerations and prevent meaningful review of the work being performed.* In general, the decision unit should be at an organizational or program level at which the manager makes major decisions on the amount of spending and the scope, direction, or quality of work to be performed. A decision unit normally should be included within a single account, be classified in only one budget subfunction, and to the extent possible, reflect existing program and organizational structures that have accounting support.

c. *Preparation of decision packages.* The decision unit manager performs two types of analyses based on the program and budget guidance received from higher level management. First, the manager examines alternative ways of accomplishing the major objectives. Such alternatives may require legislation and may have been identified and developed as a result of a major reexamination of the program or activity. In other instances the alternatives identified may not be fully developed, but will serve as a basis for reexamining the program at a later date. In still other instances, the alternatives identified may be the first steps toward more significant changes that will take longer than one year to accomplish. Normally, the best alternative is then selected and used as the basis for the second type of analysis—the identification of different levels of funding, activity, or performance. The purpose of identifying these different levels is to provide information on: (1) where reduction from the total request may be made, (2) the increased benefits that can be achieved through additional or alternative spending plans, and (3) the effect of such additions and reductions. Again, legislation may be required to put into effect some level of funding or performance.

However, nothing in this process should inhibit or prohibit any decisionmaker from submitting, requesting, or reviewing any information needed for analyses and decisionmaking. For example, separate decision package sets may be prepared to examine the impact of different alternatives. Also, packages reflecting increased performance or funding levels may introduce alternative methods of accomplishment that were not feasible at a lower level.

The guidance received from higher level management may determine the specific service, performance, output, or funding levels and the objectives to be discussed. This helps to insure that information provided in the decision package is broken down and arrayed in a manner conducive to higher level review of issues concerning the decision unit and also covering more than one decision unit. However, in all instances the decision package set should include:

(1) A minimum level. In all instances, the minimum level should be below the current level (unless it is clearly not feasible to operate below the current level); and

(2) A current level (unless the total requested for the decision unit is below the current level).

The decision package set may also include, when appropriate:

(1) A level or levels between the minimum and current levels; and

(2) Any additional increments desired above the current level.

Proposed changes (supplementals, amendments, rescissions) in current year amounts should be shown in packages separate from the packages described above. However, the above packages should include any budget year effect of current year changes. New programs or activities (e.g., those resulting from new legislative authority or a new major objective) will be proposed in a separate decision package set. Proposals for abolition of current programs or activities normally will not be reflected in a decision package set. However, such proposals should be highlighted, as appropriate, in another part of the agency justification.

The decision unit manager prepares a decision package set that includes decision packages reflecting incremental levels of funding and performance, so the cumulative amount of all packages represents the total potential budget request of the decision unit. Each package shows the effect of that funding and performance level on meeting the assigned objectives. The decision packages serve as the primary tool for budgetary review, analysis, and decision-making, although additional material may also be made available or requested for review.

Generally, a *series of packages* should be prepared for all programs and activities where, through legislative or administrative means, there is discretion as to the amount of funds to be spent or the appropriate method or level of activity. This does not mean that where a spending level is mandatory under existing substantive law, only one level will be identified. There are many instances in which the decision on whether to propose legislative changes is made during the preparation of the budget. There are also instances in which changes in regulations or program administration can affect the amount of resources needed to carry out a mandatory program. In these instances, packages should be prepared that analyze the effects of different funding or performance levels or alternative methods of accomplishing the objectives. In any instance where there is clearly no discretion in the amounts of funds to be spent or the appropriate method or level of activity, at least one decision package should be prepared that summarizes the analysis and decision-making that resulted in that request. That decision package should support the conclusion that only one funding or activity level can be considered during the budget process.

d. *Ranking of decision packages.* Completed decision packages should be ranked initially by the decision unit manager. At higher management levels, the rankings of each subordinate manager are reviewed and formed into a consolidated ranking. This consolidation process is illustrated in Exhibit 1. [Not included— eds.] The ranking shows the relative priority that discrete increments of services or other outputs have in relation to other increments of services or other outputs. The process is explicitly designed to allow higher level managers the opportunity to bring their broader perspectives to bear on program priorities by allowing them to rank the decision packages and make program trade-offs.

Agencies may use whatever review and ranking techniques appropriate to their needs. However, the minimum level for a decision unit is always ranked higher than any increment for the same unit, since it represents the level below which the activities can no longer be conducted effectively. However, the minimum level package for a given decision unit need not be ranked higher than an incremental level of some other decision unit. A minimum level for a decision unit may be ranked so low in comparison to incremental levels of other decision units that the funding level for the agency may exclude that minimum level package. This would signify the loss of funding for that decision unit.

Decision packages or decision package sets may be prepared to examine the effect of alternative ways to meet an objective (see Section 6.c.). In these instances, only those decision packages that are part of the unit's request should be ranked. The other decision packages should accompany the submission, however, so higher review levels may examine the alternatives and have an opportunity to replace the requested packages with those representing an alternative thus far not recommended.

e. *Higher level review*. In all instances, the use of decision packages and priority ranking are the major tools for analysis, review, and decisionmaking. At each higher management level:

—decision packages may be revised, deleted, or added; and

—rankings submitted by subordinate managers may be revised.

(1) *Consolidation of decision packages*. In some small agencies, it may be desirable for each higher management level to review every decision package prepared by each decision unit. In other instances, however, higher level management's decisionmaking needs may better be met by recasting all or some of the initial decision packages into a lesser number of consolidated decision packages. The consolidated packages would be based upon the more detailed information in the initial packages, but the information would be recast or reinterpreted in a broader frame of reference to focus on significant program alternatives or issues. The objectives may be redefined to reflect the higher level manager's program perspective.

This consolidation process may also be used to reduce what would otherwise be an excessive paperwork and review burden at higher levels. The agency head or his designee should determine at which review level(s) all or some of the packages will be consolidated into a lesser number of packages before submission to the next higher review level (see Exhibit 1). This consolidation should be based on natural groupings of subordinate decision units. Decision units in different budget subfunctions generally should not be consolidated. The consolidated package will summarize the more detailed information contained in the individual packages and identify the subordinate decision units covered.

In all instances a minimum level consolidated decision package will be prepared. This package may or may not include each of the minimum level packages from the decision package sets being consolidated. There will be instances when the preparation of a current level consolidated package is not feasible (e.g., when a decision package for a new program or activity is ranked higher than a current level package). When appropriate, there should also be a level or levels identified between the minimum and current levels.

(2) *Type of review*. The review can be conducted more effectively at each management level if the type of review is determined beforehand. This is especially important in the mid and higher levels in the agency, where the review workload may be significant, even with consolidation of packages. As a means of increasing the effectiveness of its review, higher level management may decide to limit its

review of the higher-ranked packages to that necessary to provide a sound basis for ranking the packages and may choose to examine in more depth only the lower-ranked packages. The lower-ranked packages would be the first to be affected by an increase or decrease in the expected budgetary resources.

7. PREPARATION OF MATERIALS. The following materials should be prepared for each decision unit.

a. *Decision unit overview.* The overview provides information necessary to evaluate and make decisions on each of the decision packages, without the need to repeat that information in each package. It should be at most two pages long, prepared in the format of Exhibit 2 [not included—eds.], and contain the following information:

(1) *Identifying information.* Include sufficient information to identify the decision unit, and the organizational and budgetary structure within which that decision unit is located. Each package should include the title of the appropriation or fund account that finances the decision unit, the account identification code (see OMB Circular No. A-11, section 21.3), and any internal agency code necessary.

(2) *Long-range goal.* When appropriate, identify the long-range goal of the decision unit. Goals should be directed toward general needs, to serve as the basis for determining the major objective(s) undertaken to work towards that goal.

(3) *Major objective(s).* Describe the major objectives of the decision unit, the requirements these objectives are intended to satisfy and the basic authorizing legislation. Major objectives normally are of a continuing nature or take relatively long periods to accomplish. Objectives should be measurable and should be those that program managers employ; they should form the basis for first determining and subsequently evaluating the accomplishments of programs or activities.

(4) *Alternatives.* Describe the feasible alternative ways to accomplish the major objectives. Identify which of the alternatives represents the method proposed for the budget year. Briefly explain how the approach selected contributes to satisfying the major objectives and the rationale for not pursuing other alternatives. This may include a discussion of organizational structure and delivery systems; longer-range cost factors; and when applicable, the unique aspects and need for the program that cannot be filled by State or local governments or the private sector (particularly for any enlarged or new proposed action).

(5) *Accomplishments.* Describe the progress of the decision unit toward meeting the major objectives. This section should include both quantitative and qualitative measures of results.

b. *Decision packages.* Each (consolidated) decision package should be no more than two pages long, be prepared in a format similar to Exhibit 3 [not included—eds.], and contain at least the following information:

(1) *Identifying information.* This information should include organizational identification (agency, bureau), appropriation or fund account title and

identification number, specific identification of the decision unit, the package number, and the internal agency code.

(2). *Activity description.* Describe the work to be performed or services provided with the incremental resources specified in the package. This section should include a discussion and evaluation of significant accomplishments planned and the *results* of benefit/cost and other analyses and evaluations that will contribute to the justification of that level.

(3) *Resource requirements.* Include appropriate information, such as obligations, offsetting collections, budget authority or outlays, and employment (full-time permanent and total), for the past, current, and budget years for the upcoming budget. The increment associated with each package should be listed, along with the cumulative totals for each measure used in that package, plus all higher ranked packages for that decision unit. At an appropriate level in the process, budget authority and outlay amounts for the four years beyond the budget year should also be included, in accordance with criteria in OMB Circular No. A–11.

(4) *Short-term objective.* State the short-term objectives (usually achievable within one year), that will be accomplished and the benefits that will result with the increment specified and the cumulative resources shown in the package. The expected results of the work performed or services provided should be identified to the maximum extent possible through the use of quantitative measures.

(5) *Impact on major objective(s).* Describe the impact on the major objective(s) or goals of both the incremental and the cumulative resources shown in the package.

(6) *Other information.* Include other information that aids in evaluating the decision package. This should include:

—explanations of any legislation needed in connection with the package;

—the impact or consequences of not approving the package;

—for the minimum level package, the effects of zero-funding for the decision unit;

—for packages below the current level, an explanation of what now is being accomplished that will not be accomplished at the lower level; and

—the relationship of the decision unit to other decision units, including the coordination that is required.

c. *Ranking sheet.* Each review level will prepare a ranking sheet to submit to the next higher review level. This ranking sheet should generally contain the information shown in Exhibit 4 [not included—eds.] for the budget year.

In instances (e.g., revolving funds) where budget authority and net outlays *are not a factor in reflecting the appropriate or priority level of performance,* managers should use other measures (e.g. total obligations, employment).

8. *OMB review and consultation.* As an important element of initiating zero-based budgeting, agencies are required this year to submit for OMB and Presidential review their proposals for:

—the program, activity, or organizational level to be the basis of the (consolidated) decision packages that will form the agency budget submission to OMB;

—current and/or budget year issues that should be highlighted through either particular decision packages or, when decision packages are not appropriate, through issue papers that ultimately tie in to one or several decision packages; and

—longer-range issues for which agencies will initiate extensive evaluations.

This identification of issues will play an integral role in OMB's spring review of agency programs, activities, and plans. Policy guidance letters to the agencies regarding the preparation of the fall budget submission will be based in part on this information.

OMB representatives will contact the agencies shortly and request these proposals.

9. Inquiries.   Should additional discussion be necessary, agencies should contact their OMB budget examiner.

Bert Lance
Director

PART IV

Strategies for Achieving Administrative Accountability: New "Checks" on the Bureaucracy

Strategies for Achieving
Administrative Accountability:
New "Checks" on the
Bureaucracy

How to control the bureaucracy has been a central issue—perhaps *the* central issue—in Public Administration since its inception as an identifiable field of study. Indeed the first essay on the subject written in the United States by a young political scientist, Woodrow Wilson (1887), "The Study of Administration,"[1] wrestled with the proper relationship between the two spheres of "politics" and "administration." Wilson's essay of course did not resolve the dilemma but certainly he can be credited with first underscoring its importance to the study of Public Administration. The accountability issue concerns essentially how to achieve effective popular control of government's activities, on the one hand, balanced, on the other hand, with the need for adequate governmental discretionary authority for the timely and effective transaction of public activities. Wilson put his finger on the heart of the administrative accountability problem, one which is still a very critical dilemma today.

While the issue of administrative accountability is an old one, one at the very center of responsible constitutional government, since the late 1960s and the early 1970s it came forcefully to the forefront of the public's attention. Events of Vietnam, Watergate, the rapid growth of government spending, government's inability to cope with crime, energy shortages, high inflation, and other pressing national questions seemed to demonstrate to many citizens that government was *out* of control or perhaps not properly *in* control. Government seemed to touch directly the lives of so many of its citizens in so many negative and very personal ways— whether by government enforcement of the 55-mile speed limit, rising portions of personal income taken for taxes, delivery of fewer services for higher cost—be it mail delivery, education, transportation, or the fight against crime, housing blight, or poverty.

---

1. Woodrow Wilson, "The Study of Administration," *Political Science Quarterly* 2 (June 1887): 197–222.

The popular debates during the 1970s over the inadequacies of government were both complex and oversimplified, but the concern of the citizenry was very real, intense, and translated into a number of significant new legislative "landmarks" aimed at achieving what many individuals perceived generally as the need for improved administrative oversight and accountability. Several of these new types of "checks" on the bureaucracy are contained in Part IV. However, it should be underscored that many of the basic documents contained in previous sections of this volume were also fundamentally "framed" with this end in mind. The executive budget was, for example (as created originally by the Budget and Accounting Act of 1921), an idea whose central purpose was to achieve better control and oversight of administrative activities within the executive branch. More recently, as Part III illustrated, the 1974 Congressional Budget and Impoundment Control Act sought to make the budget a more effective instrument for legislative control of the executive branch through a number of very important procedural and institutional reforms. As Frederick C. Mosher has written:

> the idea of accountability is probably as ancient as organized government itself—or at least any government in which there is or was some form of delegation of authority. . . . it is difficult to imagine how a responsible democratic polity could survive without the principle and some tools of accountability.[2]

The "tools of accountability," however, during the 1970s were sharpened and diversified as reflected by the documents contained in Part IV: first, the Legislative Reorganization Act of 1970 significantly increased the numerical size and scope of duties of congressional committee staffs as well as enhanced the oversight capabilities of existing legislative oversight bodies; particularly the General Accounting Office (GAO) and Congressional Reference Service (CRS). As was pointed out in Part III, the 1974 Congressional Budget Act further built upon this Reorganization Act's earlier expansion of legislative oversight capabilities by establishing the Congressional Budget Office (CBO) as well as by providing a number of other new important "tools" for better budgetary oversight. Second, new expenditure controls in the form of annual rather than the traditional multiyear appropriations were exercised on a far broader scale by Congress beginning with the 1971 Foreign Assistance Act. This particular act for the first time made a cabinet-level department, the State Department, subject to annual appropriations authorization. These stiffer expenditure controls were further developed in the 1974 Congressional Budget Act (see Part III).

---

2. Frederick C. Mosher, *The GAO: The Quest for Accountability in American Government* (Boulder, CO: Westview Press, 1979), p. 234.

Third, the War Powers Resolution of 1973 forced the executive branch to be far more "consultative" with regard to its use of troops abroad. The resolution required the president "in every possible instance" to consult with Congress before engaging the armed forces in combat. A fourth strategy was through better means of access to information. The 1974 amendment to the 1967 Freedom of Information Act (dubbed "sunshine laws") substantially served to extend the public's access to governmental information and to open up previously "closed" government meetings. A fifth route was by means of a required periodic review of administrative activities. Colorado State in 1976 adopted the first "sunset legislation" and soon many other states and localities followed suit (though not the federal government). The Colorado law required regular review of all or most administrative units of its state governments. Agency termination followed if no reasonable justification could be found for its continuation.

Still another oversight innovation in the 1970s occurred with the enactment of the Office of the Inspector General (IG) for the U.S Department of Health Education and Welfare (HEW) in 1976. While the IG had been a formal part of the military internal review processes for many years, President Carter extended the office of the Inspector General for the first time to civilian agencies beginning at HEW in order to "promote economy and efficiency in the administration . . . and to prevent and detect fraud and abuse in such programs and operations . . ."

Finally, Proposition 13 became an amendment to the California State Constitution in July 1978 and symbolized a growing grass-roots national "tax revolt" aimed at drastically curbing government local revenues. Proposition 13's strategy essentially sought to control government's overall growth by limiting its means of raising revenues. Proposition 13's emphasis upon "revenue controls" rather than "expenditure controls" marked an important new and highly controversial direction in the quest for achieving effective administrative accountability.

1. *The Legislative Reorganization Act of 1970* (October 26, 1970)

The Legislative Reorganization Act of 1946 underscored an important role for each standing committee of Congress ". . . to exercise continuous watchfulness of the execution by administrative agencies concerned with any law. . . ." The 1970 Legislative Reorganization Act put teeth into this frequently neglected legislative oversight responsibility by (1) requiring biennial committee reports on their oversight actions, (2) increasing the numerical size and level of professionalization of the regular committee staffs, and (3) broadening both the scope of oversight duties of the General Accounting Office as well as the Congressional Reference Service, the key staff arms of Congress. To be specific, the GAO was not merely asked to audit the expenditures of agencies, the Legislative Reorganization Act of 1970 asked GAO to evaluate "the results" of agency activities. The Congressional Reference Service's scope and depth of research capabilities were impressively expanded by the act as well. Within a few years Congress would add the Congressional Budget Office and Office of Technology Assessment to extend further its professional oversight competencies in the budgetary and scientific fields.[3]

2. *War Powers Resolution* (November 7, 1973)

Concerned with its inability to stop American involvement in "future-Vietnam Wars," Congress passed the War Powers Resolution of 1973. In essence, the resolution established formal requirements for extensive consultation between the executive and legislative branches prior to the engagement combat forces in extended foreign hostilities. The 1973 resolution sought to place stricter, more precise, and narrower limits on presidential war-making powers by these "consultative requirements." Several critics have since argued that such restrictions were far too binding on executive authority in foreign policy.

The resolution symbolized the growing use of the Congressional veto during the 1970s—that is, a legislative oversight tool that requires Congressional approval of an executive action prior to or during its initiation. The Congressional veto device was first enacted in the Economy Act of 1932, but its use during the 1970s accelerated dramatically. Between 1970–1975, 89 laws and 163 provisions for Congressional vetoes were enacted, or more than one-half of all the "congressional veto" provisions that were legislated since the first one in 1932.

3. *The Freedom of Information Act* (As amended November 21, 1974)

"Sunshine laws" were enacted by various state and local governments throughout the United States during the 1970s and proved to be especially important vehicles for "opening up" public meetings and access to information inside the bureaucracy. On the federal level the Freedom of Information Act (FOI) of 1967 replaced the 1946 Administrative Procedures Act's "need to know criteria" by giving considerably more general presumption in favor of disclosure except in certain specific areas of national security and personal privacy. The 1967 FOI was further broadened by 1974 amendments to the act that expanded private access to public records and placed both strict deadlines and penalties on administrative agencies in order to achieve prompt compliance with the act. This "sunshine model" has since been copied by various state and local governments though not without substantial controversies ensuing over its potential damage to personal

3. For an excellent study of the influence of increased staff size and professional expertise upon Congress, see Harrison W. Fox and Susan W. Hammond, *Congressional Staffs: The Invisible Force in American Lawmaking* (New York: Free Press, 1977).

privacy, national security and law enforcement functions, largely due to the considerable degree of secrecy required by those governmental activities.

4. *An Act Concerning Regulatory Agencies, and Establishing a System for the Periodic Review and for the Termination, Continuation, or Reestablishment Thereof* (Colorado State House Bill No. 1088, enacted April 22, 1976)

"Sunset laws" are an example of a grass-roots reform "to get government off our backs" that began in the West at the state level and spread across the country. Eventually sunset laws were proposed on several occasions in the U.S. Congress (these federal bills all died in committees). The sunset law is best exemplified in the Colorado model (which was the first of its kind) since it required periodic reviews by the legislature of all or most government agencies ". . . to evaluate the need for the continued existence of existing and future regulatory bodies." Clearly, as this law suggests, in its opening statement, the purpose of the "sunset concept" was to check ". . . a substantial increase in numbers of agencies, growth of programs and proliferation of rules and regulation . . ." While more than a dozen states have enacted sunset laws since 1976, with few notable exceptions these laws have proved to have more symbolic than real effect upon reducing the overall size and expenditure levels of governmental activity in those states where they have been enacted.

5. *Title II—Office of Inspector General* (October 15, 1976)

The Office of the Inspector General was instituted for the Department of Health Education and Welfare (HEW) in 1976 but was hardly a new invention. The military had had an elaborate IG system for many years as an "internal" and very effective check on administrative misconduct and abuse within its own chain of command. However, its debut in the civilian world occurred with its implementation at HEW in 1976. The IG as a device for administrative accountability later was extended by President Carter to all other federal departments.

Like the "military model," IGs were established: (1) "in order to create an independent and objective unit . . ." (2) "to conduct and supervise audits and investigations . . ." (3) "to provide leadership and coordination . . ." (4) to promote economy and efficiency in administration . . ." (5) "to provide a means for keeping the Secretary [of HEW] and Congress fully and currently informed about problems and deficiencies relating to the administrations of such programs . . ."

The HEW IG was given broad authority over making independent investigations, gaining access to information, and reporting the findings on an independent basis to the secretary of HEW and Congress. The future of this office depends to a large part upon who the incumbents are as well as their support from Congress and the executive branch. It should be noted, however, that "integrity and demonstrated ability and without regard to political affiliation" is the main criteria for the IG's appointment. Important too, the post required Senate confirmation as did an increasing number of top-level executive appointments in the 1970s.

6. *Proposition 13* (Article 13A, California State Constitution, effective July 1, 1978)

Proposition 13, which was enacted as Article 13A of the California State Constitution on July 1, 1978, marked the beginning of a major national grass-roots drive by tax reformer Howard Jarvis to limit local property tax revenues. Rapid inflationary trends that automatically escalated homeowners' assessed property values and subsequently their property tax rates fostered support for the passage of Proposition 13 in California and similar state initiatives elsewhere (for example, No. 2½ in Massachusetts). The measures required substantial and immediate reductions in local property tax revenues, but in turn they also resulted in sharp reductions in many basic public services. However, increased use of federal and state aid as well as new types of "user" taxes bailed out at least temporarily many local jurisdictions. The measures were accompanied by a firestorm of controversy from critics who charged the measures brought tax relief for the rich at the expense of the poor. Whatever the results of their "distributory effects," the measures, where enacted, served as very real limitations on government growth at the local level.

1. Legislative Reorganization Act of 1970

An Act

To improve the operation of the legislative branch of the Federal Government, and for other purposes.

Be it enacted by the Senate and House of Representatives of the United States of America in Congress assembled, That this Act, divided into titles, parts, and sections according to the following table of contents, may be cited as the "Legislative Reorganization Act of 1970".

TITLE II—FISCAL CONTROLS

Part 1—Budgetary and Fiscal Information and Data

BUDGETARY AND FISCAL DATA PROCESSING SYSTEM

Sec. 201. The Secretary of the Treasury and the Director of the Office of Management and Budget, in cooperation with the Comptroller General of the United States, shall develop, establish, and maintain, insofar as practicable, for use by all Federal agencies, a standardized information and data processing system for budgetary and fiscal data.

BUDGET STANDARD CLASSIFICATIONS

Sec. 202. (a) The Secretary of the Treasury and the Director of the Office of Management and Budget, in cooperation with the Comptroller General, shall develop, establish, and maintain standard classifications of programs, activities, receipts, and expenditures of Federal agencies in order—

    (1) to meet the needs of the various branches of the Government; and

    (2) to facilitate the development, establishment, and maintenance of the data processing system under section 201 through the utilization of modern automatic data processing techniques.

Public Law 91–510 (October 26, 1970). Only Title II and III covering Fiscal Controls and Sources of Information, are included here. Title I (the Committee System) Title IV (Congress as an Institution), Title V (Legislative Counsel's Office) and Title VI (Effective Dates) were deleted.

The initial classifications under this subsection shall be established on or before December 31, 1971.

(b) The Secretary of the Treasury and the Director of the Office of Management and Budget shall submit a report to the Senate and the House of Representatives on or before September 1 of each year, commencing with 1971, with respect to the performance during the preceding fiscal year of the functions and duties imposed on them by section 201 and subsection (a) of this section. The reports made under this subsection in 1971 and 1972 shall set forth the progress achieved in the development of classifications under subsection (a) of this section. The reports made in years thereafter shall include information with respect to changes in, and additions to, classifications previously established. Each such report shall include such comments of the Comptroller General as he deems necessary or advisable.

AVAILABILITY TO CONGRESS OF BUDGETARY, FISCAL, AND RELATED DATA

Sec. 203. Upon request of any committee of either House, or of any joint committee of the two Houses, the Secretary of the Treasury and the Director of the Office of Management and Budget shall—

(1) furnish to such committee or joint committee information as to the location and nature of data available in the various Federal agencies with respect to programs, activities, receipts, and expenditures of such agencies; and

(2) to the extent feasible, prepare for such committee or joint committee summary tables of such data.

ASSISTANCE TO CONGRESS BY GENERAL ACCOUNTING OFFICE

Sec. 204. (a) The Comptroller General shall review and analyze the results of Government programs and activities carried on under existing law, including the making of cost benefit studies, when ordered by either House of Congress, or upon his own initiative, or when requested by any committee of the House of Representatives or the Senate, or any joint committee of the two Houses, having jurisdiction over such programs and activities.

(b) The Comptroller General shall have available in the General Accounting Office employees who are expert in analyzing and conducting cost benefit studies of Government programs. Upon request of any committee of either House or any joint committee of the two Houses, the Comptroller General shall assist such committee or joint committee, or the staff of such committee or joint committee—

(1) in analyzing cost benefit studies furnished by any Federal agency to such committee or joint committee; or

(2) in conducting cost benefit studies of programs under the jurisdiction of such committee or joint committee.

POWER AND DUTIES OF COMPTROLLER GENERAL IN CONNECTION WITH BUDGETARY, FISCAL, AND RELATED MATTERS

Sec. 205. (a) The Comptroller General shall establish within the General Accounting Office such office or division, or such offices or divisions, as he considers necessary to carry out the functions and duties imposed on him by the provisions of this title.

(b) The Comptroller General shall include in his annual report to the Congress information with respect to the performance of the functions and duties imposed on him by the provisions of this title.

TITLE III—SOURCES OF INFORMATION

Part 1—Staffs of Senate and House Standing Committees

INCREASE IN PROFESSIONAL STAFFS OF SENATE STANDING COMMITTEES; SENATE MINORITY PROFESSIONAL AND CLERICAL STAFFS; FAIR TREATMENT FOR SENATE MINORITY STAFFS

Sec. 301. (a) Section 202(a) of the Legislative Reorganization Act of 1946, as amended (2 U.S.C. 72a(a)), is amended to read as follows:

"(a) Each standing committee of the Senate (other than the Committee on Appropriations) is authorized to appoint, by majority vote of the committee, not more than six professional staff members in addition to the clerical staffs. Such professional staff members shall be assigned to the chairman and the ranking minority member of such committee as the committee may deem advisable, except that whenever a majority of the minority members of such committee so request, two of such professional staff members may be selected for appointment by majority vote of the minority members and the committee shall appoint any staff members so selected. A staff member or members appointed pursuant to a request by the minority members of the committee shall be assigned to such committee business as such minority members deem advisable. Services of professional staff members appointed by majority vote of the committee may be terminated by a majority vote of the committee and services of professional staff members appointed pursuant to a request by the minority members of the committee shall be terminated by the committee when a majority of such minority members so request. Professional staff members authorized by this subsection shall be appointed on a permanent basis, without regard to political affiliation, and solely on the basis of fitness to perform the duties of their respective positions. Such professional staff members shall not engage in any work other than committee business and no other duties may be assigned to them.".

(b) Section 202(c) of the Legislative Reorganization Act of 1946, as amended (2 U.S.C. 72a(c)), is amended to read as follows:

"(c) The clerical staff of each standing committee of the Senate (other than the Committee on Appropriations), which shall be appointed by a majority vote of the committee, shall consist of not more than six clerks to be attached to the office of the chairman, to the ranking minority member, and to the professional staff, as the committee may deem advisable, except that whenever a majority of the minority members of such committee so requests, one of the members of the clerical staff may be selected for appointment by majority vote of such minority members and the committee shall appoint any staff member so selected. The clerical staff shall handle committee correspondence and stenographic work, both for the committee staff and for the chairman and ranking minority member on matters related to committee work, except that if a member of the clerical staff is appointed pursuant to a request by the minority members of the committee, such clerical staff member shall handle committee correspondence and stenographic work for the minority members of the committee and for any members of the committee staff appointed under subsection(a) pursuant to request by such minority members, on matters related to committee work. Services of clerical staff members appointed by majority vote of the committee may be terminated by majority vote of the committee and services of clerical staff members appointed pursuant to a request by the minority members of the committee shall be terminated by the committee when a majority of such minority members so request.".

(c) Section 202 of the Legislative Reorganization Act of 1946, as amended (2 U.S.C. 72a), is amended by striking out subsection (h) and by adding after subsection (f) the following new subsections:

"(g) In any case in which a request for the appointment of a minority staff member under subsection (a) or subsection (c) is made at any time when no vacancy exists to which the appointment requested may be made, the person appointed pursuant to such request may serve in addition to any other staff members authorized by such subsections and may be paid from the contingent fund of the Senate until such time as such a vacancy occurs, at which time such person shall be considered to have been appointed to such vacancy.

"(h) Staff members appointed pursuant to a request by minority members of a committee under subsection (a) or subsection (c), and staff members appointed to assist minority members of subcommittees pursuant to authority of Senate resolution, shall be accorded equitable treatment with respect to the fixing of salary rates, the assignment of facilities, and the accessibility of committee records.".

(d) Nothing in the amendments made by subsections (a) and (b) of this section shall be construed—

> (1) to require a reduction in—
>
>> (A) the number of staff members authorized, prior to January 1, 1971, to be employed by any committee of the Senate, by statute or by annual or permanent resolution, or
>>
>> (B) the number of such staff members on such date assigned to, or authorized to be selected for appointment by or with the approval of, the minority members of any such committee; or
>
> (2) to authorize the selection for appointment of staff members by the minority members of a committee in any case in which two or more professional staff members or one or more clerical staff members, as the case may be, who are satisfactory to a majority of such minority members, are otherwise assigned to assist such minority members.

(e) The additional professional staff members authorized to be employed by a committee by the amendment made by subsection (a) of this section shall be in addition to any other additional staff members authorized, prior to January 1, 1971, to be employed by any such committee.

INCREASE IN PROFESSIONAL STAFFS OF HOUSE STANDING COMMITTEES; HOUSE MINORITY PROFESSIONAL AND CLERICAL STAFFS; FAIR TREATMENT FOR HOUSE MINORITY STAFFS

Sec. 302. (a) This section is enacted as an exercise of the rulemaking power of the House of Representatives, subject to and with full recognition of the power of the House of Representatives to enact or change any Rule of the House at any time in its exercise of its constitutional right to determine the rules of its proceedings.

(b) Paragraphs (a) and (b) of clause 29 of Rule XI of the Rules of the House of Representatives are amended to read as follows:

"(a)(1) Subject to subparagraph (2) of this paragraph and paragraph (f) of this clause, each standing committee may appoint, by majority vote of the committee, not more than six professional staff members. Each professional staff member appointed under this subparagraph shall be assigned to the chairman and the ranking minority party member of such committee, as the committee considers advisable.

"(2) Subject to paragraph (f) of this clause, whenever a majority of the minority party members of a standing committee (except the Committee on Standards of Official Conduct) so request, not more than two persons may be selected, by majority vote of the minority party members, for appointment by the committee as professional staff members from among the number authorized by subparagraph (1) of this paragraph. The committee shall appoint any persons so selected whose character and qualifications are acceptable to a majority of the committee. If the committee determines that the character and qualifications of any person so selected are unacceptable to the committee, a majority of the minority party members may select other persons for appointment by the committee to the professional staff until such appointment is made. Each professional staff member appointed under this subparagraph shall be assigned to such committee business as the minority party members of the committee consider advisable.

"(3) The professional staff members of each standing committee—

"(A) shall be appointed on a permanent basis, without regard to political affiliation, and solely on the basis of fitness to perform the duties of their respective positions;

"(B) shall not engage in any work other than committee business;

"(C) shall not be assigned any duties other than those pertaining to committee business.

"(4) Services of the professional staff members of each standing committee may be terminated by majority vote of the committee.

"(5) The foregoing provisions of this paragraph do not apply to the Committee on Appropriations.

"(b)(1) The clerical staff of each standing committee shall consist of not more than six clerks, to be attached to the office of the chairman, to the ranking minority party member, and to the professional staff, as the committee considers advisable. Subject to subparagraph (2) of this paragraph and paragraph (f) of this clause, the clerical staff shall be appointed by majority vote of the committee. Except as provided by subparagraph (2) of this paragraph, the clerical staff shall handle committee correspondence and stenographic work both for the committee staff and for the chairman and the ranking minority party member on matters related to committee work.

"(2) Subject to paragraph (f) of this clause, whenever a majority of the minority party members of a standing committee (except the Committee on Standards of Official Conduct) so request, one person may be selected, by majority vote of the minority party members, for appointment by the committee to a position on the clerical staff from among the number of clerks authorized by subparagraph (1) of this paragraph. The committee shall appoint to that position any person so selected whose character and qualifications are acceptable to a majority of the committee. If the committee determines that the character and qualifications of any person so selected are unacceptable to the committee, a majority of the minority party members may select other persons for appointment by the committee to that position on the clerical staff until such appointment is made. Each clerk appointed under this subparagraph shall handle committee correspondence and stenographic work for the minority party members of the committee and for any members of the professional staff appointed under subparagraph (2) of paragraph (a) of this clause on matters related to committee work.

"(3) Services of the clerical staff members of each standing committee may be terminated by majority vote of the committee.

"(4) The foregoing provisions of this paragraph do not apply to the Committee on Appropriations .".

(c) Clause 29 of Rule XI of the Rules of the House of Representatives, as amended by this Act, is further amended by adding at the end of such clause the following new paragraphs:

"(f) If a request for the appointment of a minority professional staff member under paragraph (a), or a minority clerical staff member under paragraph (b), of this clause, is made when no vacancy exists to which that appointment may be made, the committee nevertheless shall appoint, under paragraph (a) or paragraph (b), as applicable, the person selected by the minority and acceptable to the committee. The person so appointed shall serve as an additional member of the professional staff or the clerical staff, as the case may be, of the committee, and shall be paid from the contingent fund, until such time as such a vacancy (other than a vacancy in the position of head of the professional staff, by whatever title designated) occurs, at which time that person shall be deemed to have been appointed to that vacancy. If such vacancy occurs on the professional staff when two persons have been so appointed who are eligible to fill that vacancy, a majority of the minority party members shall designate which of those persons shall fill that vacancy.

"(g) Each staff member appointed pursuant to a request by minority party members under paragraph (a) or (b) of this clause, and each staff member appointed to assist minority party members of a committee pursuant to House resolution, shall be accorded equitable treatment with respect to the fixing of his rate of pay, the assignment to him of work facilities, and the accessibility to him of committee records.

"(h) Paragraphs (a) and (b) of this clause shall not be construed to authorize the appointment of additional professional or clerical staff members of a committee pursuant to request under either of such paragraphs by the minority party members of that committee if two or more professional staff members or one or more clerical staff members, provided for in paragraph (a)(1) or paragraph (b)(1) of this clause, as the case may be, who are satisfactory to a majority of the minority party members, are otherwise assigned to assist the minority party members.".

(d) Nothing in the amendments made by this section shall be construed to require a reduction in—

> (1) the number of staff members otherwise authorized prior to January 1, 1971, to be employed by any committee of the House of Representatives by statute or by annual or permanent resolution, or

> (2) the number of such staff members on such date assigned to, or authorized to be selected for appointment by or with the approval of, the minority members of any such committee.

(e) The additional professional staff members authorized to be employed by a committee by the amendment made by subsection (a) of this section shall be in addition to any other additional staff members otherwise authorized, prior to January 1, 1971, to be employed by any such committee.

PROCUREMENT OF TEMPORARY OR INTERMITTENT SERVICES OF CONSULTANTS FOR SENATE AND HOUSE STANDING COMMITTEES

Sec. 303. Section 202 of the Legislative Reorganization Act of 1946 (2 U.S.C. 72a), as amended by this Act, is further amended by adding at the end thereof the following new subsection:

"(i)(1) Each standing committee of the Senate or House of Representatives is authorized, with the approval of the Committee on Rules and Administration in the case of standing committees of the Senate, or the Committee on House Administration in the case of standing committees of the House of Representatives, within the limits of funds made available from the contingent funds of the respective Houses pursuant to resolutions, which shall specify the maximum amounts which may be used for such purpose, approved by such respective Houses, to procure the temporary services (not in excess of one year) or intermittent services of individual consultants, or organizations thereof, to make studies or advise the committee with respect to any matter within its jurisdiction.

"(2) Such services in the case of individuals or organizations may be procured by contract as independent contractors, or in the case of individuals by employment at daily rates of compensation not in excess of the per diem equivalent of the highest gross rate of compensation which may be paid to a regular employee of the committee. Such contracts shall not be subject to the provisions of section 3709 of the Revised Statutes (41 U.S.C. 5) or any other provision of law requiring advertising.

"(3) With respect to the standing committees of the Senate, any such consultant or organization shall be selected by the chairman and ranking minority member of the committee, acting jointly. With respect to the standing committees of the House of Representatives, the standing committee concerned shall select such consultant or organization. The committee shall submit to the Committee on Rules and Administration in the case of standing committees of the Senate, and the Committee on House Administration in the case of standing committees of the House of Representatives, information bearing on the qualifications of each consultant whose services are procured pursuant to this subsection, including organizations, and such information shall be retained by that committee and shall be made available for public inspection upon request.".

SPECIALIZED TRAINING FOR PROFESSIONAL STAFFS OF SENATE AND HOUSE STANDING COMMITTEES

Sec. 304. Section 202 of the Legislative Reorganization Act of 1946 (2 U.S.C. 72a), as amended by this Act, is further amended by adding at the end thereof the following new subsection:

"(j)(1) Each standing committee of the Senate or House of Representatives is authorized, with the approval of the Committee on Rules and Administration in the case of standing committees of the Senate, and the Committee on House Administration in the case of standing committees of the House of Representatives, and within the limits of funds made available from the contingent funds of the respective Houses pursuant to resolutions, which shall specify the maximum amounts which may be used for such purpose, approved by such respective Houses, to provide assistance for members of its professional staff in obtaining specialized training, whenever that committee determines that such training will aid the committee in the discharge of its responsibilities.

"(2) Such assistance may be in the form of continuance of pay during periods of training or grants of funds to pay tuition, fees, or such other expenses of training, or both, as may be approved by the Committee on Rules and Administration or the Committee on House Administration, as the case may be.

"(3) A committee providing assistance under this subsection shall obtain from any employee receiving such assistance such agreement with respect to continued employment with the committee as the committee may deem necessary to assure that it will receive the benefits of such employee's services upon completion of his training.

"(4) During any period for which an employee is separated from employment with a committee for the purpose of undergoing training under this subsection, such employee shall be considered to have performed service (in a nonpay status) as an employee of the committee at the rate of compensation received immediately prior to commencing such training (including any increases in compensation provided by law during the period of training) for the purposes of—

"(A) subchapter III (relating to civil service retirement) of chapter 83 ot title 5, United States Code,

"(B) chapter 87 (relating to Federal employees group life insurance) of title 5, United States Code, and

"(C) chapter 89 (relating to Federal employees group health insurance) of title 5, United States Code.".

Part 2—Congressional Research Service

IMPROVEMENT OF RESEARCH FACILITIES OF CONGRESS

Sec. 321. (a) Section 203 of the Legislative Reorganization Act of 1946, as amended (2 U.S.C. 166) is amended to read as follows:

"CONGRESSIONAL RESEARCH SERVICE

"Sec. 203. (a) The Legislative Reference Service in the Library of Congress is hereby continued as a separate department in the Library of Congress and is redesignated the 'Congressional Research Service'.

"(b) It is the policy of Congress that—

"(1) the Librarian of Congress shall, in every possible way, encourage, assist, and promote the Congressional Research Service

"(A) rendering to Congress the most effective and efficient service,

"(B) responding most expeditiously, effectively, and efficiently to the special needs of Congress, and

"(C) discharging its responsibilities to Congress; and

"(2) the Librarian of Congress shall grant and accord to the Congressional Research Service complete research independence and the maximum practicable administrative independence consistent with these objectives.

"(c)(1) After consultation with the Joint Committee on the Library, the Librarian of Congress shall appoint the Director of the Congressional Research Service. The basic pay of the Director shall be at a per annum rate equal to the rate of basic pay provided for level V of the Executive Schedule contained in section 5316 of title 5, United States Code.

"(2) The Librarian of Congress, upon the recommendation of the Director, shall appoint a Deputy Director of the Congressional Research Service and all other necessary personnel thereof. The basic pay of the Deputy Director shall be fixed in accordance with chapter 51 (relating to classification) and subchapter III (relating to General Schedule pay rates) of chapter 53 of title 5, United States Code, but without regard to section 5108(a) of such title. The basic pay of all other necessary personnel of the Congressional Research Service shall be fixed in accordance with chapter 51 (relating to classification) and subchapter III (relating to General Schedule pay rates) of chapter 53 of title 5, United States Code, except that—

"(A) the grade of Senior Specialist in each field within the purview of subsection (e) of this section shall not be less than the highest grade in the executive branch of the Government to which research analysts and consultants, without supervisory responsibility, are currently assigned; and

"(B) the positions of Specialist and Senior Specialist in the Congressional Research Service may be placed in GS-16, 17, and 18 of the General Schedule of section 5332 of title 5, United States Code, without regard to section 5108(a) of such title, subject to the prior approval of the Joint Committee on the Library, of the placement of each such position in any of such grades.

"(3) Each appointment made under paragraphs (1) and (2) of this subsection and subsection (e) of this section shall be without regard to the civil service laws, without regard to political affiliation, and solely on the basis of fitness to perform the duties of the position.

"(d) It shall be the duty of the Congressional Research Service, without partisan bias—

"(1) upon request, to advise and assist any committee of the Senate or House of Representatives and any joint committee of Congress in the analysis, appraisal, and evaluation of legislative proposals within that committee's jurisdiction, or of recommendations submitted to Congress, by the President or any executive agency, so as to assist the committee in—

"(A) determining the advisability of enacting such proposals;

"(B) estimating the probable results of such proposals and alternatives thereto; and

"(C) evaluating alternative methods for accomplishing those results; and, by providing such other research and analytical services as the committee considers appropriate for these purposes, otherwise to assist in furnishing a basis for the proper evaluation and determination of legislative proposals and recommendations generally; and in the performance of this duty the Service shall have authority, when so authorized by a committee and acting as the agent of that committee, to request of any department or agency of the United States the production of such books, records, correspondence, memoranda, papers, and documents as the Service considers necessary, and such department or agency of the United States shall comply with such request; and, further, in the performance of this and any other relevant duty, the Service shall maintain continuous liaison with all committees;

"(2) to make available to each committee of the Senate and House of Representatives and each joint committee of the two Houses, at the opening of a new Congress, a list of programs and activities being carried out under existing law scheduled to terminate during the current Congress, which are within the jurisdiction of the committee;

"(3) to make available to each committee of the Senate and House of Representatives and each joint committee of the two Houses, at the opening of a new Congress, a list of subjects and policy areas which the committee might profitably analyze in depth;

"(4) upon request, or upon its own initiative in anticipation of requests, to collect, classify, and analyze in the form of studies, reports, compilations, digests, bulletins, indexes, translations, and otherwise, data having a bearing on legislation, and to make such data available and serviceable to committees and Members of the Senate and House of Representatives and joint committees of Congress;

"(5) upon request, or upon its own initiative in anticipation of requests, to prepare and provide information, research, and reference materials and services to committees and Members of the Senate and House of Representatives and joint committees of Congress to assist them in their legislative and representative functions;

"(6) to prepare summaries and digests of bills and resolutions of a public general nature introduced in the Senate or House of Representatives;

"(7) upon request made by any committee or Member of the Congress, to prepare and transmit to such committee or Member a concise memorandum with respect to one or more legislative measures upon which hearings by any committee of the Congress have been announced, which memorandum shall contain a statement of the purpose and effect of each such measure, a description of other relevant measures of similar purpose or effect previously introduced in the Congress, and a recitation of all action taken theretofore by or within the Congress with respect to each such other measure; and

"(8) to develop and maintain an information and research capability, to include Senior Specialists, Specialists, other employees, and consultants, as necessary, to perform the functions provided for in this subsection.

"(e) The Librarian of Congress is authorized to appoint in the Congressional Research Service, upon the recommendation of the Director, Specialists and Senior Specialists in the following broad fields:

"(1) agriculture;

"(2) American government and public administration;

"(3) American public law;

"(4) conservation;

"(5) education;

"(6) engineering and public works;

"(7) housing;

"(8) industrial organization and corporation finance;

"(9) international affairs;

"(10) international trade and economic geography;

"(11) labor and employment;

"(12) mineral economics;

"(13) money and banking;

"(14) national defense;

"(15) price economics;

"(16) science;

"(17) social welfare;

"(18) taxation and fiscal policy;

"(19) technology;

"(20) transportation and communications;

"(21) urban affairs;

"(22) veterans' affairs; and

"(23) such other broad fields as the Director may consider appropriate.

Such Specialists and Senior Specialists, together with such other employees of the Congressional Research Service as may be necessary, shall be available for special work with the committees and Members of the Senate and House of Representatives and the joint committees of Congress for any of the purposes of subsection (d) of this section.

"(f) The Director is authorized—

"(1) to classify, organize, arrange, group, and divide, from time to time, as he considers advisable, the requests for advice, assistance, and other services submitted to the Congressional Research Service by committees and Members of the Senate and House of Representatives and joint committees of Congress, into such classes and categories as he considers necessary to—

"(A) expedite and facilitate the handling of the individual requests submitted by Members of the Senate and House of Representatives,

"(B) promote efficiency in the performance of services for committees of the Senate and House of Representatives and joint committees of Congress, and

"(C) provide a basis for the efficient performance by the Congressional Research Service of its legislative research and related functions generally,
and

"(2) to establish and change, from time to time, as he considers advisable, within the Congressional Research Service, such research and reference divisions or other organizational units, or both, as he considers necessary to accomplish the purposes of this section.

"(g) In order to facilitate the study, consideration, evaluation, and determination by the Congress of the budget requirements of the Congressional Research Service for each fiscal year, the Librarian of Congress shall receive from the Director and submit, for inclusion in the Volumes of the United States Government the budget estimates of the Congressional Research Service which shall be prepared separately by the Director in detail for each fiscal year as a separate item of the budget estimates of the Library of Congress for such fiscal year.

"(h)(1) The Director of the Congressional Research Service may procure the temporary or intermittent assistance of individual experts or consultants (including stenographic reporters) and of persons learned in particular or specialized fields of knowledge—

"(A) by nonpersonal service contract, without regard to any provision of law requiring advertising for contract bids, with the individual expert, consultant, or other person concerned, as an independent contractor, for the furnishing by him to the Congressional Research Service of a written study, treatise, theme, discourse, dissertation, thesis, summary, advisory opinion, or other end product; or

"(B) by employment (for a period of not more than one year) in the Congressional Research Service of the individual expert, consultant, or other person concerned, by personal service contract or otherwise, without regard to the position classification laws, at a rate of pay not in excess of the per diem equivalent of the highest rate of basic pay then currently in effect for the General Schedule of section 5332 of title 5, United States Code, including payment of such rate for necessary travel time.

"(2) The Director of the Congressional Research Service may procure by contract, without regard to any provision of law requiring advertising for contract bids, the temporary (for respective periods not in excess of one year) or intermittent assistance of educational, research, or other organizations of experts and consultants (including stenographic reporters) and of educational, research, and other organizations of persons learned in particular or specialized fields of knowledge.

"(i) The director of the Congressional Research Service shall prepare and file with the Joint Committee on the Library at the beginning of each regular session of

Congress a separate and special report covering, in summary and in detail, all phases of activity of the Congressional Research Service for the immediately preceding fiscal year.

"(j) There are hereby authorized to be appropriated to the Congressional Research Service each fiscal year such sums as may be necessary to carry out the work of the Service.".

2. War Powers Resolution (1973)

Joint Resolution

Concerning the war powers of Congress and the President.

Resolved by the Senate and House of Representatives of the United States of America in Congress assembled,

SHORT TITLE

Section 1. This joint resolution may be cited as the "War Powers Resolution".

PURPOSE AND POLICY

Sec. 2. (a) It is the purpose of this joint resolution to fulfill the intent of the framers of the Constitution of the United States and insure that the collective judgment of both the Congress and the President will apply to the introduction of United States Armed Forces into hostilities, or into situations where imminent involvement in hostilities is clearly indicated by the circumstances, and to the continued use of such forces in hostilities or in such situations.

(b) Under article I, section 8, of the Constitution, it is specifically provided that the Congress shall have the power to make all laws necessary and proper for carrying into execution, not only its own powers but also all other powers vested by the Constitution in the Government of the United States, or in any department or officer thereof.

(c) The constitutional powers of the President as Commander-in-Chief to introduce United States Armed Forces into hostilities, or into situations where imminent involvement in hostilities is clearly indicated by the circumstances, are exercised only pursuant to (1) a declaration of war, (2) specific statutory authorization, or (3) a national emergency created by attack upon the United States, its territories or possessions, or its armed forces.

CONSULTATION

Sec. 3. The President in every possible instance shall consult with Congress before introducing United States Armed Forces into hostilities or into situations

Public Law 93–148 (November 7, 1973).

where imminent involvement in hostilities is clearly indicated by the circumstances, and after every such introduction shall consult regularly with the Congress until United States Armed Forces are no longer engaged in hostilities or have been removed from such situations.

REPORTING

Sec. 4. (a) In the absence of a declaration of war, in any case in which United States Armed Forces are introduced—

(1) into hostilities or into situations where imminent involvement in hostilities is clearly indicated by the circumstances;

(2) into the territory, airspace or waters of a foreign nation, while equipped for combat, except for deployments which relate solely to supply, replacement, repair, or training of such forces; or

(3) in numbers which substantially enlarge United States Armed Forces equipped for combat already located in a foreign nation;

the President shall submit within 48 hours to the Speaker of the House of Representatives and to the President pro tempore of the Senate a report, in writing, setting forth—

(A) the circumstances necessitating the introduction of United States Armed Forces;

(B) the constitutional and legislative authority under which such introduction took place; and

(C) the estimated scope and duration of the hostilities or involvement.

(b) The President shall provide such other information as the Congress may request in the fulfillment of its constitutional responsibilities with respect to committing the Nation to war and to the use of United States Armed Forces abroad.

(c) Whenever United States Armed Forces are introduced into hostilities or into any situation described in subsection (a) of this section, the President shall, so long as such armed forces continue to be engaged in such hostilities or situation, report to the Congress periodically on the status of such hostilities or situation as well as on the scope and duration of such hostilities or situation, but in no event shall he report to the Congress less often than once every six months.

CONGRESSIONAL ACTION

Sec. 5. (a) Each report submitted pursuant to section 4(a)(1) shall be transmitted to the Speaker of the House of Representatives and to the President pro tempore of the Senate on the same calendar day. Each report so transmitted shall be referred to the Committee on Foreign Affairs of the House of Representatives and to the Committee on Foreign Relations of the Senate for appropriate action. If, when the report is transmitted, the Congress has adjourned sine die or has adjourned for any period in excess of three calendar days, the Speaker of the House of Representatives and the President pro tempore of the Senate, if they deem it advisable (or if petitioned by at least 30 percent of the membership of their respective Houses) shall jointly request the President to convene Congress in order that it may consider the report and take appropriate action pursuant to this section.

(b) Within sixty calendar days after a report is submitted or is required to be submitted pursuant to section 4(a)(1), whichever is earlier, the President shall terminate any use of United States Armed Forces with respect to which such report was submitted (or required to be submitted), unless the Congress (1) has declared war or has enacted a specific authorization for such use of United States Armed Forces, (2) has extended by law such sixty-day period, or (3) is physically unable to meet as a result of an armed attack upon the United States. Such sixty-day period shall be extended for not more than an additional thirty days if the President determines and certifies to the Congress in writing that unavoidable military necessity respecting the safety of United States Armed Forces requires the continued use of such armed forces in the course of bringing about a prompt removal of such forces.

(c) Notwithstanding subsection (b), at any time that United States Armed Forces are engaged in hostilities outside the territory of the United States, its possessions and territories without a declaration of war or specific statutory authorization, such forces shall be removed by the President if the Congress so directs by concurrent resolution.

CONGRESSIONAL PRIORITY PROCEDURES FOR JOINT RESOLUTION OR BILL

Sec. 6. (a) Any joint resolution or bill introduced pursuant to section 5(b) at least thirty calendar days before the expiration of the sixty-day period specified in such section shall be referred to the Committee on Foreign Affairs of the House of Representatives or the Committee on Foreign Relations of the Senate, as the case may be, and such committee shall report one such joint resolution or bill, together with its recommendations, not later than twenty-four calendar days before the expiration of the sixty-day period specified in such section, unless such House shall otherwise determine by the yeas and nays.

(b) Any joint resolution or bill so reported shall become the pending business of the House in question (in the case of the Senate the time for debate shall be equally divided between the proponents and the opponents), and shall be voted on within three calendar days thereafter, unless such House shall otherwise determine by yeas and nays.

(c) Such a joint resolution or bill passed by one House shall be referred to the committee of the other House named in subsection (a) and shall be reported out not later than fourteen calendar days before the expiration of the sixty-day period specified in section 5(b). The joint resolution or bill so reported shall become the pending business of the House in question and shall be voted on within three calendar days after it has been reported, unless such House shall otherwise determine by yeas and nays.

(d) In the case of any disagreement between the two Houses of Congress with respect to a joint resolution or bill passed by both Houses, conferees shall be promptly appointed and the committee of conference shall make and file a report with respect to such resolution or bill not later than four calendar days before the expiration of the sixty-day period specified in section 5(b). In the event the conferees are unable to agree within 48 hours, they shall report back to their respective Houses in disagreement. Notwithsanding any rule in either House concerning the printing of conference reports in the Record or concerning any delay in the consideration of such reports, such report shall be acted on by both Houses not later than the expiration of such sixty-day period.

CONGRESSIONAL PRIORITY PROCEDURES FOR CONCURRENT RESOLUTION

Sec. 7. (a) Any concurrent resolution introduced pursuant to section 5(c) shall be referred to the Committee on Foreign Affairs of the House of Representatives or the Committee on Foreign Relations of the Senate, as the case may be, and one such concurrent resolution shall be reported out by such committee together with its recommendations within fifteen calendar days, unless such House shall otherwise determine by the yeas and nays.

(b) Any concurrent resolution so reported shall become the pending business of the House in question (in the case of the Senate the time for debate shall be equally divided between the proponents and the opponents) and shall be voted on within three calendar days thereafter, unless such House shall otherwise determine by yeas and nays.

(c) Such a concurrent resolution passed by one House shall be referred to the committee of the other House named in subsection (a) and shall be reported out by such committee together with its recommendations within fifteen calendar days and shall thereupon become the pending business of such House and shall be voted upon within three calendar days, unless such House shall otherwise determine by yeas and nays.

(d) In the case of any disagreement between the two Houses of Congress with respect to a concurrent resolution passed by both Houses, conferees shall be promptly appointed and the committee of conference shall make and file a report with respect to such concurrent resolution within six calendar days after the legislation is referred to the committee of conference. Notwithstanding any rule in either House concerning the printing of conference reports in the Record or concerning any delay in the consideration of such reports, such report shall be acted on by both Houses not later then six calendar days after the conference report is filed. In the event the conferees are unable to agree within 48 hours, they shall report back to their respective Houses in disagreement.

INTERPRETATION OF JOINT RESOLUTION

Sec. 8. (a) Authority to introduce United States Armed Forces into hostilities or into situations wherein involvement in hostilities is clearly indicated by the circumstances shall not be inferred—

(1) from any provision of law (whether or not in effect before the date of the enactment of this joint resolution), including any provision contained in any appropriation Act, unless such provision specifically authorizes the introduction of United States Armed Forces into hostilities or into such situations and states that it is intended to constitute specific statutory authorization within the meaning of this joint resolution; or

(2) from any treaty heretofore or hereafter ratified unless such treaty is implemented by legislation specifically authorizing the introduction of United States Armed Forces into hostilities or into such situations and stating that it is intended to constitute specific statutory authorization within the meaning of this joint resolution.

(b) Nothing in this joint resolution shall be construed to require any further specific statutory authorization to permit members of United States Armed Forces to participate jointly with members of the armed forces of one or more foreign countries in the headquarters operations of high-level military commands which were established prior to the date of enactment of this joint resolution and pursuant to the United Nations Charter or any treaty ratified by the United States prior to such date.

(c) For purposes of this joint resolution, the term "introduction of United States Armed Forces" includes the assignment of members of such armed forces to command, coordinate, participate in the movement of, or accompany the regular or irregular military forces of any foreign country or government when such military forces are engaged, or there exists an imminent threat that such forces will become engaged, in hostilities.

(d) Nothing in this joint resolution—

(1) is intended to alter the constitutional authority of the Congress or of the President, or the provisions of existing treaties; or

(2) shall be construed as granting any authority to the President with respect

to the introduction of United States Armed Forces into hostilities or into situations wherein involvement in hostilities is clearly indicated by the circumstances which authority he would not have had in the absence of this joint resolution.

SEPARABILITY CLAUSE

Sec. 9. If any provision of this joint resolution or the application thereof to any person or circumstance is held invalid, the remainder of the joint resolution and the application of such provision to any person or circumstance shall not be affected thereby.

EFFECTIVE DATE

Sec. 10. This joint resolution shall take effect on the date of its enactment.

3. The Freedom of Information Act as Amended in 1974 by Public Law 93–502

§ 552. *Public information; agency rules, opinions, orders, records, and proceedings*

(a) Each agency shall make available to the public information as follows:

(1) Each agency shall separately state and currently publish in the Federal Register for the guidance of the public—

> (A) descriptions of its central and field organization and the established places at which, the employees (and in the case of a uniformed service, the members) from whom, and the methods whereby, the public may obtain information, make submittals or requests, or obtain decisions;
>
> (B) statements of the general course and method by which its functions are channeled and determined, including the nature and requirements of all formal and informal procedures available;
>
> (C) rules of procedure, descriptions of forms available or the places at which forms may be obtained, and instructions as to the scope and contents of all papers, reports, or examinations;
>
> (D) substantive rules of general applicability adopted as authorized by law, and statements of general policy or interpretations of general applicability formulated and adopted by the agency; and
>
> (E) each amendment, revision, or repeal of the foregoing.

Except to the extent that a person has actual and timely notice of the terms thereof, a person may not in any manner be required to resort to, or be adversely affected by, a matter required to be published in the Federal Register and not so published. For the purpose of this paragraph, matter reasonably available to the class of persons affected thereby is deemed published in the Federal Register when incorporated by reference therein with the approval of the Director of the Federal Register.

(2) Each agency, in accordance with published rules, shall make available for public inspection and copying—

> (A) final opinions, including concurring and dissenting opinions, as well as orders, made in the adjudication of cases;

Public Law 90–23 (June 5, 1967) with amendments contained in Public Law 93–502 (November 21, 1974)—both amended Section 552 of Title 5, United States Code.

(B) those statements of policy and interpretations which have been adopted by the agency and are not published in the Federal Register; and

(C) administrative staff manuals and instructions to staff that affect a member of the public;

unless the materials are promptly published and copies offered for sale. To the extent required to prevent a clearly unwarranted invasion of personal privacy, an agency may delete identifying details when it makes available or publishes an opinion, statement of policy, interpretation, or staff manual or instruction. However, in each case the justification for the deletion shall be explained fully in writing. Each agency shall also maintain and make available for public inspection and copying current indexes providing identifying information for the public as to any matter issued, adopted, or promulgated after July 4, 1967, and required by this paragraph to be made available or published. Each agency shall promptly publish, quarterly or more frequently, and distribute (by sale or otherwise) copies of each index or supplements thereto unless it determines by order published in the Federal Register that the publication would be unnecessary and impracticable, in which case, the agency shall nonetheless provide copies of such index on request at a cost not to exceed the direct cost of duplication. A final order, opinion, statement of policy, interpretation, or staff manual or instruction that affects a member of the public may be relied on, used, or cited as precedent by an agency against a party other than an agency only if—

(i) it has been indexed and either made available or published as provided by this paragraph; or

(ii) the party has actual and timely notice of the terms thereof.

(3) Except with respect to the records made available under paragraphs (1) and (2) of this subsection, each agency, upon any request for records which (A) reasonably describes such records and (B) is made in accordance with published rules stating the time, place, fees (if any), and procedures to be followed, shall make the records promptly available to any person.

(4)(A) In order to carry out the provisions of this section, each agency shall promulgate regulations, pursuant to notice and receipt of public comment, specifying a uniform schedule of fees applicable to all constituent units of such agency. Such fees shall be limited to reasonable standard charges for document search and duplication and provide for recovery of only the direct costs of such search and duplication. Documents shall be furnished without charge or at a reduced charge where the agency determines that waiver or reduction of the fee is in the public interest because furnishing the information can be considered as primarily benefiting the general public.

(B) On complaint, the district court of the United States in the district in which the complainant resides, or has his principal place of business, or in which the agency records are situated, or in the District of Columbia, has jurisdiction to enjoin the agency from withholding agency records and to order the production of any agency records improperly withheld from the complainant. In such a case the court shall determine the matter de novo, and may examine the contents of such agency records in camera to determine whether such records or any part thereof shall be withheld under any of the exemptions set forth in subsection (b) of this section, and the burden is on the agency to sustain its action.

(C) Notwithstanding any other provision of law, the defendant shall serve an answer or otherwise plead to any complaint made under this subsection within thirty days after service upon the defendant of the pleading in which such complaint is made, unless the court otherwise directs for good cause shown.

(D) Except as to cases the court considers of greater importance, proceedings before the district court, as authorized by this subsection, and appeals therefrom, take precedence on the docket over all cases and shall be assigned for hearing and trial or for argument at the earliest practicable date and expedited in every way.

(E) The court may assess against the United States reasonable attorney fees and other litigation costs reasonably incurred in any case under this section in which the complainant has substantially prevailed.

(F) Whenever the court orders the production of any agency records improperly withheld from the complainant and assesses against the United States reasonable attorney fees and other litigation costs, and the court additionally issues a written finding that the circumstances surrounding the withholding raise questions whether agency personnel acted arbitrarily or capriciously with respect to the withholding, the Civil Service Commission shall promptly initiate a proceeding to determine whether disciplinary action is warranted against the officer or employee who was primarily responsible for the withholding. The Commission, after investigation and consideration of the evidence submitted, shall submit its findings and recommendations to the administrative authority of the agency concerned and shall send copies of the findings and recommendations to the officer or employee or his representative. The administrative authority shall take the corrective action that the Commission recommends.

(G) In the event of noncompliance with the order of the court, the district court may punish for contempt the responsible employee, and in the case of a uniformed service, the responsible member.

(5) Each agency having more than one member shall maintain and make available for public inspection a record of the final votes of each member in every agency proceeding.

(6)(A) Each agency, upon any request for records made under paragraph (1), (2), or (3) of this subsection, shall—

(i) determine within two days (excepting Saturdays, Sundays, and legal public holidays) after the receipt of any such request whether to comply with such request and shall immediately notify the person making such request of such determination and the reasons therefor, and of the right of such person to appeal to the head of the agency any adverse determination; and

(ii) make a determination with respect to any appeal within twenty days (excepting Saturdays, Sundays, and legal public holidays) after the receipt of such appeal. If on appeal the denial of the request for records is in whole or in part upheld, the agency shall notify the person making such request of the provisions for judicial review of that determination under paragraph (4) of this subsection.

(B) In unusual circumstances as specified in this subparagraph, the time limits prescribed in either clause (i) or clause (ii) of subparagraph (A) may be extended by written notice to the person making such request setting forth the reasons for such extension and the date on which a determination is expected to be dispatched. No such notice shall specify a date that would result in an extension for more than ten working days. As used in this subparagraph, "unusual circumstances" means, but only to the extent reasonably necessary to the proper processing of the particular request—

(i) the need to search for and collect the requested records from field facilities or other establishments that are separate from the office processing the request;

(ii) the need to search for, collect, and appropriately examine a voluminous amount of separate and distinct records which are demanded in a single request; or

(iii) the need for consultation, which shall be conducted with all practicable speed, with another agency having a substantial interest in the determination of the request or among two or more components of the agency having substantial subject-matter interest therein.

(C) Any person making a request to any agency for records under paragraph (1), (2), or (3) of this subsection shall be deemed to have exhausted his administrative remedies with respect to such request if the agency fails to comply with the applicable time limit provisions of this paragraph. If the Government can show exceptional circumstances exist and that the agency is exercising due diligence in responding to the request, the court may retain jurisdiction and allow the agency additional time to complete its review of the records. Upon any determination by an agency to comply with a request for records, the records shall be made promptly available to such person making such request. Any notification of denial of any request for records under this subsection shall set forth the names and titles or positions of each person responsible for the denial of such request.

(b) This section does not apply to matters that are—

(1)(A) specifically authorized under criteria established by an Executive order to be kept secret in the interest of national defense or foreign policy and (B) are in fact properly classified pursuant to such Executive order;

(2) related solely to the internal personnel rules and practices of an agency;

(3) specifically exempted from disclosure by statute;

(4) trade secrets and commercial or financial information obtained from a person and privileged or confidential;

(5) inter-agency or intra-agency memorandums or letters which would not be available by law to a party other than an agency in litigation with the agency;

(6) personnel and medical files and similar files the disclosure of which would constitute a clearly unwarranted invasion of personal privacy;

(7) investigatory records compiled for law enforcement purposes, but only to the extent that the production of such records would (A) interfere with enforcement proceedings, (B) deprive a person of a right to a fair trial or an impartial adjudication, (C) constitute an unwarranted invasion of personal privacy, (D) disclose the identity of a confidential source and, in the case of a record compiled by a criminal law enforcement authority in the course of a criminal investigation, or by an agency conducting a lawful national security intelligence investigation, confidential information furnished only by the confidential source, (E) disclose investigative techniques and procedures, or (F) endanger the life or physical safety of law enforcement personnel;

(8) contained in or related to examination, operating, or condition reports prepared by, on behalf of, or for the use of an agency responsible for the regulation or supervision of financial institutions; or

(9) geological and geophysical information and data, including maps, concerning wells.

Any reasonably segregable portion of a record shall be provided to any person requesting such record after deletion of the portions which are exempt under this subsection.

(c) This section does not authorize withholding of information or limit, the availability of records to the public, except as specifically stated in this section. This section is not authority to withhold information from Congress.

(d) On or before March 1 of each calendar year, each agency shall submit a report covering the preceding calendar year to the Speaker of the House of Representatives and President of the Senate for referral to the appropriate committees of the Congress. The report shall include—

(1) the number of determinations made by such agency not to comply with requests for records made to such agency under subsection (a) and the reasons for each such determination;

(2) the number of appeals made by persons under subsection (a)(6), the result of such appeals, and the reason for the action upon each appeal that results in a denial of information;

(3) the names and titles or positions of each person responsible for the denial of records requested under this section, and the number of instances of participation for each;

(4) the results of each proceeding conducted pursuant to subsection (a)(4)(F), including a report of the disciplinary action taken against the officer or employee who was primarily responsible for improperly withholding records or an explanation of why disciplinary action was not taken;

(5) a copy of every rule made by such agency regarding this section;

(6) a copy of the fee schedule and the total amount of fees collected by the agency for making records available under this section; and

(7) such other information as indicates efforts to administer fully this section.

The Attorney General shall submit an annual report on or before March 1 of each calendar year which shall include for the prior calendar year a listing of the number of cases arising under this section, the exemption involved in each case, the disposition of such case, and the cost, fees, and penalties assessed under subsections (a)(4)(E)(F), and (G). Such report shall also include a description of the efforts undertaken by the Department of Justice to encourage agency compliance with this section.

(e) For purposes of this section, the term "agency" as defined in section 551(1) of this title includes any executive department, military department, Government corporation, Government controlled corporation, or other establishment in the executive branch of the Government (including the Executive Office of the President), or any independent regulatory agency.

4.   An Act
Concerning Regulatory Agencies, and Establishing a System for the Periodic Review and for the Termination, Continuation, or Reestablishment Thereof. (1976)

Be it enacted by the General Assembly of the State of Colorado:

Section 1. Part 1 of article 34 of title 24, Colorado Revised Statutes 1973, as amended, is amended BY THE ADDITION OF A NEW SECTION to read:

24–34–104. General assembly review of regulatory agencies for termination, continuation, or reestablishment. (1) The general assembly finds that state government actions have produced a substantial increase in numbers of agencies, growth of programs, and proliferation of rules and regulations and that the whole process developed without sufficient legislative oversight, regulatory accountability, or a system of checks and balances. The general assembly further finds that by establishing a system for the termination, continuation, or reestablishment of such agencies, it will be in a better position to evaluate the need for the continued existence of existing and future regulatory bodies.

(2)(a) The following divisions in the department of regulatory agencies shall terminate on July 1, 1977:

. . . .

(5) Upon termination, each division, board, or agency shall continue in existence until July 1 of the next succeeding year for the purpose of winding up its affairs. During the wind-up period, termination shall not reduce or otherwise limit the powers or authority of each respective agency. Upon the expiration of the one year after termination, each respective agency shall cease all activities.

(6) The life of any division, board, or agency scheduled for termination under this section may be continued or reestablished by the general assembly for periods not to exceed six years. Any newly created division, board, or agency in the department of regulatory agencies shall have a life not to exceed six years and shall be subject to the provisions of this section.

(7) The legislative audit committee shall cause to be conducted a performance audit of each division, board, or agency scheduled for termination under this

Colorado State House Bill No. 1088 (April 22, 1976). Specific references to the dates and schedule for review of specific state agencies and units of government were deleted.

section. The performance audit shall be completed at least three months prior to the date established by this section for termination. In conducting the audit, the legislative audit committee shall take into consideration, but not be limited to considering, the factors listed in paragraph (b) of subsection (8) of this section. Upon completion of the audit report, the legislative audit committee shall hold a public hearing for purposes of review of the report. A copy of the report shall be made available to each member of the general assembly.

(8)(a) Prior to the termination, continuation, or reestablishment of any such agency, a committee of reference in each house of the general assembly shall hold a public hearing, receiving testimony from the public and the executive director of the department of regulatory agencies and the agency involved, and in such a hearing the agency shall have the burden of demonstrating a public need for its continued existence and the extent to which a change in the type of transfer of the agency may increase the efficiency of administration or operation of the agency.

(b) In such hearings, the determination as to whether an agency has demonstrated a public need for its continued existence shall take into consideration the following factors, among others:

(I) The extent to which the division, agency, or board has permitted qualified applicants to serve the public;

(II) the extent to which affirmative action requirements of state and federal statutes and constitutions have been complied with by the agency or the industry it regulates;

(III) The extent to which the division, board, or agency has operated in the public interest, and the extent to which its operation has been impeded or enhanced by existing statutes, procedures, and practices of the department of regulatory agencies, and any other circumstances, including budgetary, resource, and personnel matters;

(IV) The extent to which the agency has recommended statutory changes to the general assembly which would benefit the public as opposed to the persons it regulates;

(V) The extent to which the agency has required the persons it regulates to report to it concerning the impact of rules and decisions of the agency on the public regarding improved service, economy of service, and availability of service;

(VI) The extent to which persons regulated by the agency have been required to assess problems in their industry which affect the public;

(VII) The extent to which the agency has encouraged participation by the public in making its rules and decisions as opposed to participation solely by the persons it regulates;

(VIII) The efficiency with which formal public complaints filed with the division, board, or agency or with the executive director of the department of regulatory agencies concerning persons subject to regulation have been processed to completion by the division, board, or agency, by the executive director of the department of regulatory agencies, by the department of law, and by any other applicable department of state government; and

(IX) The extent to which changes are necessary in the enabling laws of the agency to adequately comply with the factors listed in this paragraph (b).

(9) If no action has been taken to extend the life of an agency because the subject was not designated in writing by the governor during the first ten days of the legislative session, pursuant to section 7 of article V of the state constitution, the agency shall continue in existence until the next subsequent odd-numbered year legislative session, at which time the general assembly shall reconsider the termination. If terminated, in no case shall an agency have less than one year to wind up its affairs.

(10) No more than one such division, board, or agency shall be continued or reestablished in any bill for an act, and such division, board, or agency shall be mentioned in the bill's title.

(11) This section shall not cause the dismissal of any claim or right of a citizen against any such agency or any claim or right of an agency terminated pursuant to this section which is subject to litigation. Said claims and rights shall be assumed by the department of regulatory agencies. Nothing in this section shall interfere with the general assembly otherwise considering legislation on any division, board, agency, or similar body existing within the department of regulatory agencies.

Section 41. **Effective date.** This act shall take effect July 1, 1976.

Section 42. **Safety clause.** The general assembly hereby finds, determines, and declares that this act is necessary for the immediate preservation of the public peace, health, and safety.

Approved: April 22, 1976.

5. Title II—Office of Inspector General (1976)

Sec. 201. In order to create an independent and objective unit—

(1) to conduct and supervise audits and investigations relating to programs and operations of the Department of Health, Education, and Welfare;

(2) to provide leadership and coordination and recommend policies for activities designed (A) to promote economy and efficiency in the administration of, and (B) to prevent and detect fraud and abuse in, such programs and operations; and

(3) to provide a means for keeping the Secretary and the Congress fully and currently informed about problems and deficiencies relating to the administration of such programs and operations and the necessity for and progress of corrective action;

there is hereby established in the Department of Health, Education, and Welfare an Office of Inspector General.

OFFICERS

Sec. 202. (a) There shall be at the head of the Office an Inspector General who shall be appointed by the President, by and with the advice and consent of the Senate, solely on the basis of integrity and demonstrated ability and without regard to political affiliation. The Inspector General shall report to and be under the general supervision of the Secretary or, to the extent such authority is delegated, the Under Secretary, but shall not be under the control of, or subject to supervision by, any other officer of the Department.

(b) There shall also be in the Office a Deputy Inspector General appointed by the President, by and with the advice and consent of the Senate, solely on the basis of integrity and demonstrated ability and without regard to political affiliation. The Deputy shall assist the Inspector General in the administration of the Office and shall, during the absence or temporary incapacity of the Inspector General, or during a vacancy in that office, act as Inspector General.

(c) The Inspector General or the Deputy may be removed from office by the

Public Law 94–505 (October 15, 1976) Title II—Office of the Inspector General—was contained within an act to convey U.S. land interests in Salt Lake City, Utah, for a charitable hospital construction, and references to this subject were deleted from the text.

President. The President shall communicate the reasons for any such removal to both Houses of Congress.

(d) The Inspector General and the Deputy shall each be subject to the provisions of subchapter III of chapter 73, title 5, United States Code, notwithstanding any exemption from such provisions which might otherwise apply.

(e) The Inspector General shall, in accordance with applicable laws and regulations governing the civil service—

> (1) appoint an Assistant Inspector General for Auditing who shall have the responsibility for supervising the performance of the functions, powers, and duties transferred by section 6(a)(1), and
>
> (2) appoint an Assistant Inspector General for Investigations who shall have the responsibility for supervising the performance of the functions, powers, and duties transferred by section 6(a)(2).

DUTIES AND RESPONSIBILITIES

Sec. 203. (a) It shall be the duty and responsibility of the Inspector General—

> (1) to supervise, coordinate, and provide policy direction for auditing and investigative activities relating to programs and operations of the Department;
>
> (2) to recommend policies for, and to conduct, supervise, or coordinate other activities carried out or financed by the Department for the purpose of promoting economy and efficiency in the administration of, or preventing and detecting fraud and abuse in, its programs and operations;
>
> (3) to recommend policies for, and to conduct, supervise, or coordinate relationships between the Department and other Federal agencies, State and local governmental agencies, and nongovernmental entities with respect to (A) all matters relating to the promotion of economy and efficiency in the administration of, or the prevention and detection of fraud and abuse in, programs and operations administered or financed by the Department, or (B) the identification and prosecution of participants in such fraud or abuse; and
>
> (4) to keep the Secretary and the Congress fully and currently informed, by means of the reports required by section 4 and otherwise, concerning fraud and other serious problems, abuses, and deficiencies relating to the administration of programs and operations administered or financed by the Department, to recommend corrective action concerning such problems, abuses, and deficiencies, and to report on the progress made in implementing such corrective action.

(b) In carrying out the responsibilities specified in subsection (a)(1), the Inspector General shall have authority to approve or disapprove the use of outside auditors or to take other appropriate steps to insure the competence and independence of such auditors.

(c) In carrying out the duties and responsibilities provided by this Act, the Inspector General shall give particular regard to the activities of the Comptroller General of the United States with a view to avoiding duplication and insuring effective coordination and cooperation.

(d) The Inspector General shall establish within his office an appropriate and adequate staff with specific responsibility for devoting their full time and attention to antifraud and antiabuse activities relating to the medicaid, medicare, renal disease, and maternal and child health programs. Such staff shall report to the Deputy.

REPORTS

Sec. 204. (a) The Inspector General shall, not later than March 31 of each year, submit a report to the Secretary and to the Congress summarizing the activities of the Office during the preceding calendar year. Such report shall include, but need not be limited to—

(1) an identification and description of significant problems, abuses, and deficiencies relating to the administration of programs and operations of the Department disclosed by such activities;

(2) a description of recommendations for corrective action made by the Office with respect to significant problems, abuses, or deficiencies identified and described under paragraph (1);

(3) an evaluation of progress made in implementing recommendations described in the report or, where appropriate, in previous reports; and

(4) a summary of matters referred to prosecutive authorities and the extent to which prosecutions and convictions have resulted.

(b) The Inspector General shall make reports on a quarterly basis to the Secretary and to the appropriate committees or subcommittees of the Congress identifying any significant problems, abuses, or deficiencies concerning which the Office has made a recommendation for corrective action and on which, in the judgment of the Inspector General, adequate progress is not being made.

(c) The Inspector General shall report immediately to the Secretary, and within seven calendar days thereafter to the appropriate committees or subcommittees of the Congress, whenever the Office becomes aware of particularly serious of flagrant problems, abuses, or deficiencies relating to the administration of programs and operations of the Department. The Deputy and Assistant Inspectors General shall have particular responsibility for informing the Inspector General of such problems, abuses, or deficiencies.

(d) The Inspector General (A) may made such additional investigations and reports relating to the administration of the programs and operations of the Department as are, in the judgment of the Inspector General, necessary or desirable, and (B) shall provide such additional information or documents as may be requested by either House of Congress or, with respect to matters within their jurisdiction, by any committee or subcommittee thereof.

(e) Notwithstanding any other provision of law, the reports, information, or documents required by or under this section shall be transmitted to the Secretary and the Congress, or committees or subcommittees thereof, by the Inspector General without further clearance or approval. The Inspector General shall, insofar as feasible, provide copies of the reports required under subsections (a) and (b) to the Secretary sufficiently in advance of the due date for their submission to Congress to provide a reasonable opportunity for comments of the Secretary to be appended to the reports when submitted to Congress.

AUTHORITY; ADMINISTRATION PROVISIONS

Sec. 205. (a) In addition to the authority otherwise provided by this Act, the Inspector General, in carrying out the provisions of this Act, is authorized—

(1) to have access to all records, reports, audits, reviews, documents, papers, recommendations, or other material available to the Department which relate to programs and operations with respect to which the Inspector General has responsibilities under this Act;

(2) to request such information or assistance as may be necessary for carrying out the duties and responsibilities provided by this Act from any Federal, State, or local governmental agency or unit thereof;

(3) to require by subpena the production of all information, documents, reports, answers, records, accounts, papers, and other data and documentary evidence necessary in the performance of the functions assigned by this Act, which subpena, in the case of contumacy or refusal to obey, shall be enforceable by order of any appropriate United States district court;

(4) to have direct and prompt access to the Secretary when necessary for any purpose pertaining to the performance of functions and responsibilities under this Act;

(5) in the event that a budget request for the Office of Inspector General is reduced, before submission to Congress, to an extent which the Inspector General deems seriously detrimental to the adequate performance of the functions mandated by this Act, the Inspector General shall so inform the Congress without delay;

(6) to select, appoint, and employ such officers and employees as may be necessary for carrying out the functions, powers, and duties of the Office

subject to the provisions of title 5, United States Code, governing appointments in the competitive service, and the provisions of chapter 51 and subchapter III of chapter 53 of such title relating to classification and General Schedule pay rates;

(7) to obtain services as authorized by section 3109 of title 5, United States Code, at daily rates not to exceed the equivalent rate prescribed for grade GS-18 of the General Schedule by section 5332 of title 5, United States Code;

(8) to the extent and in such amounts as may be provided in advance by appropriations Acts, to enter into contracts and other arrangements for audits, studies, analyses, and other services with public agencies and with private persons, and to make such payments as may be necessary to carry out the provisions of this Act.

(b)(1) Upon request of the Inspector General for information or assistance under subsection (a)(2), the head of any Federal agency involved shall, insofar as is practicable, and not in contravention of any existing statutory restriction, or regulation of the Federal agency from which the information is requested, furnish to the Inspector General, or to an authorized designee, such information or assistance.

(2) Whenever information or assistance requested under subsection (a)(1) or (a)(2) is, in the judgment of the Inspector General, unreasonably refused or not provided, the Inspector General shall report the circumstances to the Secretary and to the appropriate committees or subcommittees of the Congress without delay.

(3) In the event any record or other information requested by the Inspector General under subsection (a)(1) or (a)(2) is not considered to be available under the provisions of section 552a(b) (1), (3), or (7) of title 5, United States Code, such record or information shall be available to the Inspector General in the same manner and to the same extent it would be available to the Comptroller General.

(c) The Secretary shall provide the Inspector General and his staff with appropriate and adequate office space at central and field office locations of the Department, together with such equipment, office supplies, and communications facilities and services as may be necessary for the operation of such offices, and shall provide necessary maintenance services for such offices and the equipment and facilities located therein.

(d)(1) The Inspector General shall receive compensation at the rate provided for level IV of the Executive Schedule by section 5315 of title 5, United States Code.

(2) The Deputy shall receive compensation at the rate provided for level V of the Executive Schedule by section 5316 of title 5, United States Code.

TRANSFER OF FUNCTIONS

Sec. 206: (a) There are hereby transferred to the Office of Inspector General the functions, powers, and duties of—

(1) the agency of the Department referred to as the "HEW Audit Agency";

(2) the office of the Department referred to as the "Office of Investigations"; and

(3) such other offices or agencies, or functions, powers, or duties thereof, as the Secretary may, with the consent of the Inspector General, determine are properly related to the functions of the Office and would, if so transferred, further the purposes of this Act.

except that there shall not be transferred to the Inspector General under clause (3) program operating responsibilities.

(b) The personnel, assets, liabilities, contracts, property, records, and unexpended balances of appropriations, authorizations, allocations, and other funds employed, held, used, arising from, available or to be made available, of any office or agency the functions, powers, and duties of which are transferred under subsection (a) are hereby transferred to the Office of Inspector General.

(c) Personnel transferred pursuant to subsection (b) shall be transferred in accordance with applicable laws and regulations relating to the transfer of functions except that the classification and compensation of such personnel shall not be reduced for one year after such transfer.

(d) In any case where all the functions, powers, and duties of any office or agency are transferred pursuant to this subsection, such office or agency shall lapse. Any person who, on the effective date of this Act, held a position compensated in accordance with the General Schedule, and who, without a break in service, is appointed in the Office to a position having duties comparable to those performed immediately preceding such appointment shall continue to be compensated in the new position at not less than the rate provided for the previous position, for the duration of service in the new position.

Approved October 15, 1976.

6.   Proposition 13
State of California Constitution (1978)

Article XIII A

*Section 1. (a) The maximum amount of any ad valorem tax on real property shall
not exceed One percent (1%) of the full cash value of such property. The one percent
(1%) tax to be collected by the counties and apportioned according to law to the
districts within the counties.*

*(b) The limitation provided for in subdivision (a) shall not apply to ad valorem
taxes or special assessments to pay the interest and redemption charges on any
indebtedness approved by the voters prior to the time this section becomes effective.*

Section 2. (a) The full cash value means the ~~County Assessors~~ *county assessor's*
valuation of real property as shown on the 1975–76 tax bill under "full cash value";
or, thereafter, the appraised value of real property when purchased, newly constructed, or a change in ownership has ~~occured~~ *occurred* after the 1975 assesse-
ment. All real property not already assessed up to the 1975–76 ~~tax levels~~ *full cash
value* may be reassessed to reflect that valuation. *For purposes of this section, the
term "newly constructed" shall not include real property which is reconstructed after
a disaster, as declared by the Governor, where the fair market value of such real
property, as reconstructed, is comparable to its fair market value prior to the disaster.*

(b) The ~~fair market~~ *full cash* value base may reflect from year to year the
inflationary rate not to exceed two *2* percent ~~(2%)~~ for any given year or reduction as
shown in the consumer price index or comparable data for the area under taxing
jurisdiction, *or may be reduced to reflect substantial damage, destruction or other
factors causing a decline in value.*

*Section 3. From and after the effective date of this article, any changes in State
taxes enacted for the purpose of increasing revenues collected pursuant thereto
whether by increased rates or changes in methods of computation must be imposed by
an Act passed by not less than two-thirds of all members elected to each of the two
houses of the Legislature, except that no new ad valorem taxes on real property, or
sales or transaction taxes on the sales of real property may be imposed.*

*Section 4. Cities, Counties and special districts, by a two-thirds vote of the
qualified electors of such district, may impose special taxes on such district, except ad*

Article XIII A of California State Constitution became effective July 1, 1978; Section 2 was amended
effective November 8, 1978. The lines through the words indicate the November 8, 1978, amendments
to Article XIII A.

valorem taxes on real property or a transaction tax or sales tax on the sale of real property within such City, County or special district.

Section 5. This article shall take effect for the tax year beginning on July 1 following the passage of this Amendment, except Section 3 which shall become effective upon the passage of this article.

Section 6. If any section, part, clause, or phrase hereof is for any reason held to be invalid or unconstitutional, the remaining sections shall not be affected but will remain in full force and effect.

About the Editor

Richard J. Stillman II is a professor of Government and Politics and teaches in the Doctoral Program in Public Administration at George Mason University (Virginia). He has published several books including *Integration of the Negro in the U.S. Armed Forces, The Rise of the City Manager, The Professions in Government* (with Frederick C. Mosher, and *Public Administration: Concepts and Cases* (2nd edition). He currently serves on the editorial boards of the *American Review of Public Administration* as well as the *Annals of Public Administration* and has been a NASA University Fellow, Public Administration Fellow, and Research Fellow at the Institute of Governmental Studies, University of California, Berkeley.